Once Upon a Tart...

Once Upon a Tart...

SOUPS, SALADS, MUFFINS, AND MORE

from New York City's Favorite Bakeshop and Café

FRANK MENTESANA AND JEROME AUDUREAU

WITH CAROLYNN CARREÑO

PHOTOGRAPHS BY FRANK MENTESANA

Alfred A. Knopf   New York   2003

This Is a Borzoi Book
Published by Alfred A. Knopf

www.aaknopf.com

Knopf, Borzoi Books, and the colophon are registered trademarks of
Random House, Inc.

ISBN: 0-375-41316-2
LCCN: 2003100385

Manufactured in Singapore
First Edition

To my parents, who inspired me, and in particular to my mother,
who taught me how to enjoy cooking
—Jerome Audureau

For my dad, who showed me the pleasures of a peach
and that anything is possible
—Frank Mentesana

CONTENTS

JEROME'S INTRODUCTION

I still remember the feeling when the Realtor pulled up the storefront gate of the space that is now Once Upon a Tart. My business partner, Frank Mentesana, and I had been looking to move our wholesale tart business, then based in Long Island City, across the East River into Manhattan. All kinds of Realtors had tried to talk us into all kinds of spaces, but none of them inspired us. Looking at them made opening a bakery/café feel like work instead of like realizing a dream.

One afternoon, I decided to hop on my bike and look for myself. I came to the corner of Prince and Sullivan Streets in what is now SoHo, a very fashionable neighborhood in downtown New York, and saw a "for rent" sign on a tiny abandoned storefront. There was a heavy gate pulled down over the place, so I couldn't really see anything. But I just knew.

I called the number on the sign, and the next day a Realtor met us at 135 Sullivan Street to show us the space. Back then, SoHo ended three blocks east of Sullivan, where the big iron loft buildings end and the tenement apartments begin. And at the time, SoHo was not like it is now. It was just a few art galleries and advertising agencies—and a lot of giant, empty warehouses. The only people living there were people who liked neighborhoods with cool architecture, good light, and low rent. Artists.

Sullivan Street was a Portuguese and Italian neighborhood. Below the tenement apartments on one side of the street were a dark little bodega and an Italian cheese shop. Not a fancy cheese shop either; they had a few cans of tomatoes on their shelves and a smoker in the basement (where, by the way, they still smoke their own mozzarella). And on the other side of the street were, in this order: a Catholic church, a sawdust-on-the-floor butcher, a new, cute little French restaurant (the only new, cute thing in a three-block radius), a Laundromat, and an abandoned storefront with a lot of potential.

The Realtor tried to sell us on the fact that there had been a bakery here ninety years before. Most recently, though, it had been the New York City meeting space for some kind of reli-

Jerome's first tart shop

gious organization based in New Jersey. The small room was painted a horrible gray with matching industrial carpeting on the floor. But the way the morning light came streaming into the storefront, I could see the potential. The place had charm. We took it right then. We hadn't even seen the basement: it was so dark and piled with junk that the real-estate agent refused to bring us downstairs.

Frank and I had met a few years before while working in management for a big hotel chain. Over dinner one night after work, I told him that I was ready to start a business on my own. I asked him if he wanted to do something together, and he did. We talked about different ideas, but I knew that I wanted to open a tart business.

I had done this before. During my last year of management school in France, I had to complete a summer "externship" and write a report about it. I didn't want to slave away behind the front desk of a hotel, so I decided to open a tart shop in Vaison la Romaine, a town near Avignon, France, where I grew up. I called it Tarte Margot, after my then two-year-old daughter.

The space where I opened Tarte Margot was a doctor's office converted into a café with a little terrace in front—twenty tables total. And the concept was simple: I sold only tarts and a salad of mesclun and Dijon vinaigrette. I made about twenty tarts a day. This may not sound like a lot, but I did everything myself. It was just me and the oven and the dishwasher and the bowl to toss the salads. I opened in June, and I went back to school in October. I wrote about the experience, charting expenditures and progression of sales. I had made a profit.

At the time Frank and I started talking about a business, I had been in New York four or five years and hadn't seen many tarts for sale—no savory tarts, and sweet tarts only in a few places. I knew people would like them. I managed to convince Frank of the idea. And so we started working on the business plan in our free time. We came up with something like seventy different kinds of tarts, and then started testing them out on our friends. That's also how we came up with the name. At night, we would sit around the table in my loft talking about tarts and different ideas for the business. One evening, we started throwing out names, and our friend, Laura, came up with Once Upon a Tart. We weren't crazy about it, but then, a few days later, another friend, Jennifer, came up with the exact same name. We figured there must be something to it—that the store was destined to be called Once Upon a Tart.

We started by selling only wholesale. We had a little menu printed up that I would take around, along with samples of the tarts, to different gourmet stores and small restaurants in the neighborhood. The tarts were so beautiful, with tomatoes arranged on top or a pretty lattice crust, that I sold them right away. Their visual appeal made them easy for the shops and restaurants to sell to their customers.

The loft where I lived was what we referred to, professionally, as our "warehouse in Long Island City." We baked all the tarts in my regular oven. It was fall, luckily, so the weather was just right for us to use the fire escape as a refrigerator. One time, we were up all night making tarts for a morning delivery. At two in the morning, the wind started blowing really hard, and cases and cases of mushrooms blew off the fire escape, three floors down onto the street. I had to run out in the middle of the night to buy more mushrooms for a 7 a.m. delivery.

During that first year, when we were only wholesale, we did all the deliveries ourselves. So many times I rode the subway carrying bags and bags of tarts. Finally, I said to Frank, "We need a car." So we bought this old beat-up car. It was the Tuesday of Thanksgiving week, and we had more deliveries that day than we'd ever had—by far. I cannot tell you how happy I was to have a car, even if it was an old clunker. I stacked so many tarts in there. The car was packed, passenger seat, backseat, the floors, the back window. I warmed up the engine and pulled away from the loft. At the first intersection, a woman ran a stoplight. I knew that if I slammed on my brakes the tarts would go flying forward. So I veered off the

Our first menu

road and hit a street lamp instead. And the tarts went flying forward, backward, everywhere. The windshield was smeared with tarts; they were all over the upholstery. Every one of them—probably a hundred in all—was destroyed.

Within a couple of months after starting the business, we had so many orders that we were just tapping our fingers on the counter waiting for tarts to come out of the oven, so we could put more in. By the end of that first year, we decided it was time to open a café. Once we found the space in SoHo, we baked tarts only in the mornings. In the afternoons, we went to Sullivan Street to fix up the store so we could open. We did all the work ourselves. We tore down walls. We ripped up carpeting—and found the most beautiful terrazzo floors. We ordered little round marble-topped tables and French bistro chairs. I designed the counters, which are all on wheels. I followed the concept of bakers' racks—these tall rectangular racks that hold twenty sheet pans and that bakers wheel around their kitchens, depending on where they need to make space.

We push the counters forward, into the café space, to give us more room during production hours, when we're stocking the product on the shelves. We push the counters back to give the café more room when it fills up with customers. People probably don't even notice the wheels, or that the counters may be in a slightly different place from one day to the next, but I think it gives the space a sense of fluidity, which the shop needs because it's so small. When things don't move, they get stagnant—like closets and cupboards that never get cleaned out.

We were going to need the basement for storage, and we wanted to build an office down there, so eventually I had to check it out. I crawled through a little opening in the sidewalk and ducked my head down the narrow staircase, and there, behind piles of boxes and trash, was a wooden door with a twisted piece of metal for a lock. I untwisted the "lock" and pushed the door open. I cannot even tell you how much stuff was piled in there: piles and piles of old, musty junk. I was sure I would find something scary, but I was loving it. I started opening boxes and unwrapping old newspaper. I couldn't believe my eyes. It was like something out of a movie. Like a fantasy. All the original fixtures from the old bakery were there: glass pedestals, the original glass shelving, a marble mortar and pestle, black-and-white photographs, light fixtures. It was unbelievable. We had everything we needed to open the store, right there.

We hung the original light fixtures (and some exact replicas of them) in the deep storefront windows on either side of the front door. And we arranged the old glass pedestals in the windows below them. We piled these high with tarts, a few sandwiches, a small selection of cookies, and the most delicious fudgy brownies that Frank's brother (not a baker but a brownie lover) invented when he was helping us get ready to open the store.

The day we opened, there were people outside waiting to come in. They had seen us working on the café and they were curious. The neighborhood was ready for us. Before we opened our doors, the only coffee for sale in the neighborhood was the terrible stuff sold at corner delis in paper cups printed with pictures of the Acropolis. There were no cafés where you could sit down and have some little thing to eat

Frank and Jerome at the counter

and a good cup of coffee. This was just unbelievable to a French person. And lucky for us, because the demand was there—and about to boom.

Our menu evolved pretty quickly as soon as we discovered what our customers wanted from us. We started making scones when we realized that people needed a place to get good coffee on their way to work—either coming into the neighborhood or leaving it. And we added soups and salads to our repertoire as we became a lunchtime destination for the few pioneering businesses that kept the neighborhood buzzing during the daytime. We continued to sell wholesale the first year we had the store—the tarts we sold around town were like an edible business card—but eventually we got too busy to do both.

Ten years later, the neighborhood has grown up. The street is filled with boutiques—the kind that sell expensive baby clothes and fancy handbags. A few of the old Italian shops remain: lucky for us, the cheese shop and the butcher are still there, and a woman named Angela still sits outside her apartment entrance next door to the café all day, every day. She's like the unofficial mayor of Sullivan Street.

Once Upon a Tart has grown up, too. We have our regular customers whom we know by name and by the muffins they order. And we have become a destination for out-of-towners who want to eat where the locals do. We have had offers to franchise our business. We have been asked by investors, on their way to Wall Street, if we want to open a store uptown or in Connecticut. But we always say no. Because then we couldn't do what we do. Frank and I both still work in the kitchen. We still put in long, exhausting days to get out the Thanksgiving orders that always come at the very last minute. And we still, occasionally, make deliveries ourselves. One of us is at the store every day of the week. We like what we do. We hope you do, too.

FRANK'S INTRODUCTION

When Jerome first mentioned tarts as an idea for a business we could start together, I have to admit, I was skeptical. I tried to steer him toward the idea of frozen prepared foods, like gourmet TV dinners. Then I went through a phase in which I thought we should start a line of condom key-chains (this was the beginning of the safe-sex movement). But Jerome stuck to tarts. And, well, Jerome can be very convincing.

I had made tarts before. Or, rather, I had made *one* tart before. And not very successfully. I was working in a hotel kitchen for a few months as part of the management program I was enrolled in at the time. And I was asked to make an apple tart. The recipe called for caramelizing the apples before putting them in the tart. So I sliced up some apples, sprinkled them with sugar, threw them in a pan with lots of butter, and started cooking, waiting for them to get nice and brown and sweet.

I kept cooking the apples. And cooking them and cooking them. And they wouldn't caramelize. I didn't want to say any-thing to my supervisor about his apples. But I remember thinking: What is wrong with these things? Finally, I tasted one and realized what I'd done. I had taken handfuls out of the salt bin instead of sugar. (Salt doesn't caramelize no mat-ter how long you cook it.) I didn't learn a lot of specifics about cooking during that stint. But I did learn that if you make a mistake you start over, try again. That was the beginning of a long and beautiful relationship with trial and error in the kitchen.

Trial and error, I learned, is at the cornerstone of opening a business as well. A bakery business anyway. Or *our* bakery business, seeing as how I was a tart novice who'd been enthused into opening a business making something I didn't know how to make. I am not a professionally trained cook. Nor is Jerome. We're just two guys who like to cook and who like good food and who have, by necessity—we had cus-tomers to feed—learned how.

The truth is, I was so excited to be out of the corporate world and to get into the kitchen, I could have been making

Frank and Jerome in the kitchen

baby food for all I cared. From the moment I got my hands in the dough, I was hooked. I would completely lose track of time and find myself after midnight still experimenting with flours, trying to get the exact texture I wanted in a crust: flaky, but with a crunch. I would get obsessed with the smallest things, like figuring out how to make an onion tart look pretty (a lattice top), or how to make a tomato tart less watery (set the tomatoes in a colander first).

I'm amazed that we managed to pull it off. We were crammed into Jerome's loft in Long Island City with this one regular oven and an apartment-size refrigerator. We had designated one of his two phone lines to be the business line. We would answer that phone, "Once Upon a Tart," like we were a real *business*. I'd tap on the keyboard in front of me while I

was taking an order; I thought our customers would be impressed that we were computerized. Meanwhile, the computer wasn't even on. We essentially created a fictitious business for people to believe in. It was up to us to make good on what we had led them to believe.

I'm not saying we weren't prepared. We had dough worked out, and for weeks we'd been using our friends as guinea pigs for the tarts. But I like to be in command of every detail before I move forward with something—I'm the kind of guy who looks at a map to figure out where I'm going *before* I get into the car. Jerome's different—more spontaneous. And he decided it was time to take samples around to various stores long before we had every detail mapped out. The first afternoon he took them around, we got one order. For forty tarts! Jerome was leaving for vacation the next day. It was the most unbelievably scary feeling, wondering if we could actually pull this off. We had to, of course. And we did.

In the ten years we've been in business, I've learned that, when it comes to cooking, you never have command of every detail. I'm always running into something new and unexpected, whether I'm in the store kitchen or at home. Recently I went to make pizzas for a dinner party for eight. I'd made pizzas before, but this time, the dough just wouldn't work—it kept tearing. I suggested ordering Chinese food, but my guests didn't want Chinese. They said they could get that at home. So I boiled up some pasta and turned what I was putting on the pizza—the sauce, the toppings, and the cheese—into a pasta dish. That's what I like about cooking. Even at the store, with some two thousand customers depending on us every week, and counting on some things to be exactly the same every time they come in, I still feel like I'm always learning, always improvising.

Which is what cooking is all about, ultimately. Over the years, many customers have asked us for our recipes—our *secrets.* The fact is, we don't have secrets. We didn't reinvent the chocolate-chip cookie. We don't even have mysterious or complicated recipes. Mysterious and complicated is not what we do, or what we've ever wanted to do. We let the fancy chefs work with the most exotic ingredients and gimmicky presentations. We have a different goal in mind when we're coming up with recipes. We want to take those things we love to eat— some things from our childhoods, and some things we've discovered along the way—and, with fresher ingredients, better bread, more vibrant condiments, make them better.

The only secret to our cooking is that we've never been afraid to try something that might not turn out. To take risks, to add something to a dish that isn't, by pre-existing standards, supposed to be there—marmalade in gingerbread, for example, or ground almonds to a creamy pea soup. We're also not afraid of the truth. We hand our experiments to whoever walks in the store at that moment and let them tell us if they like it or not.

I am pleased to be handing over these recipes to a public that has been so good to us. But I hope that we've also provided enough information about ingredients and techniques that you'll feel comfortable ignoring us every once in a while, and confident enough to start tinkering with our recipes, making them your own.

EQUIPMENT

We're not big into equipment, but there are a few tools we like, things we'd call necessities.

- **A rolling pastry cutter** gives a nice fluted edge to lattice strips. If you don't have one, a pizza cutter or a knife will do fine.
- **A pastry cutter** is an old-fashioned tool for cutting butter into flour. Two knives pulled in a crisscross motion work just as well.
- **A food processor** is the one piece of kitchen equipment we'd save in a fire. We use only the steel blade. Use it for puréeing soups and making all kinds of doughs, vinaigrettes, and mayonnaise.
- We love **rolling pins**. We use tapered pins for pie and tart dough, and straight pins for cookie dough, to get an even thickness. No matter what the pin is made of (marble or wood) or what kind of dough you're rolling, you need to dust the pin with flour or your dough will stick to it.
- We use **tart pans with removable bottoms**. It makes taking the tart out of the pan so easy. This way, we rarely break a crust.
- You must use **pie weights** to weigh down a tart or pie crust when you're "blind baking" it (baking the crust without a filling). You can buy the weights specifically for this purpose. Or you can use dried beans: kidney, garbanzo, black beans, anything you like. Keep your designated pie weights in a mason jar or some other container, and reuse them. But don't try to cook with them.
- We love **rubber spatulas**. We can't believe it when we go into someone else's kitchen and don't find any rubber spatulas. They're one of our favorite kitchen utensils, and they're so inexpensive. Some rubber spatulas are heatproof.

Our version of heavy equipment: an industrial immersion blender

They're worth the extra cost, because you can use them to stir things on the stovetop.

- We don't like to be sticklers when it comes to tools, but we do believe in the appropriate **knife** for the appropriate task. Serrated knives for slicing bread, small paring knives for coring fruits and vegetables, and big chef's knives for chopping. It's important to keep your knives sharp. A dull knife is more dangerous than a sharp one—because you have to apply so much pressure to make it work.

- A **mandoline** is a pretty expensive little machine used for slicing vegetables to a uniform thickness—or thinness—depending on how you adjust it. You can buy a cheap mandoline, but it won't be as sturdy.

- We don't know what we'd do without a **salad spinner**—at the store or in our homes. There's just nothing better for getting the water off lettuce. And getting the water off is essential to getting vinaigrette to cling to the lettuce. We wash lettuce directly in the spinner.

- We use two kinds of **colanders**: a basic one for draining pasta and most beans and grains, and a mesh colander for draining smaller beans and grains, like lentils and quinoa, which would fall right through the holes of a regular colander.

- It's essential to use **dry measuring cups** for measuring dry ingredients, because with them you can scoop up your flour, for instance, then scrape it off. There is a different dry measuring cup for every measure.

- A **liquid measuring cup** has a spout and a handle and is for measuring liquid ingredients. The correct way to use it is to set the cup on the counter and pour your liquid in until it reaches the line. Ideally, for the most accurate measure, you should crouch down so that you are looking at the cup dead-on.

- There is a difference between a **sheet pan** and **a baking sheet.** A sheet pan has edges; a baking sheet is flat all the way around. Sheet pans are standard in professional baking. You might remember ordering birthday "sheet cakes," in whole-, half-, or quarter-sheet pan sizes. Some say baking sheets allow cookies to bake more evenly—because they're not sunk down below the edges of a sheet pan. Our cookies aren't so delicate that we notice a difference. Use what you have.

- An **immersion blender** looks like a plastic battery-powered baton with a whirling blade at one end. If you like to make puréed soups, you may want to invest in one. It makes puréeing so simple. Just stick the immersion blender in the pot, turn it on, and move it around so that it touches the entire batch of soup. In a few minutes you've transformed a bunch of vegetables into a beautiful, smooth soup. No ladle, no food processor, and no soup dribbled on the counter.

- We like a **four-sided grater** for shredding and grating soft cheeses, like cheddar, and vegetables, like carrots. We use a smaller **handheld grater** for grating lemon rinds and hard cheeses, like Parmesan, because it's easier to clean.
- The purpose of a **double boiler** is to keep whatever you're cooking, like custards and chocolate, away from the direct flame, and thereby prevent burning. If you don't have a double boiler, use a stainless-steel bowl set over a pot of boiling water.
- A **grill pan** is a nice way to get grill marks on your meat, as well as add flavor, without going outside. We like cast iron, because it heats up nice and hot, just like a grill.
- We're not big fans of one-task tools, but we do use a **potato brush.** Potatoes can be muddy and dirty, and we really like to scrub them. Besides, a potato brush doesn't have to be saved just for potatoes. We use it for carrots and other root vegetables, too.
- We like the kind of **vegetable peeler** that is shaped something like a slingshot. It swivels and makes peeling so much easier.
- There's just something about **nesting bowls.** We love them because we have everything at our fingertips: a small bowl for eggs, larger bowls for flour, or for mixing wet and dry ingredients.
- We use a big **citrus press** at the store and in our homes—it makes juicing so quick and painless. If you don't have one, an **old-fashioned glass juicer** works fine.
- We don't recommend you go out and buy any **pots and pans** just because the recipes in this book call for something you don't have. But if you want to buy pots and pans and you're using our recipes as an excuse, keep in mind that you

are less likely to burn things in a heavy-gauge pan. Cast iron is relatively inexpensive and very useful. Stainless-steel copper-bottomed pots are our favorite. We love the weight of them, and also the way they look—beautiful but not fancy. If you don't want to spend a lot of money, any heavy-gauge pot will work, and you can get them pretty inexpensively at a kitchen-supply store. If you don't have a heavy-bottomed saucepan, use the best you've got and be sure to keep a close eye on it. With a thinner pot you'll have to stir more frequently and lower the flame and maybe even add a bit of water if you find what's cooking is sticking to the bottom.

- **Parchment paper** is a heavy, nonstick paper that we use for lining sheet pans or cookie sheets in baking. We love it, because it guarantees that whatever we're baking is going to come right off the pan. And, assuming we didn't drip any batter underneath the parchment on the pan itself, when we're done we just lift up the parchment and throw it out, then wipe off the pan with a paper towel. You can find parchment paper at most grocery stores. Cut it to fit the pan you're lining and lay the parchment on the pan. To make sure the parchment doesn't slide around, dab the pan with a tiny bit of butter in two or three places.

- We're pleased to introduce you to a nifty little tool that we love, called a **bench knife.** Ours is a 3-by-6-inch sturdy metal rectangle with a dull blade on one of the longer sides and a wooden handle on the other. It is a simple little thing, made for cutting dough and also for scraping dough off your work surface—and nothing works better.

Once Upon a Tart...

Once Upon a ...
SAVORY TART

Crunchy Savory Tart Crust
Rosemary–Whole Wheat Tart Crust
Provençal Tart with Gruyère and Herbes de Provence
Granny's Tomato Tart
Frank's Tomato Tart
Zucchini Tart with Curried Custard and Dried Currants
Sautéed Spinach-and-Mushroom Tart with Ricotta Cheese
Roasted-Potato Tart with Fresh Tarragon, Sautéed Mushrooms, and Melted Gruyère
Caramelized-Leek-and-Celery Tart
Roasted Red Pepper Tart with Black Olive Tapenade and Parmesan Cheese
Roasted-Eggplant-and-Tomato Tart with Basil
Sweet-Onion Tart with Black Olives in a Rosemary–Whole Wheat Crust
Roasted-Ratatouille Tart with Herbes de Provence
Caramelized-Fennel Tart in a Rosemary–Whole Wheat Crust
Classic Potato-and-Onion Frittata
Variations on Our Classic Frittata
Variation: Frittata Sandwiches

We started our business selling only tarts; thus the name. Jerome had run a little *tarterie* one summer as an assignment for the management school he attended in France. We met working for a big hotel chain in New York City. And we were both ready to do something on our own. "I showed Frank pictures of Tarte Margot—just to tempt him," Jerome says. Jerome then dragged Frank to Paris for the sole purpose of looking at tarts. (Poor Frank.)

"When I introduced Frank to tarts," Jerome says, "he couldn't tell the difference between a tart and a quiche." A quiche is about four times as thick as a tart. That thickness is all custard. Quiches had come into style in America and gone out of style just as quickly, maybe because they have so much cream and egg yolk in them. That was when people started worrying about how much fat they were eating. Quiche was so passé, it was like a joke. We didn't want to be in the business of selling something that would make Americans think: Quiche! Ha-ha-ha. (Even though they were wrong.)

Frank had been to France, but he had never given tarts a second thought. Once he started looking around, he was shocked to notice how common tarts were. We went to lunch our first day and, sure enough, there were people at table after table eating a leek tart and green salad dressed with Dijon vinaigrette. Granted, in France, cafés and restaurants tend to specialize, and this happened to be a café that sold tarts. "Eating a tart in France is like eating a hamburger here," Frank says, still incredulous. He liked the idea of tarts enough to quit his job and go into selling them full-time.

We tried to work out as much of the business as possible while we still had money coming in from our jobs. The first thing we did was start playing with dough. We knew that without a good crust it didn't really matter what was inside. And vice versa—with a flaky, buttery crust, the tart would be delicious with just about any filling.

We tested different types of flours in combination with unbleached white flour to find out the effect they would have on the baked crust. Cornmeal made it crunchier. Whole wheat made it denser and gave it that nutty whole-wheatness. We ultimately decided to put just a little semolina flour, the flour commonly used to make most pasta, in our dough. We got the idea from a tart-baker we'd met in Avignon, the walled city in the south of France where Jerome grew up. The semolina added a nice crunch to the crust without the grainy texture we got from cornmeal. It also gave the crust a longer shelf life, so that our customers could buy a tart on, say, Sunday and eat the last of it on Tuesday.

While we were still working days at the hotel, we had dinner parties in the evenings where we'd serve nothing but tarts—some with inspired fillings, and some with fillings that turned out to be just plain weird. We tested them on our friends (when you ask friends for their opinion, boy, do they give it). This was not your typical dinner party, where at a certain point one guest pauses, puts down his fork, and tells the cook how good the food is, and the other guests chime in. Our friends told us what they thought of each and every tart in no uncertain terms. A curry tart didn't have enough curry. The onion tart was ugly. "I remember specifically one friend insisting that two tarts we'd made were too similar," Frank says. "Once he said it, everyone at the table decided he was right. And we were forced to take one off our tentative menu." Talk about tough customers.

We decided to sell tarts wholesale before opening a café, to make sure people would buy them—and also to make some money. We determined that our challenge was to convince people that tarts were the French equivalent of pizza: you didn't have to use a knife and fork to eat a tart, you could just pick it up and take a bite. Convincing New Yorkers, however, that you could treat this buttery, fluted crust filled with things like caramelized leeks or curry and zucchini in the same way you treat a pizza, was another thing altogether. We never quite did it, but we did manage to build a whole identity and successful business around our tarts.

THINGS TO KNOW

The tart recipes we give you are for our basics at the store, but you could put pretty much anything in a tart shell. And, trust us, we have. When we were developing our menu of tarts, we stepped out of the tart paradigm and instead thought: meal-in-a-crust. Don't be afraid to do the same: to step out of these recipes and use different vegetables or cheeses in place of those we call for. Our tarts are all vegetarian, because we started out as a vegetarian café. At home, Jerome makes the leek tart with ham, which is how it's made in France. And the spinach-and-mushroom tart is good with chopped-up chicken or bacon. Use your imagination.

We use one standard custard for all our savory tarts. The recipe is based on a simple ratio of 1 large egg to ⅛ cup cream. (We use light cream, but heavy cream works just as well.) We give specific amounts of custard for each recipe, but the amount you need may vary, because vegetable sizes vary. Ideally, you want the custard to come ¼ to ⅛ inch from the top edge of the crust. If you have leftover custard, don't worry about it, just dump it, or save it for your next tart if you're going to make another tart in the next few days. And if you happen to need more custard (we don't think you will), that's not a problem either. Just pour in a little bit of cream. Or whip up another whole portion and pour it on in. We use a large measuring cup in place of a bowl when making the custard. The spout on the measuring cup makes it easy to pour the eggs right over the vegetables.

These tarts are done cooking when the custard is "set," which means it is cooked and has firmed up. There are two ways to test this. You can press the center of the tart—because the center is the last part to cook—with your finger to feel whether or not the custard is firm to the touch. This requires you know what firm custard feels like. (Remember Jell-O? It feels like that.) After you make a tart or two, it'll be obvious. The custard will be hot to the touch, so be careful: touch it lightly and quickly. Another way to test whether or not it's set is to shake the pan. If it jiggles, it needs more time.

We have one standard crust, the one with semolina. Occasionally we use a rosemary–whole wheat crust. We call for a particular crust in all our tart recipes, but there's no reason you can't put one filling in another type of crust.

These tarts will keep, refrigerated, for a few days. If you want to make one in advance, you can reheat it. Throw it in a preheated 375-degree oven for 10 minutes or so, right before you're ready to serve it.

DOUGH LESSONS

Making crust can be intimidating to those who haven't done it. A fluted-edge tart crust only makes it more so. But a crust is a crust is a crust. And a crust, no matter what kind of pan it's baked in, is not the least bit difficult to make. Here's how.

I. Cutting Butter (and Shortening) into Flour

Cutting butter and shortening into flour is the first step in making crust and the most important to get right. The hows and whys of cutting butter into flour are what make the difference between a hard, dense crust, what's known as "tough," and a light and flaky crust, what's known as "tender." The key: *keep the ingredients cold and don't overwork them.*

We start out with the butter chilled because when the butter and shortening in your dough melt in the oven as opposed to on your countertop, they cause the flour to form thin layers—what's known to the layman as "flake." A flaky crust is the goal.

We chop the butter into small pieces because small pieces require less working to cut into flour than do big pieces. At this point, we turn to the food processor. There's nothing quite like that fast-moving metal blade and the incremental control of the pulse button for cutting butter and shortening into flour. We use the pulse button so that we don't overmix them. This can happen so quickly, and it's imperative that it not happen. So just pulse.

To get started, dump your flour and salt into the bowl of a food processor fitted with a metal blade, and use the pulse button to evenly distribute the salt. Then add the shortening and butter all at once, and pulse until the butter is no longer visible as butter but has integrated into the flour and looks like what many recipes describe as "coarse meal." We don't know what coarse meal is exactly, so we just want you to know that it will be grainy, like small, wet-looking crumbs. You do not want to mix it until the two form a paste or dough. Take the blade out of the food processor and dump the mixture (you may have to knock it a bit) into a big bowl.

A tart slice served on a plate with a simple salad—Boston lettuce or mesclun tossed with a Dijon vinaigrette—makes a perfect and pretty meal. That's how we offer our tarts at the store, that's how we eat them in our homes, and that's how they've been served in France since, well . . . since the invention of the tart, we suppose.

7

II. Cutting Butter into Flour the Old-Fashioned Way

Making crust is one of the few instances in baking where technology actually works better than Grandma's way. Of course, good crust was around long before the invention of the whirring metal blade. So, if you don't have a food processor, don't give up. Just dump the flour, salt, butter, and shortening into the biggest bowl you have. Then take two table knives and, beginning with the knives crossed in the center like scissors, pull them away from each other toward the edges of the bowl. Repeat this motion until the butter and flour mixture looks like big moist crumbs. This method takes a lot more effort (and more time, during which the butter melts some) than using a food processor, but it works just fine.

III. What's Up with the Ice Water?

Now let's talk about that most mysterious element of crust-making, the ice water. Water is what turns your flour and butter from "moist crumbs" to dough—and the reason for the ice is to keep the butter as cold as possible before it gets into the oven. Some recipes call for a specific amount of ice water. We just ask you to have a glass of it nearby. You'll be adding the water until the dough looks a certain way—and that amount will vary significantly depending on the weather, the flour, and other mysteries of nature that we have yet to identify. You want to add the smallest amount of water necessary to get those crumbs to come together into a ball. For our recipes you'll start by adding 4 tablespoons water (¼ cup). Spoon 1 tablespoon at a time over the pile of crumbs in the big bowl.

To bring the crumbs together into a ball of dough, you can either stir around the edges of the bowl with a wooden spoon, as Frank does, or you can use your hands, like you were making a snowball. Jerome uses his hands. (Jerome uses his hands any chance he gets; he says it makes him feel like a real baker.) The first few times you make tart dough and begin working the ice water into the dry and crumbly flour mixture, you'll swear it will never come together. You'll want to dump more water on it. Resist the temptation. Understand the dough needs to barely come together. Pat it into a ball with your hands. A few crumbs or chunks might even fall off your ball of dough. This is preferable to getting the dough so wet that it's sticky. If it turns white in color or sticks to your fingers, you've put in too much water. This is not the end of the dough-making world. If your dough is too wet, pat a little flour onto the outside. This will dry it out.

Next, put the dough ball on your work surface and cut it in half using a bench knife or any big knife. Roll each half into a ball and wrap each ball in plastic wrap. Press the ball down with the heel of your hand to form a disk. Refrigerate the disks for 30 minutes or more. This allows the butter and shortening to chill, which makes for easier rolling—warm dough clings tenaciously to the rolling pin—and helps the crust hold its shape when it bakes. If you don't chill the dough, the butter and shortening will melt the moment they hit the warm oven, and the crust will flop. A floppy-sided crust is mostly an aesthetic problem, but nice upright edges do allow more filling to be poured into them. We refrigerate our dough overnight, so we're always using "yesterday's" dough.

Our dough recipes make enough to line two 9-inch tart pans. Unless you're making a tart with a lattice top, you'll need only one ball of dough per tart. You can refrigerate the other for 3 to 4 days, or freeze it for 2 months. Move frozen dough to the refrigerator the night before you need it, or leave it on the countertop for a few hours to thaw.

IV. Rolling Out Tart Dough

When you're rolling out tart dough, the goal is to get the dough into a round that's big enough to line both the bottom and the sides of a tart pan—again, without working it too much. We roll our dough to ¼ inch thick. We wouldn't expect you to have a ruler out on the counter, but it might not be a bad idea the first couple of times. Though it's not difficult, if you've never done it before rolling out dough may be a bit awkward.

The ideal surface for rolling out dough is a slab of marble, granite, or stainless steel. Something cool. Of course, whatever kind of kitchen countertops you have will work, as long as they're flat. Get out a bag of flour, toss a handful of it on your work surface, and spread the flour around with your fingers in a light layer. Plunk your disk of dough right down in the center of the flour. If the dough is chilled through, let it rest on the countertop for 10 minutes or so to soften it slightly. Put your hands back in the flour and rub them together, then up and down your rolling pin, so that it's covered with flour, too. Now you're ready to roll.

Holding the pin with both hands, lay it across the disk, and begin rolling outward, from the center toward twelve o'clock, toward one o'clock, two o'clock, three o'clock; then work

toward the left, moving the pin toward eleven o'clock, ten o'clock, nine o'clock. Be gentle with the rolling pin; apply a constant, even pressure. You're not smashing the dough down, but instead letting the dough roll out from the pressure and motion of the pin. You're also not moving back and forth with the pin on the dough. You move outward, pick up the pin, rest it in the center, and move it outward again.

Next, pick up the dough and give it a quarter-turn. (Turning helps you to roll the dough out evenly and keeps the dough from sticking to the work surface.) You'll want to sprinkle some more flour on the counter, the dough, and your rolling pin. Don't be afraid of using too much flour. It's what your dough is made of anyway. And it makes rolling that much easier. If the dough is sticking to the pin or to your work surface, use a pastry cutter to loosen it or sprinkle more flour on your work surface. Roll from the center outward again. Continue to give the dough quarter-turns, rolling it until it's big enough to line the pan and its sides. The finished tart

dough will need to be at least 1½ inches bigger than the tart pan, in order to allow room for the creases and tucks in the sidewall of the pan.

V. Getting Dough into the Tart Pan

To get your nice ¼-inch-thick sheet of dough into your tart pan, first loosely fold it in half. This makes it easier to move without breaking it, and if you want to fold it again, into quarters, you can do that, too. Take your dough and place it in the center of the tart pan, with the folded side across the center of the pan. Unfold the dough so that it is now lying in and hanging over the edges of your tart pan.

Next, you need to fit the dough into the pan. You'll need to use both hands: one to lift the dough and the other to press the dough (probably with your thumb) into the creases and fluted edges of the pan. Do this until you work your way around the perimeter of the pan.

When you're finished, you will have tart dough fitted against the bottom and sides of the pan and also flapping over

its sides. Pinch the excess flaps of dough off between your thumb and forefinger. Now your tart shell is officially prepared. Place your prepared tart shell in the refrigerator for at least ½ hour. Otherwise the sides of your tart shell will collapse when you bake your tart.

You can save any extra bits of dough to decorate the top (using "sugared pastry leaves," as on the Pumpkin Tart on page 227). Or roll the dough into sticks about 4 inches long; twist and sprinkle them with a lot of sugar, or cinnamon and sugar, and bake 10 minutes or so, until they're golden brown. They're delicious with ice cream.

VI. Making a Lattice Top
We use a lattice crust when we want to dress up a less-than-attractive (but tasty, of course!) filling.

To make a lattice, roll a ball of dough out onto a sheet of parchment paper to ¼ inch thick and until it is roughly 9 inches in diameter. Refrigerate for at least 30 minutes while you assemble your tart. If you don't have room in your refrig-

erator for a big sheet of rolled-out dough, loosely fold it in half or into quarters.

When you're ready to make the lattice, take the dough out of the refrigerator and lay it, parchment side up, on a floured countertop. Peel the parchment away, and cut strips ¾ inch wide using a pastry cutter or a small knife. Lay the dough strips in parallel lines with a 1-inch space between them. Lay another set of strips at a 60-degree angle to the first set of strips. (You could do it at any angle you wanted to; we just happen to like the argyle look of the 60-degree angle.) For a proper lattice crust, the strips are woven, under-over-under-over. So do that if you want, but be forewarned: it's tricky, and it will take a lot more time. We don't think it makes a big enough difference, so we forgo the weaving.

VII. Par-Baking Tart Shells
Every one of our savory tarts calls for a par-baked crust, which refers to the fact that it's partially baked. Par-baking ensures that the crust will be nice and crispy when the tart is

done. The fillings themselves don't need to be baked for as long as the crust does, so par-baking essentially gives the crust a head start.

To par-bake a crust, pierce the dough in your lined tart pan with the tines of a fork. This keeps the crust from puffing up when it's baked. Then place a sheet of aluminum foil or parchment paper on top of the dough. Next, weigh the dough down, also to prevent the crust from puffing up. Specialty stores sell little metal or ceramic "pie weights" made just for this purpose, but since we're not into one-task tools, we keep a big jar of dried garbanzo beans around for this purpose. (You can use the beans again and again as weights, but, no, you can't eat them once they've been used this way.) Place the tart shell on the center rack in the oven, and bake for 10 minutes at 400 degrees. Remove the pan from the oven, and remove weights and foil or parchment paper. Return the tart shell to the oven and bake for another 5–10 minutes, or until the floor of the tart shell looks and feels dry.

VIII. Getting the Tart out of the Pan

We like to remove the tarts from their pans about 10 minutes after taking them out of the oven, to give them time to cool slightly. We wouldn't even think about using tart pans without removable bottoms. Getting the tarts out of the pans in one piece is our main priority. And removable-bottom pans make this easy and eliminate pretty much all the risk. At the store, we place the tart on what in professional kitchens is known as a number 10 can. It's a big, giant can, bigger than any can you'd ever want in your house but smaller than a tart pan. At home, we like to use a big can of tomatoes. With the tart up on the can, we pull the sides of the pan down around it (like a hula hoop falling off the hips) and then slide the tart off the bottom portion of the pan and onto a rimless serving dish or a cutting board. We do the same thing at home, substituting any big can or a sturdy glass for the number 10 can. If the tart seems to be sticking to the bottom, it's probably because the filling has leaked out of the crust and hardened between the crust and the pan. If you remove the tart from the pan while it's still warm, you'll avoid this problem altogether. Otherwise, take the biggest knife you have—it doesn't need to be sharp—and slide it between the two to cut the sticky stuff away.

Crunchy Savory Tart Crust

MAKES ENOUGH FOR TWO 9-INCH TART CRUSTS

For more detailed method, see Dough Lessons (page 6).

1. Position oven racks so that one is in the center and preheat oven to 400 degrees.
2. Put the flours and salt in the bowl of a food processor fitted with a metal blade, and pulse a couple of times just to integrate the flours and salt.
3. Add the butter and shortening all at once and pulse quite a few times, until the mixture forms little balls, like moist crumbs, and no chunks of butter or shortening remain. You have to pulse, not *run,* the food processor. The worst thing that can happen at this stage of the crust-making game is for the flours and fats to come together into a paste.
4. Remove the blade from the food processor and dump the dough crumbs into a big bowl. Fill a tablespoon with ice water and sprinkle over the surface of the dough. Repeat with 3 more tablespoonsful.
5. Use your hands or a wooden spoon to bring the dough together into a ball, adding more water if needed, 1 tablespoon at a time. The dough should be just past crumbly, but holding together. You don't want it to be so wet that it sticks together or turns white in color.
6. Cut the dough in half, and wrap each half in plastic wrap. Press each half with the palm of your hand to form a disk. Refrigerate at least 30 minutes before rolling out.
7. Roll out 1 disk of dough to ¼ inch thick. Fit it into your tart pan (see Dough Lessons, page 10) and chill for 30 minutes. Then use the tines of a fork to prick holes over the bottom of the tart. Line the dough with parchment paper or aluminum foil, and weigh down with pie weights or dried beans.
8. Place the tart shell on the center rack in the oven, and bake for 10 minutes. Remove the paper and weights from the pan. Return it to the oven, and bake

2½ cups unbleached all-purpose flour

3 tablespoons semolina flour

1 teaspoon salt

12 tablespoons (1½ sticks) cold unsalted butter, cut into ¼-inch cubes

3 tablespoons cold solid vegetable shortening

A glass of ice water

until the crust is golden brown and toasted all over, 5–10 more minutes for a par-baked tart shell. For a fully baked tart shell, bake for another 15 minutes at 400 degrees or until it's golden brown all over. Remove the tart shell from the oven and set it on a wire rack to cool.

Rosemary–Whole Wheat Tart Crust

MAKES ENOUGH FOR TWO 9-INCH TART CRUSTS

2 cups unbleached all-purpose flour
½ cup whole wheat flour
1 teaspoon salt
12 tablespoons (1½ sticks) cold unsalted butter, cut into ¼-inch cubes
3 tablespoons cold solid vegetable shortening
1 tablespoon chopped fresh rosemary
A glass of ice water

Prepare crust using the method for the Crunchy Savory Tart Crust (above). Sprinkle the rosemary over the moist crumbs after you've cut the butter into the flour.

Provençal Tart with Gruyère and Herbes de Provence

MAKES ONE 9-INCH TART

12–15 plum tomatoes (2½ pounds), cored and cut into ¼-inch-thick rounds

2 tablespoons Dijon mustard

1 par-baked 9-inch Crunchy Savory Tart Crust (page 15)

1 cup coarsely grated Gruyère cheese

1 teaspoon *herbes de Provence*

2 large eggs

¼ cup light cream

1 teaspoon salt

A few turns of freshly ground black pepper

This is our idea of good picnic food. We use plum tomatoes for this tart; of the tomatoes available year-round, they're the best. They also tend to be less watery, which is important when you're making a tart. Any tasty tomato will work as long as you let the slices sit in a colander to drain.

1. Position your oven racks so that one is in the center, and preheat the oven to 375 degrees.
2. Put the tomato slices in a colander, and place it in the sink. Let the tomatoes sit for 15 minutes to drain off any excess liquid.
3. Spread the mustard evenly over the tart shell with a rubber spatula or the back of a spoon. Sprinkle the cheese over the mustard, and sprinkle the *herbes de Provence* over the cheese.
4. Working from the outside in, lay the drained tomato slices in overlapping concentric circles, making sure the crust is covered entirely.
5. Whisk the eggs in a small bowl, or a large measuring cup with a spout, to break up the egg yolks. Whisk in the cream, salt, and pepper. This is your custard. Pour the custard evenly over the tomatoes until it comes to about ¼ inch from the top edge of the crust. (If you have extra, don't worry about it; if you don't have enough, pour a little cream on top.)
6. Place the tart on the center rack in the oven, and bake for 1 hour to 1 hour and 20 minutes, or until the custard is set. Set custard won't jiggle when you shake the pan and will be firm when you touch it. (The custard will also be hot, so touch it lightly.) The tomatoes in this tart may give off a lot of liquid; don't con-

fuse this with uncooked eggs and accidentally overcook your tart. The liquid will evaporate as the tart cools.

7. Remove the tart from the oven and set it on a wire rack. Allow the tart to cool slightly.

8. To remove the tart from the pan, rest it on a big can. Make sure the tart is steady and balanced. Slide the outside ring of the pan down off the tart. Then place the tart on your work surface, and slide it off the bottom of the pan and onto a rimless serving dish or a cutting board. Serve warm or at room temperature.

Before we do anything else, we slice our tomatoes. We always use a serrated knife. It makes it easier to get perfect rounds.

What is Herbes de Provence?

Herbes de Provence is a combination of herbs used in the south of France for cooking. The herbs include basil, fennel seed, lavender, marjoram, rosemary, sage, summer savory, and thyme. You can buy the combination here in cute little clay containers (usually imported from Provence, where they have a thing for pottery). The herbs give roasted meats and vegetables a very specific French flavor that you'll probably recognize when you use them. If you don't have *herbes de Provence* and you don't feel like buying it, use a combination of the herbs you do have. Just note that thyme, rosemary, marjoram, and basil (all dried) are the most prominent flavors you're looking for.

Granny's Tomato Tart

A traditional tomato tart in France does not contain custard. Jerome's grandmother used to make them often in the summer. In fact, she wouldn't think about making one at any other time. In the small town in the south of France where she lives, there is still such a thing as a season for fruits and vegetables. Nowadays you might find a tomato there in December, but not one Granny would use.

To make a tomato tart the way Granny does, roll out a full recipe of dough and fit it into an 8-by-10-inch rectangular sheet pan. Prick the bottom with the tines of a fork. Fully bake the crust: 10–15 minutes at 400 degrees with the weights in, and another 15–20 minutes after you've removed the weights. Remove the crust from the oven, and let it cool to room temperature. Spread Dijon mustard in a thin layer over the bottom of the crust. Grate Gruyère cheese in a thin layer over the mustard. Slice about 4 pounds of plum tomatoes, and put them in a colander set in the sink to drain off any excess liquid. Arrange the tomatoes in one layer, like rows of fallen dominoes, down the length of the crust. Sprinkle with *herbes de Provence,* and bake the tart in a 400-degree oven until the tomatoes begin to shrivel and the cheese melts, about 10 minutes.

Frank's Tomato Tart

Frank often makes Granny's tart on weekends in the country when he can't find enough ways to use up all the tomatoes he's grown in his kitchen garden.

Sometimes he spreads the crust with Basil Pesto (page 164) instead of mustard, changes the cheese to grated smoked mozzarella, and uses fresh basil or parsley instead of the *herbes de Provence.* Tarts are flexible. They're really just a platform for good ingredients. And good ideas.

Zucchini Tart with Curried Custard and Dried Currants

4 medium zucchini (1¾ pounds),
sliced into ¼-inch-thick rounds

2 tablespoons olive oil

2 garlic cloves, peeled and minced
(page 23)

Salt and freshly ground black
pepper (for the zucchini)

½ cup dried currants

1 par-baked 9-inch Crunchy Savory
Tart Crust (page 15)

2 large eggs

¼ cup light cream

½ teaspoon salt

A few turns of freshly ground black
pepper

1 tablespoon Madras curry powder

Jerome served a version of this at his original Tarte Margot in France. Curry is not very common in France, but he was inspired by a curried meat pie he tasted at the English tea shop in Avignon, the town where he grew up. Zucchini is probably the blandest vegetable grown. It takes on the flavor of whatever it's cooked with, so it's a good one to combine with curry. The sweet dried currants in this recipe bring out the curry flavor.

1. Position your oven racks so that one is in the center, and preheat the oven to 450 degrees.
2. Toss the zucchini with the olive oil, garlic, a sprinkling of salt (¼ teaspoon), and a few turns of freshly ground black pepper in a big bowl. Spread the zucchini out on a sheet pan, and bake until the zucchini soften a bit and begin to brown, about 10 minutes. Be careful not to cook them so much that they fall apart. Remove the pan from the oven, and lower the oven temperature to 375. Allow the zucchini to cool to room temperature on the sheet pan before assembling the tart. Otherwise their heat will cook the eggs, and you'll end up with scrambled eggs in your tart shell.
3. Sprinkle the currants evenly over the tart shell. Arrange the cooled zucchini slices in the tart shell by placing them in overlapping concentric circles. Work from the outside in, packing the zucchini slices as tightly as you can, and making sure the crust is covered entirely.
4. Whisk the eggs in a small bowl, or a large measuring cup with a spout, to break up the yolks. Whisk in the cream, salt, pepper, and curry powder. This is your

custard. Pour the custard evenly over the zucchini slices until it comes to about ¼ inch from the top edge of the crust.

5. Place the tart on the center rack in the oven and bake for 1 hour, or until the custard is set. Set custard won't jiggle when you shake the pan and will feel firm when you touch it. (It will also be hot, so touch it lightly and quickly.)

6. Remove the tart from the oven and set it on a wire rack. Allow the tart to cool slightly.

7. To remove the tart from the pan, rest it on a big can. Make sure the tart is steady and balanced. Slide the outside ring of the pan down off the tart. Then place the tart on your work surface, and slide it off the bottom of the pan and onto a rimless serving dish or a cutting board. Serve warm or at room temperature.

How to Deal with Garlic

We don't use a garlic press. It's just one more kitchen gadget to have around and to have to find. Besides, we hate the idea of cleaning it. Do you use a toothbrush to get that stuff out of there? Garlic is so easy to chop by hand. Cut off the root end of the garlic. Place a big chef's knife on its side over the garlic clove and slam down on the knife with the heel of your hand. You now have what we refer to in these recipes as "smashed" garlic. The smashing breaks the garlic into little pieces and makes it easy to slip the skin right off. This is how Frank's grandmother did it—only she used a big can to smash it. We take smashed garlic cloves and sometimes use them just like that, as in some recipes for sautéed vegetables. This gives you the surface area to impart lots of garlic flavor to the oil without the risk of burning, or even browning, the garlic, which makes it bitter. "Coarsely chopped" garlic means you take the smashed garlic clove and give it a few runs with a knife in either direction. "Minced" garlic means you give it a few more runs with the knife in both directions. It's crude compared with the tiny, perfect mince, the product of meticulous knife skills you might see in a professional French kitchen. But it's minced enough for us.

"I've never measured ground pepper in my life. I wouldn't even know how. I only use pepper from a peppermill—how are you supposed to grind that into a tiny measuring spoon? Grind the pepper mill over your food until it has the amount of pepper you want it to have."
—Jerome

Sautéed Spinach-and-Mushroom Tart with Ricotta Cheese

MAKES ONE 9-INCH TART

½ recipe raw dough for Crunchy Savory Tart Crust (page 15), chilled (for the lattice top)

2 tablespoons unsalted butter

2 tablespoons olive oil

1 pound fresh spinach (or 1 box defrosted frozen spinach, drained in a colander, excess water squeezed out)

3 garlic cloves, peeled and minced (page 23)

½ pound white mushrooms, cleaned, trimmed, and thinly sliced (page 25)

2 large eggs

¼ cup light cream

1 cup ricotta cheese

½ cup grated Pecorino or Parmesan cheese

½ teaspoon nutmeg

⅛ teaspoon crushed red-pepper flakes   *continued*

We added cheese to this tart in an effort to convince people it was some kind of French pizza. We're not sure if our reasoning worked, but people bought the tarts anyway, and they came back for more. We cover this tart with a lattice crust to hide the sautéed spinach, which tastes a lot better than it looks.

1. Position your oven racks so that one is in the center, and preheat the oven to 375 degrees.

2. Roll the chilled dough out on a sheet of parchment paper. Roll it into a round that is at least 9 inches in diameter and ¼ inch thick. Refrigerate the dough for at least 30 minutes.

3. Heat 1 tablespoon of the butter and 1 tablespoon of the olive oil together in a large sauté pan over high heat. Add the fresh spinach a handful at a time (because it won't all fit in the pan at first), stirring as you go. Keep adding the spinach, stirring so that it cooks evenly, until all the spinach is wilted and dark green. Remove the pan from the heat, and dump the spinach into a big bowl.

4. Lower the heat to medium, and return the pan to the stove. Heat the rest of the butter and olive oil with the chopped garlic until the garlic becomes translucent. (Don't overcook the garlic or it will become bitter.) Add the sliced mushrooms, and sauté them for 5 minutes, until they look glossy and dark, like sautéed mushrooms you'd want to eat by the forkful. Remove the mushrooms from the heat, and toss them in the bowl with the spinach.

5. Whisk the eggs in a small bowl, or a large measuring cup with a spout, to break up the yolks. Whisk in the cream, cheeses, nutmeg, red-pepper flakes, salt, and

pepper. This is your custard. Stir the custard into the bowl with the spinach and mushrooms until it is evenly distributed. Spoon this filling into the tart shell, using a rubber spatula to get it all out of the bowl. Use the spatula to level off the filling in the tart shell.

6. Take the rolled-out dough from the refrigerator and lay it, parchment side up, on a floured work surface. Peel off the parchment paper. Using a pastry cutter, a pizza cutter, or a small knife, cut the dough into ¾-inch-wide strips.

7. To make the lattice top, lay the strips in parallel lines with 1-inch spaces between them. Lay another set of strips in the opposite direction. (We do it at a 60-degree angle, because we like the way it looks.) Tuck the ends of the lattice strips into the filling where it meets the edges of the tart. Using a pastry brush or a scrunched-up paper towel, brush the crust with egg wash.

8. Place the tart on the center rack in the oven, and bake it for 1 hour to 1 hour and 10 minutes, until the filling is puffed up and firm to the touch and the lattice is golden brown.

9. Remove the tart from the oven and set it on a wire rack. Allow the tart to cool slightly.

10. To remove the tart from the pan, rest it on a big can. Make sure the tart is steady and balanced. Slide the outside ring of the pan down off the tart. Then place the tart on your work surface and slide it off the bottom of the pan and onto a rimless serving dish or a cutting board. Serve warm or at room temperature.

1 teaspoon salt
A few turns of freshly ground black pepper
1 par-baked 9-inch Crunchy Savory Tart Crust (page 15)

FOR THE EGG WASH
1 egg whisked with 1 tablespoon cream or milk

How to Clean a Mushroom

Mushrooms are like sponges—they'll get soggy or heavy if you wash them. We use a damp towel or paper towel to wipe them down. There are things called "mushroom brushes," too. We never use them. A towel works just as well. We cut off the very ends of mushroom stems, because they tend to be dry and filled with dirt. But otherwise we use the stems. There's no reason not to. They taste the same as any other part of the mushroom.

Roasted-Potato Tart with Fresh Tarragon, Sautéed Mushrooms, and Melted Gruyère

MAKES ONE 9-INCH TART

1 pound red-skinned potatoes (4
  medium-size), well scrubbed,
  cut into ½-inch disks
½ big yellow onion, diced fine
¼ cup olive oil
2 garlic cloves, peeled and minced
  (page 23)
Salt and freshly ground black
  pepper (for roasting)
1 par-baked 9-inch Crunchy Savory
  Tart Crust (page 15)
2 teaspoons chopped fresh tarragon
  leaves (page 162)
4 large eggs
½ cup (4 ounces) light cream
1 teaspoon salt
A few turns of freshly ground black
  pepper
1½–1¼ pound white mushrooms or
  mix of white and wild mushrooms, cleaned, trimmed, and
  thinly sliced (page 25)
½ cup grated Gruyère cheese or
  your favorite sharp melting
  cheese (such as cheddar)

We think of this as an omelet in a tart shell, what with the potatoes, mushrooms, cheese, and eggs. It's important to cut the potatoes thin, so that you don't bite into a whole chunk of potato with nothing around it to give it flavor. At home, Frank substitutes wild mushrooms, such as shiitakes or chanterelles, for half of the white mushrooms.

1. Position your oven racks so that one is in the center, and preheat the oven to 450 degrees.

2. Toss the potatoes and onion with half of the olive oil, the garlic, a sprinkling of salt (¼ teaspoon), and a few turns of freshly ground black pepper. Spread the potatoes and onion out on a sheet pan, and roast them until the onion is translucent and the potatoes are golden brown and tender to the

bite or when pierced with a fork, about 15–20 minutes. Remove the sheet pan from the oven and allow the vegetables to cool slightly. Reduce the oven temperature to 375.

3. Sprinkle the tart shell with the chopped tarragon. Scrape the cooled potatoes and onion evenly into the tart shell.

4. Whisk the eggs in a small bowl, or a large measuring cup with a spout, to break

up the yolks. Whisk in the cream, salt, and pepper. This is your custard. Pour the custard over the potatoes and onion until it comes to within ¼ inch from the top edge of the crust.

5. Place the tart on the center rack in the oven, and bake for 55 minutes to 1 hour, or until the custard is set. Set custard won't jiggle when you shake it and will feel firm to the touch. (It will also feel hot, so touch it quickly and lightly.)

6. While the tart is baking, warm the remaining olive oil in a large sauté pan over high heat until the oil is almost at smoking point. Add the mushrooms, and stir to coat them with the oil. Sauté the mushrooms, stirring (or tossing, if you're that kind of cook) occasionally, for 5–10 minutes, until mushrooms are glossy and dark. Then sprinkle with salt and stir again. Remove the pan from the heat.

7. Remove the tart from the oven. While the tart is still warm, sprinkle the cheese evenly over the tart filling.

8. Dump the mushrooms on top of the cheese, and use your fingers or a fork to spread them in an even blanket over the cheese.

9. Return the tart to the oven, and bake it until the cheese just melts, 5–10 minutes.

10. Remove the tart from the oven and set it on a wire rack. Allow the tart to cool slightly.

11. To remove the tart from the pan, rest it on a big can. Make sure the tart is steady and balanced. Slide the outside ring of the pan down off the tart. Then place the tart on your work surface and slide it off the bottom of the pan and onto a rimless serving dish or a cutting board. Serve warm or at room temperature.

"I always cook red potatoes with tarragon. My mom uses it with chicken. A lot of herbs are only flavorful if you eat the herb itself. If you cook something with tarragon, though, the whole dish is flavored with tarragon. You have to be careful not to use too much."
—Jerome

"Gruyère is a specific kind of Swiss cheese. It happens to be my favorite. I find it nuttier, sweeter, just better than any other Swiss. None of the recipes that call for Gruyère would suffer because you used another Swiss, like Emmentaler."
—Frank

Caramelized-Leek-and-Celery Tart

MAKES ONE 9-INCH TART

½ recipe raw dough for Crunchy Savory Tart Crust (page 15), chilled (for the lattice top)

2 tablespoons unsalted butter

2 tablespoons olive oil

6 leeks (2 pounds), whites and light-green parts only, washed and sliced into ¼-inch-thick rounds (page 29)

1 teaspoon ground ginger

6 celery stalks, cut into ¼-inch slices

3 large eggs

⅜ cup (3 ounces) light cream

2 tablespoons French-Style Grainy Mustard (page 161, or from a jar)

1 teaspoon salt

½ teaspoon freshly ground black pepper

1 par-baked 9-inch Crunchy Savory Tart Crust (page 15)

continued

This is our version of a classic leek tart from Belgium, called a *flamiche,* with celery added for crunch. It's one of our favorite tarts. A lot of people are unfamiliar with leeks—they're basically big mild onions that, when cooked like these are, just melt in your mouth. Powdered ginger has a nice, spicy sort of taste that heightens the flavor of the leeks in this tart.

1. Position your oven racks so that one is in the center, and preheat the oven to 375 degrees.

2. Roll the chilled dough out on a sheet of parchment paper. Roll it into a round that is at least 9 inches in diameter and ¼ inch thick. Refrigerate the dough for at least 30 minutes.

3. Heat 1 tablespoon of the butter and 1 tablespoon of the olive oil in a large sauté pan over high heat. Add the leeks. When the leeks begin to wilt slightly (after about 5 minutes), reduce the heat to medium and continue to sauté the leeks for about an hour, until they are tender and caramelized. Stir the leeks occasionally to keep them from sticking to the bottom and burning. You may need to splash a little water over the leeks—this basically buys you cooking time. Add the ginger, and continue cooking for a few more minutes to integrate the flavors. Remove the pan from the heat, and let the vegetables cool to room temperature. Dump the leeks into a large mixing bowl, and wipe the pan clean.

4. In the same pan, sauté the celery in the remaining butter and olive oil over high heat until the celery is tender and translucent. Add the celery to the bowl with the leeks. Allow the celery and leeks to cool to room temperature.

5. Whisk the eggs in a small bowl, or a large measuring cup with a spout, to break up the yolks. Whisk in the cream, mustard, salt, and pepper. This is your cus-

tard. Stir the custard into the bowl with the cooled leeks and celery, and use a rubber spatula to scrape this filling into your tart shell.

6. Take the rolled-out dough from the refrigerator and lay it, parchment side up, on a floured work surface. Peel the parchment off the dough. Using a pastry cutter, a pizza cutter, or a small knife, cut the dough into ¾-inch-wide strips.

7. To make the lattice top, lay the strips in parallel lines with a 1-inch space between them. Lay another set of strips in the opposite direction. (We do it at a 60-degree angle because we like the way it looks). Tuck the ends of the lattice strips into the filling where it meets the edges of the tart. Using a pastry brush or a scrunched-up paper towel, brush the crust with egg wash.

8. Place the tart on the center rack in the oven, and bake for about 40 minutes, or until the lattice is golden brown and the filling is puffed up and firm to the touch.

9. Remove the tart from the oven, and set it on a wire rack to cool slightly.

10. To remove the tart from the pan, rest it on a big can. Make sure the tart is steady and balanced. Slide the outside ring of the pan down off the tart. Then place the tart on your work surface and slide it off the bottom of the pan and onto a rimless serving dish or a cutting board. Serve warm or at room temperature.

FOR THE EGG WASH
1 large egg whisked with 1 tablespoon cream or milk

How to Wash a Leek

You have to wash leeks very thoroughly. They grow in dirt, after all. And they consist of tight concentric rings. So dirt that gets in there really stays in there, unless . . . The best way to get the grit out of your leeks is to slice them into rounds, from just above the root end to the top, then soak them in a sink (or a large bowl) full of cold water. Use your fingers to separate the rings. Then let them rest. The dirt will fall to the bottom. Scoop the leeks out with your hands (or run them through a colander), and repeat the process until you are no longer finding sand at the bottom of your sink (or bowl).

What Exactly Does "Caramelize" Mean?

Caramelization is a process wherein you cook something, like a vegetable, to within an inch of its vegetable life. The said vegetable breaks down and releases sugar, thereby becoming sweet. Thus the word "caramel" in "caramelize." You can caramelize things to different degrees. When you sauté onions for 10 minutes, they're already sweeter. That's on the road to caramelizing. But if you continue for an hour, what you end up with is brown and gooey, and the onions themselves almost melted—like a jam or chutney. That is caramelized. Basically, when you're caramelizing, you can't cook the vegetables too long. But you want to make sure not to burn them. That's a different taste altogether.

29

Roasted Red Pepper Tart with Black Olive Tapenade and Parmesan Cheese

MAKES ONE 9-INCH TART

6 red bell peppers, julienned (page 152)

1 big yellow onion, quartered and sliced thin

2 garlic cloves, peeled and minced (page 23)

2 tablespoons olive oil

Salt and freshly ground black pepper (for roasting)

3 tablespoons Black Olive Tapenade (page 169) or black olive paste from a jar

1 par-baked 9-inch Crunchy Savory Tart Crust (page 15)

¼ cup grated Parmesan cheese

2 large eggs

¼ cup light cream

1 teaspoon salt

A few turns of freshly ground black pepper

½ cup whole fresh basil leaves, cut into thin strips (page 162)

Of all our tarts, this one has the densest flavor. Jerome claims it's too rich. Frank doesn't believe there's any such thing.

1. Position your oven racks so that one is in the center, and preheat the oven to 450 degrees.
2. Toss the peppers in a big bowl with the onion, garlic, olive oil, a sprinkling of salt (¼ teaspoon), and a few turns of freshly ground black pepper. Scatter the vegetables onto a sheet pan, and roast for about 40–50 minutes, until the edges of the peppers begin to blacken. (If you find the peppers cooking unevenly, move them around with a metal spatula or by shaking the pan.)
3. Remove the peppers and onion from the oven, and use a metal spatula to scrape them (including any pan scraps and juices) into a medium-size bowl. Allow the peppers and onions to cook. Lower the oven temperature to 350.
4. Spread the tapenade evenly over the tart shell with a rubber spatula. Sprinkle the cheese evenly over the tapenade.
5. Whisk the eggs in a small bowl, or a large measuring cup with a spout, to break up the yolks. Whisk in the cream, salt, pepper, and half of the basil. This is your custard. Stir the custard into the bowl with the peppers and onions, and use a rubber spatula to scrape this filling into your tart shell. Place the tart in the oven, and bake for 50–55 minutes, or until custard is set. Set custard won't jiggle when you shake the pan and will be firm to the touch. (It will also be hot, so touch it lightly and quickly.)
6. Remove the tart from the oven and set it on a wire rack. Allow the tart to cool slightly.

7. To remove the tart from the pan, rest it on a big can. Make sure the tart is steady and balanced. Slide the outside ring of the pan down off the tart. Then place the tart on your work surface and slide it off the bottom of the pan and onto a rimless serving dish or a cutting board.

8. Sprinkle the tart with the remaining basil. Serve warm or at room temperature.

Roasted-Eggplant-and-Tomato Tart with Basil

MAKES ONE 9-INCH TART

1 large or 2 small eggplants or
    Japanese eggplants (1 pound),
    cut into ¼-inch-thick rounds
Salt (for sweating the eggplant)
2 garlic cloves, peeled and minced
    (page 23)
2 tablespoons olive oil
A few turns of freshly ground black
    pepper, plus more for the
    custard
8 or 9 plum tomatoes (1½ pounds),
    cored and cut into ¼-inch-thick
    rounds
¼ cup grated Parmesan cheese
¼ cup whole fresh basil leaves,
    plus ¼ cup fresh basil leaves cut
    into thin strips (to top the tart)
    (page 162)
1 par-baked 9-inch Crunchy Savory
    Tart Crust (page 15)
2 large eggs
¼ cup light cream
1 teaspoon salt

This is one of Jerome's recipes from Tarte Margot. We often substitute a pound of zucchini, sliced ¼ inch thin, for the eggplant in this tart.

1. Position your oven racks so that one is in the center, and preheat the oven to 450 degrees.
2. Put the eggplant slices in a colander, and place the colander in the sink. Sprinkle the eggplant with a generous coat of salt. Toss so that the salt coats all sides of the eggplant. Let the eggplant rest for at least 20 minutes to sweat the bitterness out (page 38).
3. After sweating, toss the eggplant slices in a medium-size bowl with the garlic, olive oil, and a few turns of freshly ground black pepper. Spread the eggplant slices on a sheet pan, and roast for about 10–15 minutes, until they begin to brown. The slices should be firm enough to hold their shape. Remove the sheet pan from the oven. Allow the eggplant slices to cool to room temperature.
4. While the eggplant is roasting, put the tomato slices in the colander and place the colander in the sink. Let the tomatoes sit for 15 minutes to drain off any excess liquid.
5. Reduce the oven temperature to 350 degrees.
6. Dump the cheese and the whole basil leaves into the bowl of a food processor (or a blender) fitted with a metal blade, and pulse until the basil is finely chopped. Using a rubber spatula, spread the basil-cheese paste evenly over the bottom of the tart shell.
7. Working from the outside in, arrange the vegetable slices—alternating between eggplant and tomato—in overlapping concentric circles in a "camellia" pat-

tern. Use the smaller pieces of eggplant or tomato to fill in any gaps, so that the crust is totally covered.

8. Whisk the eggs in a small bowl, or a large measuring cup with a spout, to break up the yolks. Whisk in the cream, salt, and pepper. This is your custard. Pour the custard over the vegetables until it comes to about ¼ inch from the top edge of the crust.

9. Place the tart in the oven, and bake for about an hour and 10 minutes, or until the custard is set. Set custard is firm to the touch and doesn't jiggle when you shake the pan. (The custard will be hot, so touch it lightly and quickly.)

10. Remove the tart from the oven, and set it on a wire rack. Allow the tart to cool slightly.

11. To remove the tart from the pan, rest it on a big can. Make sure the tart is steady and balanced. Slide the outside ring of the pan down off the tart. Then place the tart on your work surface and slide it off the bottom of the pan and onto a rimless serving dish or a cutting board. Sprinkle the thin strips of basil over the tart. Serve warm or at room temperature.

Sweet-Onion Tart with Black Olives in a Rosemary–Whole Wheat Crust

MAKES ONE 9-INCH TART

4 big yellow onions (3½ pounds),
  quartered and cut into ¼-inch
  slices
3 tablespoons olive oil
2 tablespoons Black Olive Tapenade
  (page 169) or black olive paste
  from a jar
1 large egg
⅛ cup light cream
1 teaspoon salt
½ teaspoon freshly ground black
  pepper
1 par-baked 9-inch
  Rosemary–Whole Wheat Tart
  Crust (page 16)
½ cup black olives (such as Moroccan oil-cured)

We really have to push this tart on our new customers. People have a hard time getting past the idea of a mouthful of onions. But, in fact, the onions in this tart are cooked to the point where they are sweet, almost like a chutney. They lose that who-will-kiss-me? onion quality entirely.

1. Position your oven racks so that one is in the center, and preheat the oven to 375 degrees.
2. Sauté the onions in the olive oil in a large sauté pan over high heat for 5–10 minutes, stirring often so they don't stick to the pan. Once they have reduced slightly and begun to soften and wilt, lower the heat to medium and continue cooking for about an hour, stirring occasionally, until the onions are browned and so soft they're almost melted (you may need to add ¼ cup of water to the pan occasionally to prevent the onions from burning or sticking to the bottom of the pan).
3. Remove the pan from the heat. Stir in the tapenade and allow the onions to cool.
4. Whisk the egg in a small bowl, or a large measuring cup with a spout, to break up the yolk. Whisk in the cream, salt, and pepper. This is your custard. Stir the custard into the pan with the cooled onions, and dump this filling into your tart shell, using a spatula or wooden spoon to get it all out and then to level out the filling in the tart shell.
5. Place the tart in the oven, and bake for 40–45 minutes, until the filling is set (firm to the touch) and very dark in color.

6. Remove the tart from the oven and set it on a wire rack. Allow the tart to cool slightly.
7. Pit the olives by pressing them between your fingers. The pit will break right through the olive and pop out. Slice the olives coarsely.
8. To remove the tart from the pan, rest it on a big can. Make sure the tart is steady and balanced. Slide the outside ring of the pan down off the tart. Then place the tart on your work surface and slide it off the bottom of the pan and onto a rimless serving dish or a cutting board. Sprinkle the sliced olives over the top of the tart. Serve warm or at room temperature.

Jerome's Caramelized Red Onions

One of my favorite vegetables is red onions, caramelized. To make them, I leave the skins on. I cut the onions in half, pour olive oil and red-wine vinegar over the onion halves, sprinkle them with salt, and put them on a sheet pan. I roast the onions in a 450-degree oven for $\frac{1}{2}$ hour, until they're starting to blacken in places. When they come out, they are so beautiful, and they're almost melted inside, like roasted eggplant. You can serve the halves just like that, with a nice steak. But usually what I do is cut each half into $\frac{1}{2}$-inch-thick slices and put them in salads or sandwiches.

Roasted-Ratatouille Tart with Herbes de Provence

Ratatouille is a classic Provençal dish made of a very Provençal combination of vegetables—eggplant, tomatoes, red peppers, zucchini, onions, and garlic—cooked so long and so slowly that the vegetables melt into one rich dish. For this tart, we cook the vegetables separately, because we have this idea that if you cook them separately you will taste the individual flavors more intensely. Ideally, you'll have more than one sheet pan so you can roast different vegetables at the same time.

1. Position your oven racks so that one is in the center, and preheat the oven to 450 degrees.
2. Put the eggplant in a colander and sprinkle it with a generous coat of salt. Toss so that the salt coats all sides of the eggplant. Place the colander in the sink and let eggplant rest for at least 20 minutes to sweat the bitterness out (page 38).
3. Toss the zucchini and yellow squash in a big bowl with a tablespoon of olive oil, a sprinkling of salt (¼ teaspoon), a few twists of freshly ground black pepper, and one-third of the garlic. Dump the zucchini and squash onto a sheet pan and spread them out evenly. Roast them until they begin to brown, 8–10 minutes. Remove the pan from the oven and, using a metal spatula, scrape the zucchini, squash, and pan scraps and juices off the sheet pan and back into another bowl. (You don't need to let the vegetables cool before scraping them off the pan. We do that when we want to keep vegetable pieces intact; in ratatouille, they'll fall apart anyway. Besides, you need the pan.) Toss the tomatoes in the first bowl with a tablespoon of olive oil, a sprinkling of salt, a few twists of freshly ground

1 large eggplant, diced (page 119)

Salt (for "sweating" the eggplant) and freshly ground black pepper (for roasting the vegetables)

1 zucchini, quartered lengthwise and cut into 1-inch pieces

1 yellow squash, quartered lengthwise and cut into 1-inch pieces

¼ cup olive oil

8 garlic cloves, peeled and minced (page 23)

4 plum tomatoes, core removed, quartered lengthwise, and cut into 1-inch pieces

1 red bell pepper, cut into 1-inch cubes (page 117)

1 small red onion, diced fine

1 teaspoon *herbes de Provence* (page 19)

2 large eggs

¼ cup light cream

1 par-baked 9-inch Crunchy Savory Tart Crust (page 15)

How to Deal with Eggplant

Prepared correctly, eggplant is creamy and delicious. Prepared incorrectly, eggplant can be bitter and not so delicious. The solution: Get the bitterness out. This requires nothing more than salting it. First, cut the eggplant how you want it—in slices or cubes or sticks—and put it in a colander. Place the colander in the sink, and then pour a lot of salt on the eggplant. You don't need cover it with a thick blanket of salt, but definitely hit all the eggplant with it. Then toss it so that the salt coats all sides. Now all you have to; do is to let the eggplant sit for 20 minutes; the salt does the rest of the work. The salt makes the eggplant "sweat," literally; you can see the liquid come out of it, which is why it's in a colander, and why the colander's in the sink. Along with the sweat goes the bitter taste. The sweat also takes the salt with it, so you don't need to worry about using too much.

black pepper, and one-third of the garlic. Scatter the tomatoes evenly on a sheet pan and roast for about 10–15 minutes, until they begin to brown around the edges. Remove the pan from the oven and scrape the tomatoes into the bowl with the zucchini and the squash.

4. While the tomatoes are roasting, toss the red pepper and onion with a tablespoon of olive oil, a sprinkling of salt (¼ teaspoon), a few turns of freshly ground black pepper, and one-third of the minced garlic in the same big mixing bowl. Spread the mixture out evenly on your sheet pan, and cook until the edges start to blacken, 10–15 minutes. Remove the pan from the oven and, using a metal spatula, scrape the peppers and onions off the sheet pan and into the bowl with the other cooked vegetables.

5. Repeat with the eggplant but without any additional salt. Spread the eggplant slices out evenly on your sheet pan, and roast them until they begin to brown.

Remove the pan from the oven, and use a spatula to scrape the eggplant into the bowl with the other vegetables. Add the *herbes de Provence,* and toss the vegetables together with a wooden spoon or whatever you have handy. Your hands will work well once the vegetables are cool enough to touch them.

6. Whisk the eggs in a small bowl, or a big glass measuring cup with a spout, to break up the yolks. Whisk in the cream. This is your custard. Stir the custard into the vegetables so that they are all coated.

7. Spoon the filling into the tart shell. Don't worry if there are so many vegetables that they are mounded high in the tart shell—the more vegetables the better.

8. Place the tart on the center rack in the oven, and bake for 50–55 minutes, or until the filling is firm to the touch.

9. Remove the tart from the oven and set it on a wire rack. Allow the tart to cool slightly.

10. To remove the tart from the pan, rest it on a big can. Make sure the tart is steady and balanced. Slide the outside ring of the pan down off the tart. Then place the tart on your work surface and slide it off the bottom of the pan and onto a rimless serving dish or a cutting board. Serve warm or at room temperature.

Using more than one sheet pan makes quick work of roasting vegetables.

Caramelized-Fennel Tart in a Rosemary–Whole Wheat Crust

4 fennel bulbs (2½–3 pounds)

1 big yellow onion, quartered and cut into ¼-inch slices

3 tablespoons olive oil

1 tablespoon chopped fresh rosemary leaves, plus whole leaves to top tart (page 162)

2 large eggs

¼ cup light cream

1 teaspoon salt

½ teaspoon freshly ground black pepper

1 par-baked 9-inch Rosemary–Whole Wheat Tart Crust (page 16)

This tart is very straightforward—it's all about the fennel. Fennel isn't used much in American cooking, and we think this recipe is a great introduction to it. Why? Because we cook the fennel until it is sweet.

1. Position your oven racks so that one is in the center, and preheat the oven to 350 degrees.
2. Prepare the fennel by cutting the stalks and feathery tops off of the bulbs. (You may want to reserve some of the feathery tops to decorate the finished tart.) Cut the fennel bulb in half lengthwise. Use a paring knife to carve out the core from both halves, then cut lengthwise into ¼-inch slices.
3. Sauté the fennel and onion in the olive oil in a large sauté pan over high heat for 5–10 minutes, until they begin to soften. Lower the heat to medium and continue cooking for about an hour, stirring frequently, until they're brown and so soft they're almost melted. (If the fennel or onion slices seem to be burning, lower the heat further or throw in a splash of water.) Remove the pan from the heat, and stir in the chopped rosemary. Allow the pan and everything in it to cool to room temperature.
4. Whisk the eggs in a small bowl, or a large measuring cup with a spout, to break up the yolks. Whisk in the cream, salt, and pepper. This is your custard. Stir the custard into the pan with the cooled fennel and onion until it is distributed throughout. Dump the filling into the tart shell, and use a wooden spoon or spatula to level it out.
5. Place the tart in the oven, and bake for 35–40 minutes, until the filling is brown and firm to the touch.

6. Remove the tart from the oven and set it on a wire rack. Allow the tart to cool slightly.
7. To remove the tart from the pan, rest it on a big can. Make sure the tart is steady and balanced. Slide the outside ring of the pan down off the tart. Then place the tart on your work surface and slide it off the bottom of the pan and onto a rimless serving dish or a cutting board. Serve warm or at room temperature.

"Occasionally customers come into the store and ask, What is fennel? Fennel has a bulb like a big light-green beet, stalks like celery, and feathery tops like fresh dill. In the south of France, fennel is used a lot. My mother uses the feathery ends of fennel when she cooks fish. It's nothing exotic."
—Jerome

"My dad used to serve fennel raw, sliced, with a bowl of olive oil topped with salt and pepper. I still love it that way."
—Frank

Classic Potato-and-Onion Frittata

MAKES ONE 9- OR 10-INCH FRITTATA

Early on in our business, there was a woman named Maria Angel who came from Barcelona, Spain, to work in the kitchen at Once Upon a Tart. Whenever she had a little time on her hands, she would take it upon herself to make a Spanish tortilla, which, in case you don't know, is nothing like the thing used to wrap up a burrito, but more like a frittata. In a cast-iron pan, she would whisk up eggs, sautéed potatoes and onions, and cook the whole thing over a low flame with the lid on. The result: a fluffy, vegetable-filled, sliceable egg dish.

Eventually, Maria left us. Happily, she left us with her frittata recipe. We bake ours, because we have more oven than stovetop space, but the result is just as good. We rarely serve things straight out of the pan, but we make an exception if the pan happens to be a cast-iron skillet. We just love the rugged look of it.

2 pounds red potatoes, scrubbed, halved, and sliced into ¼-inch-thick half-rounds

2 big yellow onions, quartered and thinly sliced

¼ cup olive oil, plus 2 tablespoons for roasting potatoes

2 teaspoons salt, plus more for sprinkling on potatoes

½ teaspoon freshly ground black pepper, plus more for sprinkling on potatoes

10 large eggs

1. Position your oven racks so that one is in the center, and preheat the oven to 450 degrees.
2. Toss the potatoes and onions in a big bowl with 2 tablespoons of the olive oil, a sprinkling of salt (¼ teaspoon), and a few turns of freshly ground black pepper. Scatter the potatoes and onions on a sheet pan, and roast them until the potatoes are brown and tender, about 25 minutes. Remove the pan from the oven and allow the potatoes and onions to cool.
3. Lower the oven temperature to 350 degrees.
4. Whisk the eggs with the salt and pepper in a big bowl.
5. Scrape the cooled potatoes and onions into the bowl with the eggs with a metal spatula. Stir everything together so that the vegetables are covered with eggs.
6. Heat the remaining olive oil (¼ cup) over high heat in a 9- or 10-inch cast-iron

pan until the oil just begins to smoke. Pour the eggs, potatoes, and onions into the pan, and cook for a minute on the stovetop. This gives the frittata a nice brown "crust" and, the hope is, prevents the frittata from sticking to the pan in the end.

7. Move the pan into the oven, and bake the frittata for 20–25 minutes, until the center is firm to the touch.

8. Remove the pan from the oven, and allow the frittata to cool slightly before slicing. You can slice the frittata in the pan, or place a plate on top of the frittata and flip the pan so the frittata falls out onto the plate. Flip it again onto another plate so that the top of the frittata is facing up. Serve warm or at room temperature.

Frank on Salt

I don't feel comfortable telling people how much salt and pepper to put in their food. How much or how little you like is a matter of personal taste. If you don't use salt, your taste buds adjust and you need less of it in your cooking. If you eat a lot of salt, you're going to want more salt in your food and you're going to use more salt in your cooking.

We decided not to write "salt to taste," as they do in some cookbooks, because we think that the average home cook uses salt too sparingly and ends up with bland food. So how to know when you've got enough salt? When your food tastes bold and flavorful, then you know you've used enough salt. If you're using fresh, quality ingredients and your food still needs a little more flavor, that often means you need a little more salt.

Kosher salt is the only salt we have at the store. We cut off the top of the box and dig right in. At home, I keep kosher salt in an old-fashioned salt box by the stove. Before the salt box, I poured it into a little bowl, which works fine. Grains of kosher salt don't fit through a salt shaker. Iodized salt does, but iodized salt tastes metallic to me. Besides, I like to touch my salt—I think it helps me know how much to use. I also use a lot of sea salt at home, especially on raw vegetables. And in salads, I often throw in some big crystals of salt. Try it. You will be enjoying the mild, cool flavor of the lettuce, and then, all of a sudden, you'll get a piece of that salt on your tongue, and you'll be like, Wow, I never knew lettuce could taste so good.

Variations on Our Classic Frittata

Frittatas are flexible. Basically, they're eggs scrambled and seasoned with salt and pepper and filled with whatever else you want to throw in. We've made frittatas with leftover pasta. And cheese, whether mixed and melted in with the eggs, or melted on top after the frittata is done, is never a bad thing. It's cheese!

Take out a portion—or all—of the potato and onion in our Classic Potato-and-Onion Frittata and add one or more of the following:

roasted eggplant
garlic-sautéed broccoli rabe and Marinated Sun-Dried Tomatoes (page 165)
roasted or sautéed sliced zucchini or yellow squash
roasted or sautéed asparagus
shredded Gruyère, sharp cheddar, or smoked mozzarella or crumbled feta
fresh herbs such as basil, thyme, oregano, or Italian parsley

To make individual-size frittatas, pour the eggs and vegetables into muffin tins smeared with olive oil, and bake until they're set.

Variation: Frittata Sandwiches

To make frittata sandwiches, slice a whole 9- or 10-inch frittata into 1-inch slices. Cut four ciabattas (or other crusty Italian rolls) in half (like hamburger buns), and lay them on your work surface with the bottoms closest to you and the matching tops directly behind. Cover bottom halves with frittata slices in overlapping layers. Spread a generous amount of Rosemary-Garlic Aïoli (page 178) on the top portion of each roll. If you don't have aïoli and don't want to make it, rub bread with a raw garlic clove and slather with mayonnaise. Place each top on respective bottom, and slice each sandwich in half.

45

Once Upon a ...
SOUP

Vegetable Stock
Frank's Chicken Stock
Frank's Roasted Chicken
Three-Onion Soup
Variation: Gooey, Cheesy Baked Onion Soup
Black-Bean-and-Pumpkin Soup with Cinnamon and Ginger
Puréed Spinach-and-Sweet-Pea Soup with Fresh Mint
Green-Lentil Soup with Coconut Milk and Indian Spices
Chilled Avocado-and-Cucumber Soup with Fresh Dill
Cream of Wild Mushroom Soup with Grated Pecorino Cheese
Smooth Garlic-and-Roasted-Red-Pepper Soup with Fresh Thyme
Vegetarian Vegetable Chili
Creamy Carrot Soup with Fresh Dill
Variation: Carrot-Ginger Soup with Curry and Orange
Chickpea-Tomato Soup with Fresh Rosemary
Sweet-Pea Soup with Fresh Ginger and Ground Toasted Almonds
Mushroom-Barley Soup with Spring Vegetables
Curried Corn Chowder with Coconut Milk
Chilled Gazpacho with Roasted Red Pepper and Fresh Dill

We were not real soup-makers when we first opened the store. Soup takes time. And Frank, well, hadn't given much time to soup since he was a kid. As for Jerome, he just didn't get the whole idea of soup as an everyday food. Growing up in France, he seldom saw soup on a menu. Soup was something your mother made on an occasional winter afternoon.

Our first lunchtime customers, however, those SoHo pioneers at the ad agencies and art galleries, were soup lovers, lucky to get 15 minutes to go out and eat. More often, they would grab something and take it right back to their desks. (The amount of food we deliver via wire baskets hinged to the front of a few rickety bicycles we've collected is testament to New Yorkers' lack of a proper lunch break.) Soup, when you need something fast, is the perfect thing. It's easy to eat, it's relatively healthy, and even the heartiest bean soup leaves you feeling good, like you can tackle the rest of the workday without needing a nap.

When we were developing our soup menu, we knew right away we weren't going to make any of the soup standards. Not that we have anything against a really good split-pea or lentil soup. But you'll find those in the soup kettles of any New York deli. You can even get decent versions of those soups out of a can. So we set out to make soups that you couldn't get out of a can even if you wanted to.

We took soup standards and tweaked them by adding other flavors that we liked. Plain ol' brown lentil became Green-Lentil Soup with Coconut Milk and Indian Spices (page 60). We took the idea of Campbell's-style tomato and made Chickpea-Tomato Soup (page 75). We added coconut milk to corn chowder, and added roasted red peppers to our gazpacho. Trust us: there isn't a deli in New York serving our kind of soup.

THINGS TO KNOW

Soup is really easy food. It would be almost impossible to mess up, unless, say, you charred the onions (and still put them in your soup). Soup is so inexact, in fact, that the entire category must have been born of kitchen scraps. Of course, there are a few things to know when making soup—not imperatives, just things to make your life easier. And your soup tastier.

A lot of soups start with sautéing onions. We often use a combination of half butter, half olive oil to sauté onions or other vegetables. We like the flavor of butter, and the olive oil has a higher burning point—so we can sauté over a hotter flame without burning the butter. We didn't invent this trick; it's very common in Italian cooking. We don't melt butter before sautéing. It will melt in the pan anyway. Since butter burns easily, we don't want to give it any more heat than we have to. We sauté onions until they are soft and translucent. The cooking actually changes the flavor of the onion—makes it sweet and removes any hint of bitterness and the strong onion flavor.

All of our soups call for stocks. You can use either vegetable or chicken stock. There's nothing like homemade stock. But if you don't have the time or inclination to make your own stock, don't let that stop you from making soup. Our soups, especially the puréed ones, are so flavorful that they even taste good when made with water or canned stock. If you use canned stock we recommend you use low-fat stocks, not because we care about fat, but because low-fat stocks contain less sodium. Look for those that don't contain MSG (monosodium glutamate), which many canned stocks do.

When we call for vegetables to be chopped a certain way, it is not arbitrary. It has to do with what we're going to do with them later. In the case of our Mushroom-Barley Soup with Spring Vegetables (page 77), we wanted them all to be on the same scale as grains of barley, so that when you take a spoonful, you get some of everything floating amidst the broth.

In the puréed-soup recipes, you'll notice that we've called for many of the vegetables to be simply "chopped." We've been purposefully vague. The soup is being puréed anyway, so there's no need to cut your onions into a perfect little dice. By "chopped," we mean roughly ½-inch pieces. When you're puréeing soup, the blade of the food processor will have a difficult time cutting through the vegetables if there's too much liquid in the food processor. Scoop the vegetables into the blender or food processor with as little broth as possible. We like to use a slotted spoon for this.

We based the number of servings on a 12-ounce portion. At the store, we serve 12-ounce portions because our customers are eating soup as a meal. If we were serving soup as an opener to a meal, we'd serve something closer to 8-ounce portions, in which case the number of servings would change.

We like to chill soup in a pitcher. It makes it easy to pour into the individual bowls we serve it in. No matter what you chill the soup in, make sure you cover the container. You don't want stuff falling into it. And you don't want it to absorb the flavor of the cat food or the Chinese takeout in the fridge.

We don't believe in the word "garnish." So often it means putting something on or around your food that doesn't belong there. We do, however, believe strongly in making our food look pretty. For soups particularly, fresh herbs are our favorite way to "decorate." Sprinkle a bit of finely chopped herbs—whatever you used in that soup—on top of each bowl. And we can't think of a single soup that wouldn't taste great with a dollop of crème fraîche and a sprinkling of finely chopped or snipped chives or Italian parsley. With any puréed soup, you can add texture and color by topping the finished soup with a handful of whole vegetables—corn to corn chowder, chopped tomatoes to gazpacho.

We've specified in each recipe whether the soup is best served right away. Bean soups all taste better the next day, so, if you're looking for something to make for a week's worth of lunches, try the Black-Bean-and-Pumpkin Soup (page 57) in the fall or the Chickpea-Tomato Soup (page 73) in the summer. At home, Frank always doubles soup recipes. He figures if he's going to be chopping all those vegetables, he might as well make enough soup to freeze for later. "I like to have my soup and eat it, too," he says.

"Soup needs salt. It's a lot of water, after all. So always taste for salt before serving."
—Frank

Vegetable Stock

2 tablespoons unsalted butter

2 tablespoons olive oil

1 big yellow onion, chopped

1 leek, root end and dark-green
  tops removed, sliced ¼ inch
  thin, and washed (page 29)

1 big potato (any kind), peeled and
  chopped

2 or 3 medium carrots, chopped

2 celery stalks, chopped

2 garlic cloves, smashed and
  peeled (page 23)

8 cups (2 quarts) cold water

1 bunch fresh Italian parsley,
  washed and chopped (page 162)

2 bay leaves

1 teaspoon salt

1 teaspoon whole peppercorns

We like vegetable stock because its flavor is subtle and doesn't over-power the flavors of the actual soup. At the store, we pile up vegetable trimmings to throw into stock—carrot peels, celery leaves and bottoms, the ends of onions and leeks. We stay away from cabbage or eggplant or asparagus, anything with a really strong, overwhelming flavor.

1. Sauté the vegetables in the butter and olive oil in a big soup pot over high heat, stirring occasionally to prevent the vegetables from sticking to the pot and burning. When the vegetables begin to soften and reduce in volume, 5–10 minutes, lower the heat to medium and continue cooking until the onions are tender and translucent, about 10 more minutes.

2. Return the heat to high. Add the water, parsley, bay leaves, salt, and peppercorns and bring to a boil. Lower the heat, and simmer until the water no longer tastes like water—but tastes like broth—at least 2 hours. Pour the stock through a colander, being careful not to let it splash, since it will be very hot. You can use the stock right away, or cool it to room temperature before putting it in the refrigerator or the freezer.

Frank's Chicken Stock

I give precise amounts for making stock below. But the truth is, at least for me, making stock is a very haphazard process. I never go to the store to buy vegetables for stock. And I would no sooner measure when I'm making stock than I would when I'm making an ice-cream sundae.

I always start with the carcass of a whole roasted chicken, because having the carcass left over from a roasted chicken dinner is what inspires me to make the stock in the first place. Then I look around for some leftover vegetables: a few stalks of celery and some root vegetables: parsnips, potatoes, carrots. (Left over, but not *old,* mind you.) I often have onion ends and carrot skins left from the onions and carrots I served with the roasted chicken. If not, I'll peel the skins off carrots right into the stockpot, and keep the carrots themselves for snacking on. But I rarely sacrifice whole vegetables for stock. At the grocery store, they sell little containers filled with chopped vegetables—carrots and celery, parsley—all wrapped in plastic. If you don't have leftovers handy, these are a good substitute.

I sauté the vegetables in a soup pot with a 50-50 mixture of butter and olive oil for 10 or 15 minutes. Once the carrots are tender and the onions translucent, I throw in the chicken carcass and the remaining ingredients and fill the pot almost to the top with water. If you don't have a leftover chicken carcass, use a whole roasting chicken cut up in place of the carcass. You can then turn that boiled chicken into a Curried Chicken Salad (page 104).

As far as seasoning my stock, I throw in some whole black peppercorns, a couple of bay leaves, and a big handful of chopped fresh Italian parsley—stems, too. I'm not very specific about the herbs—I might also pull some chives or oregano or thyme out of the garden. The one thing I don't use is rosemary, because its flavor is too strong, and I like to keep the herb flavor light. The most important thing about chicken stock is the chicken flavor.

I bring the stock to a boil, lower the heat, and let it simmer for 2 or 3 hours. It

2 tablespoons unsalted butter
2 tablespoons olive oil
1 big yellow onion, chopped
2 or 3 medium carrots, chopped
2 celery stalks, chopped
12 cups (3 quarts) cold water
2 bay leaves
1 teaspoon whole black peppercorns
1 bunch fresh Italian parsley, chopped (page 162)
1 whole roasted chicken carcass

could even be 4 hours, depending on what else I'm doing around the house at the time. Then I start tasting it. When the stock no longer tastes like water with a faint hint of chicken, but more like something I would want to sip from a bowl all by itself, then it's done. I strain the stock through a fine-mesh colander, but, honestly, I'm not very concerned about little pieces of vegetable or chicken getting through the holes in the colander. And I never strain the fat from my stock. Fat is where the flavor is. My recipe for roasting the chicken follows below.

Frank's Roasted Chicken

At home, I roast a chicken just about every week. A roasted chicken is everything I want in a meal: it's easy to make, and tasty, and there is always the guarantee of leftovers. I've gotten so addicted to the leftovers that sometimes, when I'm roasting a chicken for dinner, I'll throw in another one just for leftovers. I make chicken sandwiches with it, or shred some chicken into the Roasted Fingerling Potato Salad (page 122) or into a Spinach-and-Mushroom Tart (page 24).

I like to serve roasted chicken with potatoes—either roasted with rosemary and garlic, or mashed with copious amounts of butter, half-and-half, and salt and pepper. And I always serve potatoes alongside a green vegetable. Whatever's in season, usually steamed or sautéed on the stovetop. I only have one oven, and the chicken's in there.

To roast a whole fryer chicken, first of all, be prepared to get your hands dirty. Preheat your oven to 400 degrees. Rinse your chicken under cold running water, and pat it dry with paper towels. Tuck a handful of fresh rosemary leaves (or tarragon or thyme) under the skin at the neck end (the larger, open end) of the chicken, where the skin separates from the flesh. If you like garlic, slide a few slices of garlic under the skin, too. Rub ¼ cup olive oil all over the chicken, and sprinkle it on all sides with salt and freshly ground black pepper. Place chicken on a roasting rack in a roasting pan (or directly on a sheet pan if you don't have a roasting rack and pan), and bake until the skin is nice and crunchy and golden brown. Figure on about 20 minutes per pound. But more important is for the meat inside to be done. To test, pierce a wing with a knife. If no liquid comes out, the chicken is done. Allow the chicken to rest for a few minutes before carving into it. To serve, I like to cut off the legs and wings with poultry shears or a sharp knife and slice the breast meat.

Three-Onion Soup

MAKES 6 SERVINGS

Frank had to do some research to prove to Jerome that what Americans call French onion soup really is from France. Jerome never saw it when he was growing up. He and the soup apparently come from different regions. We caramelize three types of onions—yellow onions, red onions, and leeks—to make this sweet, hearty soup. At the store, we don't do the whole melted-cheese top thing that characterizes French onion soup, so we didn't think it deserved that name. Three-onion soup is even better the next day. Serve it with French bread, of course.

2 big yellow onions, quartered and thinly sliced

2 red onions, quartered and thinly sliced

4 leeks, root end and dark-green tops removed, sliced ¼ inch thin, and washed (page 29)

1 tablespoon unsalted butter

1 tablespoon olive oil

2 tablespoons unbleached all-purpose flour

8 cups vegetable or chicken stock (pages 50, 51)

1 tablespoon Worcestershire sauce

1 teaspoon salt

½ teaspoon freshly ground black pepper

½ cup grated Parmesan cheese

1. Sauté the yellow and red onions and the leeks in the butter and olive oil in a large soup pot over high heat for 5–10 minutes, stirring occasionally to keep the onions from sticking to the bottom of the pot and burning.
2. When the onions have begun to soften slightly and reduce in volume, 5–10 minutes, lower the heat to medium and continue to sauté them for about an hour, until they are caramel in color and almost melted. You don't want the onions to burn, so, if it looks like they're heading in that direction, lower the flame even more, or splash a little bit of water over them—this buys you some cooking time.
3. Sprinkle the onions with the flour, stirring all the while so the flour doesn't clump. Sauté for another 5 minutes to cook off the floury taste.
4. Pour the stock over the onions and bring it to a boil over high heat. Reduce the heat and simmer for 30 minutes. Stir in the Worcestershire sauce, salt, and pepper.
5. Just before you're ready to serve the soup, whisk in the cheese. It's important to whisk in the cheese at the last minute, or else the cheese will fall to the bottom of the pot and burn. Serve warm.

Variation: Gooey, Cheesy Baked Onion Soup

When Frank was 10 years old, he "borrowed" a French cookbook from the Livingston Public Library. (In fact, he still has that book and still uses it.) He found a recipe for French onion soup in the book that he loved to make for his family. It seemed foreign to him, and fancy. His mom was so pleased with his initiative that she went out and bought proper crocks for him to serve the soup in. And his dad would come home from his grocery-shopping trips to New York City with big chunks of Gruyère cheese, even though, being Italian, this was not something he would ever have bought if it weren't for Frank and his soup thing.

Preheat your oven to 350 degrees. Slice stale bread, brush the slices with olive oil, scatter them on a sheet pan, and bake until the bread dries out and the edges are golden brown. Ladle the warm Three-Onion Soup into heatproof bowls, and lay a slice of the baked bread over each bowl. Grate a layer of Gruyère cheese over the bread, and place the crocks under the broiler until the cheese bubbles and browns.

Black-Bean-and-Pumpkin Soup
with Cinnamon and Ginger

MAKES 6 SERVINGS

This is a cold-weather soup. Period. We wouldn't even think about serving it in the spring or summer. The pumpkin, the beans, the cumin—they are rich, warming flavors. This, like all bean soups, is even better the next day. You can turn this soup into a meal by pouring it over a bed of steamed white or yellow rice. Serve it with tortilla chips and a simple green salad dressed up with cubes of ripe avocado, thinly sliced red onion, and a little bit of chopped fresh cilantro.

1. Drain and rinse the soaked beans in a colander. Bring the water and the beans to a boil in a large soup pot over high heat. Lower the heat and simmer, uncovered, for about an hour, until the beans are soft to the bite but not falling apart or splitting. Drain the beans in a colander.

2. Sauté the onion and garlic in the olive oil in a large soup pot over high heat, stirring frequently so that they don't stick to the bottom of the pan, until the onion begins to soften, 5–10 minutes. Lower the heat to medium and continue to sauté, stirring occasionally, for about 10 more minutes, until the onion is tender and translucent.

3. Add the tomatoes, cumin, cinnamon, ginger, salt, and pepper to the soup pot, and sauté until the tomatoes begin to break down and give off juices, 5–10 minutes. Pour in the stock, pumpkin purée, vinegar, and beans.

4. Bring the soup to a boil. Lower the heat and simmer for about 15 minutes, allowing the flavors to meld.

5. Remove the soup from the heat to purée. Puréeing makes it a thick, smooth, more cohesive soup, but you still want the texture of the black beans, so don't

1½ cups dried black beans, picked through, rinsed and soaked overnight (page 61)

6 cups cold unsalted water (for simmering the beans)

½ big yellow onion, diced

1 garlic clove, peeled and minced (page 23)

2 tablespoons olive oil

¾ pound plum tomatoes (6–8), peeled and diced (page 76)

1 tablespoon cumin

½ teaspoon cinnamon

1 teaspoon ground ginger

1 teaspoon salt

½ teaspoon freshly ground black pepper

4 cups (1 quart) vegetable or chicken stock (pages 50, 51)

1 cup canned or fresh pumpkin purée

1 tablespoon red-wine vinegar

Be careful when you're using an immersion blender—if the walls of the pot aren't high enough, or you don't immerse the blender deep enough, you'll end up with more soup (or whatever you're puréeing) on the walls of your kitchen than in the pot.

purée it all. If you're using an immersion blender, purée one-third of the soup right in the pot. Serve warm.

6. If you don't have an immersion blender, wait until the soup cools, then scoop up some with a ladle, or a heatproof measuring cup with a handle, and pour it into the bowl of a food processor (or a blender) fitted with a metal blade. Process in batches until you have puréed about one-third of the soup. Serve warm.

Frank on Spinach

When I'm making a spinach salad or garlic-sautéed spinach, I buy the baby spinach that's sold loose (preferably organic). It's much more tender than the big leaf spinach sold in bags. But in a soup, where it's all getting cooked down and puréed, it doesn't really make a difference, so I use the stuff in bags. I just love that I don't have to worry about getting all that sand out—it's already done. Frozen spinach, however, has a different flavor altogether. Use it only in emergencies.

Puréed Spinach-and-Sweet-Pea Soup with Fresh Mint

MAKES 6 SERVINGS

Peas and mint are a classic combination and one we both love. This soup is best served the day you make it. If you keep it more than a day, the bright-green color of the vegetables will begin to dull and brown. Try it chilled on a summer day.

1. Sauté the onions in the butter in a large soup pot over high heat, stirring occasionally to prevent the onions from sticking and burning, until they begin to soften and reduce in volume, 5–10 minutes. Lower the heat to medium and continue to sauté for another 10–15 minutes, until the onions are tender and translucent. Stir in the spinach and sauté until the spinach is wilted, about 5 minutes.

2. Add the peas and the stock to the pot, and bring it all to a boil over high heat. Lower the heat and simmer, uncovered, for 10–15 minutes.

3. Remove the soup from the heat to purée. If you're using an immersion blender, you can purée the soup in the pot. Otherwise, wait a few minutes, until the soup cools.

4. If you don't have an immersion blender, scoop up some of the soup with a ladle or a measuring cup with a handle. Pour it into the bowl of a food processor (or a blender) fitted with a metal blade. Blend until the soup is smooth. Pour the puréed soup into a bowl while you purée the remaining soup in batches.

5. Return the puréed soup to the soup pot, and warm it over medium heat. Slowly whisk in the cream. Using the whisk, stir in half of the mint, and the salt and pepper. Serve warm or chilled. Sprinkle the remaining mint over the individual servings.

3 tablespoons unsalted butter

2 big yellow onions, quartered and coarsely chopped (roughly ½-inch pieces)

2 10-ounce bags (or the equivalent) of fresh spinach, rinsed

2½ cups frozen petite peas

3 cups vegetable or chicken stock (pages 50, 51)

½ cup light cream

½ cup fresh mint, cut into thin strips (page 162)

1 tablespoon salt

A few turns of freshly ground black pepper

Green-Lentil Soup with Coconut Milk and Indian Spices

MAKES 6 SERVINGS

1 big yellow onion, diced fine

2 garlic cloves, peeled and minced (page 23)

3 tablespoons unsalted butter

2½ teaspoons fresh thyme (or 1 teaspoon dried)

1½ teaspoons turmeric

6 cups vegetable or chicken stock (pages 50, 51)

1½ cups French green lentils (*lentilles de Puy*), picked through and rinsed (page 119)

3 tablespoons unsalted butter, clarified, or ghee (page 61)

½ teaspoon cardamom

¼ teaspoon cinnamon

¼ teaspoon ground cloves

A pinch of nutmeg

A few turns of freshly ground black pepper

1 cup canned coconut milk

Jerome invented this soup during an Indian-food phase he was going through. Jerome loves coconut milk. And he uses only French green lentils—not because they're French, but because he likes that they hold their shape better than brown lentils. You could use either here. Serve warm today or tomorrow. (Or the next day.)

1. Sauté the onions and garlic in the butter in a large soup pot over high heat, stirring occasionally to keep them from sticking to the bottom of the pot and burning. When the onions have begun to reduce in volume, about 5–10 minutes, lower the heat to medium, add the thyme and the turmeric, and continue sautéing, stirring from time to time, for 10–15 more minutes, until the onions are tender and translucent.

2. Add the stock and the lentils, and simmer for 25–30 minutes, until the lentils are soft. The best way to test lentils is to take one out of the pot and bite into it. It should be tender.

3. Warm the clarified butter in a small saucepan over medium heat. Add the cardamom, cinnamon, cloves, nutmeg, and pepper, and sauté until the warmth from the butter brings out the aroma of the spices, 2–3 minutes.

4. Add the clarified butter and spices to the soup. Stir in the coconut milk, and cook for about 15 minutes over medium heat, so the flavors blend together.

"In my cupboard, I have big old-fashioned cookie jars full of all kinds of beans and grains. They're a nice thing to have around for the proverbial rainy (i.e., soup-friendly) day."

—Frank

What Is Clarified Butter?

Clarified butter is butter without the milk solids. Regular butter burns at a low temperature. Clarified butter cooks at a higher temperature without burning. Ghee, which is commonly used in Indian cooking (and sold in jars in Indian and some grocery stores), is clarified butter that has been browned; it can be used in place of clarified butter in any of our recipes.

To make clarified butter, melt your butter in a small heavy-bottomed saucepan over medium heat. Skim the foam off the top. What you'll have left is clarified butter and white sediment at the bottom, which is the milk solids. Carefully pour the clarified butter into a glass measuring cup (or any other heatproof container), leaving the sediment in the pan.

How to Deal with Dried Beans

We always pick through beans to look for little stones or unattractive-looking beans that might have sneaked in with them. One trick we have for picking through beans is to spread them out on a sheet pan lined with parchment paper. When we're ready to rinse them, we just lift the paper up by either side and pour the beans into the colander. No spilling.

We soak all of our beans (except lentils) before we cook them. It shortens cooking time. We've also heard that soaking beans helps to reduce beans' tendency to cause gas, but this we don't know.

To soak beans, put them in a bowl with a ratio of 1 part beans to 3 parts water. The exact amount isn't as important as making sure the beans are entirely covered with water. We don't salt the water when soaking or cooking beans. Salt inhibits the beans from absorbing water, and it's the absorption of water that softens them, which is the whole point of soaking and cooking them. Let the beans sit for 6–8 hours or overnight.

But if you want to make a recipe that calls for soaked beans and you haven't soaked them, it's not the end of your bean-eating world. It just means you'll have to cook the beans a little longer.

If you didn't plan far enough ahead to soak your beans overnight, you can do what's called a "quick-soak." Place the beans in a big pot of unsalted water over high heat. When the water comes to a boil, turn off the heat, cover the pot, and let the beans soak, or steam, really, for an hour. At this point they're the same as beans that have been soaked overnight. Drain and rinse the beans in a colander, and move on with the recipe.

Chilled Avocado-and-Cucumber Soup
with Fresh Dill

MAKES 4 SERVINGS

This chilled summer soup is quick and easy to make. Nothing in the soup is even cooked, so the finished product will only taste as good as your raw ingredients. When Frank makes this at home, he dices some extra cucumbers and avocado and sprinkles this on top of each bowl, along with a dollop of sour cream. This soup is best served the same day you make it.

1. Put the garlic, cucumber, and avocado into the bowl of a food processor (or a blender) fitted with a metal blade, and purée. If some bits cling to the sides, scrape them down with a rubber spatula and purée again. Add the buttermilk, water, dill, salt, peppers, and half the orange juice, and blend until you have a smooth soup.
2. Taste the soup, and add the remaining orange juice in increments until you have the flavor you want.
3. Pour the soup into a serving bowl or pitcher. Cover, and refrigerate until ready to serve. Taste for salt before serving. Serve chilled.

2 garlic cloves, smashed and peeled (page 23)

1 cucumber, peeled, halved, seeded, and coarsely chopped (page 117)

1 ripe avocado, halved and pitted

¼ cup cold buttermilk

¾ cup water

2 tablespoons fresh dill

2 teaspoons salt

A pinch of cayenne pepper

A few turns of freshly ground black pepper

1½ cups freshly squeezed orange juice

Frank on How to Peel, Slice, and Otherwise Deal with an Avocado

If you grew up in California, you know how to slice an avocado just like you know how to peel an orange. But I didn't grow up in California. Which means that I made a real mess the first few times I sliced an avocado. The way I do it now is, I take a chef's knife, cut the avocado in half, and pull the halves apart by twisting them gently, in opposite directions, with my hands. Then, with the same knife, I hit the pit and lift it out. (This is fun and sort of samurai-like, but be careful.) If I want to slice the avocado, what I do next is, with a paring knife, score each half in half and peel back the skin. The good thing about this method is that I now have two neat halves that I can slice. Or, if I'm planning to mash or spread the avocado, I simply slice it in half and scoop the meat out with a big spoon. Either way, if you don't use the whole avocado, leave the pit in the half that remains, and squeeze lemon or lime juice over the exposed avocado.

Cream of Wild Mushroom Soup
with Grated Pecorino Cheese

MAKES 6 SERVINGS

2 big yellow onions, coarsely
    chopped (roughly ½-inch pieces)

2 tablespoons unsalted butter

2 tablespoons olive oil

½ pound white mushrooms

½ pound assorted wild mushrooms
    (chanterelles, shiitakes, porto-
    bellos), cleaned, stems trimmed
    (page 25)

1 big russet potato, peeled and
    coarsely chopped

1 tablespoon coarsely chopped
    fresh Italian parsley (page 162)

2 teaspoons salt

A few turns of freshly ground black
    pepper

4 cups (1 quart) vegetable or
    chicken stock (pages 50, 51)

2 teaspoons Worcestershire sauce

½ cup light cream

½ cup grated Pecorino cheese (or
    any hard, sharp grating cheese,
    like Parmesan)

We use a combination of white and wild mushrooms in this soup. It's a great way to get the taste of wild mushrooms without making a million-dollar soup. Plus we like the mild flavor of the whites opposite the intensity of the wilds. We don't purée the soup completely, because we like to bite into chunks of mushrooms. This soup is best served the day you make it.

1. Sauté the onions in the butter and olive oil in a large soup pot over high heat, stirring occasionally to keep the onions from sticking to the bottom and burning. When the onions have begun to reduce in volume, about 5–10 minutes, lower the heat to medium and continue cooking for about 10 more minutes, until the onions are tender and translucent.

2. Add the mushrooms and sauté, covered, for 10–15 minutes, or until the mushrooms look glossy and dark. Add the potato, parsley, salt, and pepper, and sauté, uncovered, for another 5 minutes.

3. Add the stock to the pot and bring it to a boil. Lower the heat and simmer with the lid only partially covering the pot until the potatoes are tender, 25–30 minutes. Be careful not to get burned by the steam when you lift the lid off the pot to check the potatoes.

4. Remove the soup from the heat to purée. If you're using an immersion blender, you can purée the soup in the pot. Otherwise, wait at least 15 minutes, until the soup cools.

5. If you don't have an immersion blender, scoop up some soup with a ladle or a measuring cup with a handle, and pour it into the bowl of a food processor (or a

blender) fitted with a metal blade. Blend until the soup is smooth. Pour the puréed soup into a bowl while you purée, in batches, all but the last quarter of the soup.

6. Return the puréed soup to the soup pot. Whisk in the Worcestershire sauce and the cream. If the soup is too thick, add a little more stock or cream. Stir in the cheese just before you're ready to serve the soup. Serve warm.

"Believe it or not, potatoes have flavor. Those just dug from the dirt will taste of the earth, and their skins will be beautifully thin. I love Yukon gold potatoes for mashed potatoes or anything where I really want the taste of a potato. But for soups, I prefer russets because they're bland. They make an ideal thickener. As for cleaning potatoes, well, just remember: they grow in dirt. They need a lot of scrubbing."
—Frank

Jerome on Cream

The most common question our customers ask about our soups is: Does it have cream in it? Every day, all day long, I hear that question. Of course, so many times they don't want the soup if it has cream. I don't understand this. Cream soups are the best kind of soups. The cream gives the soup such a nice texture and richness. I know our customers are worried about their diets. But do you know how much cream is in a cup of soup? By the time you divide the total cream in a soup by the number of servings, it's not much. The Creamy Carrot Soup (page 71), the Cream of Wild Mushroom Soup (page 64)—they taste really creamy and they only have 1½ tablespoons of cream in each serving. It's so little. Besides, the same people who refuse to eat that soup will eat a muffin made with butter and drink a giant cappuccino that's full of milk. To me this makes no sense at all.

Smooth Garlic-and-Roasted-Red-Pepper Soup with Fresh Thyme

MAKES 6 SERVINGS

6 red bell peppers, cored, seeded, and chopped

1 big bulb garlic (20 cloves), smashed (page 23)

4 tablespoons olive oil

¼ teaspoon salt

1 big yellow onion, coarsely chopped

1 big russet potato, peeled and coarsely chopped

7 cups vegetable or chicken stock (pages 50, 51)

1 teaspoon fresh or ½ teaspoon dried thyme (page 162)

2 teaspoons salt

½ teaspoon freshly ground black pepper

A simple soup for roasted-red-pepper lovers. Teacups full of this (or any) soup are a nice way to add a course to a meal—whether it's a sit-down, a buffet, or a cocktail party—while leaving your guests with an appetite for the meal to come. This soup is best served the day it's made.

1. Position your oven racks so that one is in the center, and preheat the oven to 400 degrees.
2. Toss the peppers in a bowl with the garlic, half of the olive oil, and a sprinkling of salt (¼ teaspoon). Spread the peppers and garlic evenly over a sheet pan, place the sheet pan on the center rack in the oven, and roast for 40–45 minutes, until the peppers and garlic are tender and black around the edges. Remove from the oven.
3. Sauté the onion and potato in the remaining olive oil in a large soup pot over high heat, stirring occasionally so that they don't stick to the bottom of the pan and burn. When the onion has begun to reduce in volume, 5–10 minutes, lower the heat to medium and continue to sauté, stirring, for about 10–15 more minutes, until the onion is tender and translucent.
4. Add the roasted peppers and garlic, stock, thyme, salt, and pepper to the soup pot, and bring it all to a boil. Lower the heat and simmer, partially covered, for about 20 minutes, until the flavors come together.
5. Remove the soup from the heat to purée. If you're using an immersion blender, you can purée the soup in the pot. Otherwise, wait a few minutes, until soup cools.

6. If you don't have an immersion blender, scoop up some soup with a ladle or a measuring cup with a handle, pour it into the bowl of a food processor (or a blender) fitted with a metal blade, and blend until the soup is smooth. You need to purée this soup well, because the peppers aren't skinned and you don't want to end up with little bits of pepper skin in your soup.

7. Pour the puréed soup into a bowl while you purée the remaining soup in batches.

8. Return the puréed soup to the soup pot and warm it over medium heat. Serve warm.

"Making soup is like going to the gym for me. I resist doing it. But when I finally get around to doing it, I'm glad I did."
—Frank

"I love making soup. I like the fact that it's a long process. I often make it at home, especially when it's cold and rainy."
—Jerome

Vegetarian Vegetable Chili

2 cups dried black beans, picked
    through, rinsed, and soaked
    overnight (page 61)

8 cups cold unsalted water (for
    simmering the beans)

1 15-ounce can kidney beans; or 1
    cup dried kidney beans, picked
    through, rinsed, and soaked
    overnight (page 61)

⅓ cup olive oil

2 garlic cloves, peeled and minced
    (page 23)

1 big yellow onion, diced

3 medium carrots, peeled and
    diced (page 119)

4 celery stalks, diced

3 red bell peppers, diced (page
    117)

1 jalapeño pepper, halved, stem
    and seeds removed, and minced

1 zucchini, diced (page 119)

1 yellow squash, diced (page 119)

1 cup frozen or canned corn, or 1–2

continued

Everyone has his or her favorite chili recipe. This happens to be Frank's. It's a staple at the café during colder months, served with Honey-Corn Muffins (page 276). At home, Frank serves it with lots of sides—marinated grilled chicken or steak cut into cubes, onions, sharp cheddar cheese, black olives, chopped fresh cilantro, sour cream. With a green salad, like the cool crunchy leaves of a Caesar-ish Salad (page 178), it's a whole meal.

1. Drain and rinse the soaked black beans in a colander. Bring the beans and water to a boil in a big soup pot over high heat. Lower the heat and simmer, uncovered, for an hour or more, until the beans are soft to the bite but not falling apart or splitting. Drain the beans in a colander.

2. For canned kidney beans, drain them in a colander and rinse them well. If you are using dried kidney beans, use the quick-soak method above.

3. In the same big soup pot, warm the oil and garlic over medium heat for a few minutes to flavor the oil. (Be careful not to overcook the garlic—if it begins to brown, turn down the heat.) Add the onion, turn the heat up to medium-high, and sauté for 5–10 minutes, until onion is tender and translucent.

4. Continue adding the chopped vegetables one at a time, letting each cook for about 5 minutes before adding the next, in this order: carrots, celery, bell and jalapeño peppers (together), zucchini and yellow squash (together), and, last, corn.

5. Once you've added and sautéed all the vegetables, add the cumin, chili powder, paprika, sugar, and coriander and cook for another 5–10 minutes, until the vegetables absorb the flavor of the spices.

6. Stir the beans, tomatoes, hot sauce, and bay leaf into the soup pot. Bring the chili to a boil over high heat. Lower the heat and simmer for an hour or more, until the chili thickens. Serve warm, with sour cream, grated cheddar cheese, and chopped red onions or scallions.

"No matter how much you want to eat it now, admit it: chili is always better the next day."
—Jerome

ears, shucked and kernels cut off the cob

2 tablespoons ground cumin

⅓ cup chili powder

2 tablespoons paprika

1 tablespoon sugar

2 tablespoons ground coriander

1 28-ounce can Italian-style tomatoes, diced

1½ pounds plum tomatoes, cored and diced

2 tablespoons hot sauce (such as Frank's Original Red Hot or Tabasco)

1 bay leaf

TO TOP THE CHILI:

1 cup sour cream

1 cup grated cheddar cheese

½ red onion, diced (page 119)

1 bunch scallions, sliced thin

Creamy Carrot Soup with Fresh Dill

Jerome invented this soup. It's his favorite. This soup tastes best the day you make it.

1. Sauté the onion in the butter and oil in a large soup pot over high heat, stirring occasionally. Lower the heat if you see the onion browning. When the onion has begun to reduce in volume, in about 5–10 minutes, lower the heat and continue cooking for 10–15 more minutes, until it is tender and translucent.
2. Add the carrots and potato and cook for 15–20 minutes, until some of the potato pieces begin to brown slightly.
3. Add the stock to the soup pot and bring to a boil over high heat. Lower the heat and simmer for 30–40 minutes, until the carrots are soft enough to mash against the side of the soup pot with a fork or wooden spoon.
4. Remove the soup from the heat to purée. If you're using an immersion blender, you can purée the soup in the pot. Otherwise, wait a few minutes, until soup cools.
5. If you don't have an immersion blender, scoop up some soup with a ladle or a measuring cup with a handle, pour it into the bowl of a food processor (or a blender) fitted with a metal blade, and blend until the soup is smooth. Pour the puréed soup into a bowl while you purée the remaining soup in batches.
6. Return the puréed soup to the soup pot. Stir in the dill, salt and pepper, and cream, and warm the soup over medium heat before serving. This soup should be thick, but not so thick that your spoon stands up in it. Add more cream or stock to thin it. Serve warm and top with chopped fresh dill.

1 big yellow onion, coarsely chopped

1 tablespoon unsalted butter

1 tablespoon olive oil

2 pounds medium carrots (8–10), peeled and coarsely chopped

1 big russet potato, peeled and diced

4 cups vegetable or chicken stock (pages 50, 51)

¼ cup chopped fresh dill, plus more to top the soup (page 162)

1 teaspoon salt

¼ teaspoon black pepper

½ cup light cream

Variation:
Carrot-Ginger Soup with Curry and Orange

Frank came up with this variation on our Creamy Carrot Soup to satisfy his love of curry. Add a tablespoon of Madras curry powder and a 2-inch piece of ginger, minced, to the sautéing onions. Then substitute equal amounts orange juice for cream and chopped fresh cilantro for dill. Purée the soup as if it were the Creamy Carrot Soup, adding more orange juice if the soup needs to be thinned or if you want more orange flavor. Serve it warm, with a dollop of sour cream and fresh cilantro leaves on top.

"When we call for 'freshly squeezed juice,' that means it really should be freshly squeezed. It makes a difference in the final flavor."
—Jerome

Chickpea-Tomato Soup with Fresh Rosemary

MAKES 6 SERVINGS

This is one of our most popular soups—and definitely the simplest to make. If we get into a bind, we can get a batch ready, start to finish, in less than an hour. And it tastes just as good the next day.

1. Drain the canned chickpeas in a colander and rinse them well. For dry chickpeas, place them in a pot with 4 cups cold unsalted water. Bring to a boil over high heat, then lower the heat and simmer, uncovered, for an hour or more, until the beans are tender and have lost their "raw bean" flavor. Drain the chickpeas and rinse them in a colander.

2. Warm the olive oil with the garlic and rosemary in a large soup pot, for 1–2 minutes. You don't want the garlic to brown; you just want it to flavor the oil. Add the tomatoes, sugar, salt and pepper, and roughly half of the chickpeas, and lastly, the stock. Bring to a boil over high heat. Lower the heat and simmer, partially covered, for 20 minutes.

3. Remove the soup from the heat to purée. If you're using an immersion blender, purée the soup in the pot. Otherwise, wait a few minutes, until the soup cools.

4. If you don't have an immersion blender, scoop up some soup with a ladle or a measuring cup with a handle, pour it into the bowl of a food processor (or a blender) fitted with a metal blade, and blend until the soup is smooth. Pour the puréed soup into a bowl while you purée the remaining soup in batches.

5. Return the puréed soup to the soup pot, add the remaining chickpeas, and warm over medium heat. Serve warm.

2 15-ounce cans chickpeas; or 2 cups dried chickpeas, picked through, rinsed, and soaked overnight (page 61)

4 tablespoons olive oil

2 garlic cloves, peeled and coarsely chopped (page 23)

2 3-inch sprigs fresh rosemary, needles removed from stem and finely chopped (page 162)

4 pounds plum tomatoes, peeled, seeded, and diced fine (page 76), or 2 20-ounce cans diced Italian plum tomatoes

A pinch of sugar

1 teaspoon salt

A few turns of freshly ground black pepper

4 cups vegetable or chicken stock (pages 50, 51)

Sweet-Pea Soup with Fresh Ginger and Ground Toasted Almonds

1½ cups blanched almonds (page 76) plus more to top the soup

2 big yellow onions, coarsely chopped

1-inch piece fresh ginger, peeled (page 75) and finely grated

4 tablespoons (½ stick) unsalted butter

1-pound bag frozen petite peas (3⅓ cups)

6 cups vegetable or chicken stock (pages 50, 51)

1 teaspoon salt

A few turns of freshly ground black pepper

Customers do a double take when they see this soup listed on our chalkboard. Almonds? In soup? We encourage people to try it, and they invariably love it. Frozen peas, especially the little petite peas, are right up there with sliced bread in terms of progress when it comes to packaged foods. We use them exclusively. We wouldn't even think about shelling our own peas for something like this soup. It would take all day. At least. It's hard to imagine anyone even made pea soup, much less a big bowl of peas for a holiday meal, in the days before frozen peas. This soup is best served the day it's made.

1. Preheat oven to 450 degrees.
2. Scatter the almonds on a sheet pan and toast them for 8–10 minutes, or until they begin to brown and to give off a nutty fragrance. Remove the almonds from the oven and allow them to cool slightly. Pour the toasted almonds into a bowl. Take 1½ cups of the almonds and pour them into the bowl of a food processor (or a blender) fitted with a metal blade. Pulse repeatedly until the nuts are coarsely ground (the size of Grape-Nuts cereal).
3. Sauté the onions and ginger in the butter in a large soup pot over high heat, stirring occasionally so that they don't stick to the bottom or burn. When the onions have begun to reduce in volume, in about 5–10 minutes, lower the heat to medium and continue cooking for 10–15 more minutes, until the onions are tender and translucent.
4. Add the peas and the stock and bring to a boil over high heat. Lower the heat and simmer, partially covered, for 20–30 minutes, until the peas begin to turn a

dull avocado-green. Add the ground nuts, salt, and pepper, and simmer for another 5 minutes to allow the flavors of the nuts to cook into the soup.

5. Remove the soup from the heat to purée. If you're using an immersion blender, purée the soup in the pot. Otherwise, wait a few minutes, until soup cools.

6. Scoop up some soup with a ladle or a measuring cup with a handle, pour it into the bowl of a food processor (or a blender) fitted with a metal blade, and blend until the soup is smooth. Pour the puréed soup into a bowl while you purée the remaining soup in batches.

7. Return the puréed soup to soup pot, and warm over medium heat. Serve warm, topped with a sprinkling of the reserved nuts, chopped.

How to Deal with Fresh Ginger

To peel ginger, cut the nubs off of the root so you have a relatively even surface to work with. Then, using a vegetable peeler, peel the skin off as much of the ginger as you're going to grate. You may want to go back and peel the little nubs that you cut off, depending on how badly you need the ginger. When you're grating ginger, the piece you're grating will become stringy after you've grated it for a while—so much so that it will be almost impossible to grate. When you notice a whole bunch of strings hanging off your ginger, stop. Cut that part off, throw it out, and start grating again.

How to Blanch Almonds

It's easiest, of course, to buy already blanched almonds. But if you have almonds with skins lying around, or if you're just curious to try blanching, it isn't difficult at all. Just bring a pot of water to a boil. Dump in the raw, unskinned nuts. In a minute or two, when you see the skins beginning to loosen from the nuts, drain them through a colander. Once they're cool enough to work with, slip the skins right off with your fingers.

How to Toast Nuts

Toasted nuts smell and taste so much better than untoasted nuts that we're tempted to say all nuts should be toasted before using them in anything. Toasting also revives nuts that may be a bit stale. Stale nuts are not to be confused with rancid nuts, which are soft and taste bitter. Toss those out, and buy some fresh ones. Depending on their size, nuts will take about 5 to 10 minutes to toast in a 450-degree oven. You have to keep an eye on the nuts and move them around either by shaking the pan or by stirring them up with a metal spatula to prevent them from burning. The nuts are done when they begin to give off a strong nutty aroma. You want to chop nuts after toasting them, not before—small pieces are too easy to burn. If you don't already have the oven on, you can also toast nuts on the stovetop. Just throw them in a sauté pan over high heat and cook for about 5 minutes, or until the nuts become fragrant, shaking the pan often to keep the nuts from burning.

How to Peel Tomatoes

No matter how long you cook a tomato, its skin will never dissolve. We know. We've tried. The good news is that peeling the skin off a tomato isn't nearly as tedious as it sounds.

Bring a big pot of water to a boil over high heat. Use a small paring knife to carve an "x" at the bottom of each tomato. Drop the tomatoes into the boiling water for 1 minute. You don't want to cook the tomatoes, you just want the skin to loosen up, which makes it easier to peel. Once the skin looks slack but not wrinkled, and the skin around the "x" is curled slightly, drain the tomatoes in a colander and run cold water over them.

Using the same small knife, cut the core out of each tomato. Grab the tomato skin (at the place where you carved the "x") between your thumb and the edge of the paring knife, which is supported by your index finger, and gently pull the skin back from the meat of the tomato. If you're lucky, you'll get the skin off in four whole quarters. If you didn't leave the tomatoes in the water quite long enough, you'll have to settle for removing bits and pieces of skin at a time. The skin is so thin it will stick to your knife and fingers, so you should have a cup of cold water handy. Dip the knife into it to clean it off as you go.

Mushroom-Barley Soup with Spring Vegetables

MAKES 6 SERVINGS

This is one of our healthier soups, although that wasn't our point in making it. We just love the chewy texture of the barley with the vegetables. We call for specific vegetables in this recipe, but soup is not science; throw whatever vegetables you want in here. This soup is best served the same day. If you serve it the next day, be warned, the longer it sits, the more the barley will absorb the stock, and the thicker the soup will become. Add more stock to thin it.

2 medium carrots, peeled and diced fine (page 119)
2 celery stalks, diced fine
4 cups cold unsalted water
¾ cup barley, picked through and rinsed
1 teaspoon salt
A few turns of freshly ground black pepper
½ pound white mushrooms (including stems), wiped clean with a damp towel or paper towel and diced (page 25)
2 leeks, relieved of root end and dark-green tops, sliced ¼ inch thin, and rinsed (page 29)
½ pound asparagus, ends trimmed, cut on the diagonal into ¼-inch slices (page 128)
1 tablespoon unsalted butter
1 cup frozen petite peas
3 cups vegetable or chicken stock (pages 50, 51)
1 tablespoon chopped fresh Italian parsley (page 162)

1. Place the carrots, celery, and water in a large soup pot over high heat. Bring to a boil, and add the barley, salt, and pepper. Return to a boil, and continue to boil until the barley has absorbed all the water, 25–30 minutes. Stir occasionally toward the end of cooking time to make sure the barley doesn't stick to the bottom of the pot. The barley should be tender but still *al dente*—with a bit of bite. You may want to taste it periodically. If it is done before the water is absorbed, drain the excess water. If it is undercooked, add a small amount of water so the barley can cook a little longer.

2. Sauté the mushrooms, leeks, and asparagus in the butter over high heat until the asparagus is tender but not mushy. It'll cook more in the soup, and there's nothing worse you can do to asparagus than overcook it.

3. Add the mushrooms, leeks, and asparagus, along with the peas, to the soup pot. Add the stock and the parsley, and continue cooking over medium heat for another 15 minutes, until the flavors come together. Serve warm.

Curried Corn Chowder with Coconut Milk

MAKES 6 SERVINGS

1 big yellow onion, diced

2 garlic cloves, peeled and minced
(page 23)

¼ teaspoon fresh or ⅛ teaspoon
dried thyme (page 162)

2 tablespoons unsalted butter

3½ cups frozen or canned corn, or
4 ears, shucked and kernels cut
off cob

4 cups vegetable or chicken stock
(pages 50, 51)

1 teaspoon sugar

2 tablespoons unsalted butter,
clarified, or ghee (page 61)

1 tablespoon Madras curry powder

¼ cup canned coconut milk

1 tablespoon chopped fresh cilantro
(page 162)

1 tablespoon salt

A few turns of freshly ground black
pepper

Absolutely our most popular soup. We use frozen corn so we can make it year-round, but if you're making this soup in the summer, when fresh corn is piled high at farm stands and markets, it tastes even better. It's best served the day it's made.

1. Sauté the onion, garlic, and thyme in 2 tablespoons butter (not clarified) in a large soup pot over high heat, stirring occasionally to keep the onions and garlic from sticking to the bottom of the pot. When the onion has begun to reduce in volume, in 5–10 minutes, lower the heat to medium and continue cooking for about 10–15 more minutes, until the onion is tender and translucent.

2. Add the corn, stock, and sugar, and bring to a boil. Lower the heat, and let the stock simmer for 30 minutes.

3. In a separate sauté pan, warm the clarified butter over medium heat. Add the curry powder, and cook until the curry becomes fragrant, 3–5 minutes.

4. Remove the soup from the heat to purée. If you're using an immersion blender, you can purée the soup in the pot. Otherwise, wait a few minutes, until the soup cools.

5. If you don't have an immersion blender, scoop up half the soup with a ladle or measuring cup with a handle, pour it into the bowl of a food processor (or a blender) fitted with a metal blade, and blend until the soup is smooth. Return the puréed soup to the soup pot.

6. Return the pot to the stove over medium heat, and stir in the curry butter. To get all the curry butter out of the pan, use a rubber spatula to scrape it down, then pour a little bit of the soup into the pan, swish it around, and dump it back in the soup pot. Stir the coconut milk, cilantro, salt, and pepper into the soup pot, and cook for another 15 minutes, until the flavors come together. Serve warm with freshly ground black pepper.

Chilled Gazpacho with Roasted Red Pepper and Fresh Dill

We use roasted red pepper to add a hint of smokiness to this cool summer classic. For an outdoor lunch, we like to serve this in a big bowl set in a bucket of crushed ice. We like to garnish this with finely chopped red pepper, tomato, cucumber, and sprigs of fresh dill. This soup is just as good the day after it's made.

1. Dump all the ingredients into the bowl of a food processor (or a blender) fitted with a metal blade, and purée until the soup is smooth. Place the soup in the refrigerator, covered, to chill. Serve chilled.

1 red bell pepper, roasted as
   instructed on page 109
6 plum tomatoes, peeled, seeded,
   and diced (page 76)
1 red onion, coarsely chopped
2 garlic cloves, peeled and coarsely
   chopped (page 23)
1 cucumber, peeled, halved,
   seeded, and coarsely chopped
   (page 117)
1 tablespoon red-wine vinegar
1 tablespoon balsamic vinegar
¼ cup olive oil
3 cups canned tomato juice
A pinch of cayenne pepper
3 tablespoons chopped fresh dill
   (page 162)
2 teaspoons salt
A few turns of freshly ground black
   pepper

Once Upon a ...
SANDWICH

Fresh Dill–Tuna Salad Sandwich with Tomatoes and Sprouts

Hummus Sandwich with Crunchy Vegetables, Sprouts, and Ginger-Curry Vinaigrette

Goat Cheese Sandwich with Artichoke Hearts and Black Olive Vinaigrette

Variations on a Goat Cheese Sandwich Theme

Fresh Mozzarella Sandwich with Oven-Roasted Tomatoes and Pesto

Variation: Toasted Melted Fresh Mozzarella Sandwich

White-Bean Spread Sandwich with Sautéed Broccoli Rabe and Sun-Dried Tomatoes

Vermont-Cheddar-and-Cucumber Sandwich with Mango Chutney Mustard

Grilled Chicken Sandwich with Artichoke Hearts and Tarragon–Lemon Vinaigrette

Grilled Chicken Breasts · Poached Chicken Breasts

Brie Cheese Sandwich with Sliced Pears, Fresh Figs, and Watercress

Leftover Turkey Sandwich with Gruyère Cheese and Tomato Chutney

Tuna-and-Eggplant-Caponata Sandwich with Arugula and Black Olive Tapenade

Curried Chicken Salad Wrapped in a Flour Tortilla

Poached Chicken Breasts

Chicken-and-Avocado Sandwich with Radish Sprouts and Vinaigrette

Chicken Caesar-ish Salad Sandwich on Toasted Country Italian Bread

Tuna Sandwich with Mascarpone Cheese, Roasted Peppers, and Arugula

Frank's Marinated Roasted Peppers

Simple Grilled Tuna Steaks

Pork Loin Sandwich with Frisée and Rosemary-Garlic Aïoli

Roasted Pork Loin

Sandwiches were the first savory item we added to the menu at Once Upon a Tart after we decided to do more than just tarts. They were the obvious thing, since sandwiches are a lunchtime basic—familiar and easy to grab on the run. We were surrounded by delis at the time. We let them take care of ham-and-cheese. We wanted to be creative, to make sandwiches with different flavors that you didn't ordinarily find in sandwiches.

We started with what we knew and liked, sandwiches like tuna salad and turkey-and-Swiss, and updated them with fresher and bolder flavors. We also took combinations of flavors that we liked on their own—brie and figs, for instance—stuck them between bread, and called it a sandwich.

The process was pretty simple. We decided on the star of the sandwich, then we chose its supporting cast. We thought about what bread would match what ingredient—in size, texture, and flavor. We picked a green that gave us crunch and as much or little flavor as we wanted. We found some kind of oil—a vinaigrette or mayonnaise or whatever—to contrast with the other ingredients. And then we added what we have come to call "that one last thing."

That one last thing is the closest thing to a "secret" we have. Something that surprises us all the time is that people often ask us what the "secret" to our sandwiches is. Customers also ask why our sandwiches are so much better than those they make at home—even when they set out to imitate ours. We really don't know the answer, but we suspect it has to do with their stopping short of the sandwich's potential. Sun-dried tomatoes, marinated artichoke hearts, chutney . . . that one last thing is what gives the sandwich an extra punch. That's what makes our sandwiches special.

THINGS TO KNOW

We think of sandwich-making as building rather than cooking. As with building, we like to start with a strong foundation: really good bread. And then pile on the quality raw (or cooked, as the case may be) materials.

For the home cook, sandwiches are a by-product of leftovers. Whether it's turkey after Thanksgiving, that little piece of fish you were bold enough to ask the waiter to wrap up after dinner last night, or a little chunk of cheese sitting all alone in the dairy drawer of your fridge, sandwiches' main ingredients likely lived a more glamorous life before. Let the main ingredient decide your sandwich, and then mix and match, using whatever else you have on hand in the way of bread, greens, condiments, and anything that could be interpreted as "that one last thing."

If you're improvising with bread, just try to find one whose shape, flavor, and texture best fit with whatever you're going to pile in the middle (page 84). As for greens, we've steered clear of iceberg lettuce because it's such a cliché. We use organic baby greens or mesclun. But if all you have in the way of greens is a head of iceberg rolling around in your crisper drawer, use it. It has great crunch factor. Jerome likes to toss greens he's putting on a sandwich with dressing. He says it moistens the sandwich without getting the bread soggy.

We like to make our sandwiches in an assembly line,

because sandwiches are about assembly. So get all your ingredients out. Clear enough space on the counter or table to put the bottoms of your sandwiches in a row closer to you. We like to keep the tops and bottoms of halved rolls together. That way we have more chance of a sandwich that's not going to have its filling spilling out. We generally only spread whatever we're moistening our sandwiches with on the top half of the bread, but if you want a really moist sandwich, spread it on both halves. Either way, don't forget the edges. If you're a lazy spreader, the first bite of your sandwiches will be dry. Also, stack the ingredients of your sandwiches as evenly as possible. The tendency is to make a pile, so the first few bites of a sandwich are practically bread-on-bread, and the middle is so fat you can't get your mouth around it. Don't do this.

Now that you've assembled a sandwich that would make a structural engineer proud, you don't want to let it all fall to pieces when you cut it in half. Hold down on the bread with one hand as you use a serrated knife to cut through it with the other. Use the knife like a saw, and be patient, let the knife cut through the bread rather than you smashing down on the bread—and squishing all the good stuff out the sides.

Beyond that, what to say? These are sandwiches. Don't get hung up because you don't have a sun-dried tomato in the house. Don't go 5 miles to the store because you happen to have romaine and not arugula. Improvise. But don't delete. If you take out one ingredient, add another, or we guarantee your sandwich will taste like, well . . . like it's missing something.

FOR EVERY BREAD, THERE IS A REASON

Sandwiches at Once Upon a Tart begin and end with really good bread. We get numerous deliveries every morning. Ciabatta comes on foot, from the Sullivan Street Bakery, right down the street; the Tom Cat truck swings by a little later with sacks of sourdough baguettes. Choosing bread for a sandwich is not arbitrary. Different breads lend themselves to different sandwich ingredients. The textures and flavors of the two should complement each other. Even color is important. That's why we use pumpernickel on our Turkey Sandwiches with Gruyère Cheese (page 100), and a roll with black sesame seeds for our Dill–Tuna Salad Sandwiches (page 87). (We wanted something to set ours apart from the plain ol' deli versions.) Ultimately, what's important is that a sandwich remain a sandwich—not a pile of sandwich insides left behind on the plate while you bring two pieces of bread to your mouth.

French Baguette: The baguette was many Americans' introduction to nonsliced bread. Its long, crusty exterior, soft interior, and mild flavor make it good for quick multiple sandwiches, made submarine-style.

Ciabatta: Ciabatta is a crusty Italian loaf, rectangular and flat, that is made in an individual size and also in a long loaf, both of which lend themselves to just about any type of sandwich. When you cut into ciabatta, it will likely have big airholes in it.

Pullman Loaf: This is the closest thing to Wonder bread as far as nonpackaged breads go. It's made in a rectangular loaf

"The best tool for cutting a sandwich is a serrated knife. You use it like a saw, so you're never pushing down on the sandwich. Hold the sandwich firmly with the whole palm and heel of one hand, and gently, patiently, saw the bread into whatever size and number of sandwiches you want."
—Frank

pan and then sliced. Pullman is perfect for tea sandwiches, especially if you can have it sliced extra-thin.

Semolina: Semolina is a pretty common Italian bread with a hard, chewy exterior. It's made out of the same flour as pasta. It has a yellowish color and is often covered with sesame seeds, which give it a distinct flavor. It's such a pretty bread, we often use it to mask not-so-pretty (but delicious, of course) sandwich fillings.

Pita: Pita is a Middle Eastern bread that, when you cut off a bit of one end or cut it in half, forms a pocket that makes a great container for messy ingredients. Pita is thin, which means you get a lower bread-to-filling ratio, which some people prefer. We like the texture of whole-wheat pita. It's a great bread to have in the freezer for sandwich emergencies.

Seven-Grain Bread: In case you ever wondered: the seven grains in this sort of bread are whole-wheat flour, oat flour, rye flour, pumpernickel flour, bulgur, rolled oats, and white buckwheat. In addition to that, grainy breads often contain sunflower seeds, which makes them nutty and sweet. We like them with sweet sandwiches, like those that have chutney or curry, and we also like them with avocado, which is a bit of a California cuisine cliché, we know.

Onion or Rosemary Focaccia: Focaccia is a square, puffy, pizzalike bread, delicious all by itself. It is floppy, though, and does not hold ingredients well. When you use it for sandwiches, make sure to use it with ingredients that are not going to spill out: chicken breasts and sliced beefsteak tomatoes work well, as do sliced Italian meats like prosciutto and salami. Tuna salad in focaccia: bad idea.

Seeded Rolls and Baguettes: Seeds aren't sprinkled on bread for looks alone. They add a nice texture, and, whether sesame, poppy, or caraway, seeds impart another flavor to sandwiches. Try them; see what you like.

Sourdough: Sourdough is sour. It has a tangy flavor that people either love or don't. We love it, especially toasted, as in Chicken Caesar-ish Salad Sandwiches (page 107).

Pumpernickel Bread: Pumpernickel is German black bread, made black and also sweet by molasses. It has a very rich, distinct flavor that goes well with mellow flavors like turkey and ham.

Country Italian Bread: This name is a bit of a generalization. We're referring to Italian breads that have a crusty, flour-dusty exterior and a chewy interior that, like ciabatta (which falls into this category), has big airholes in it. You'll most often see it in big, round, domed loaves. Country Italian bread has probably single-handedly raised the bar on American bread standards. You could make any one of our sandwiches on it.

Fresh Dill–Tuna Salad Sandwich with Tomatoes and Sprouts on Black-Sesame-Seed Roll

MAKES 4 SANDWICHES

The loyal following that this sandwich has is a mystery to us. We have customers who eat it every day of the week, and some who insist there must be some secret as to how we make it. But it truly is just a tuna-salad sandwich—with mayonnaise, onions, salt, and pepper. (Okay, we add fresh dill.) Jerome believes it's about Americans' obsession with tuna-salad sandwiches in general. We use black-sesame-seed rolls, but any seeded roll, such as a kaiser roll, is fine.

1. Dump the tuna into a medium-size bowl, and use a fork to mash it until it is fine. Add the lemon juice, mayonnaise, dill, and onion, and mash it all together.
2. Slice the rolls in half like a hamburger bun and lay them on your work surface with the bottoms closer to you and their respective tops directly behind them. Spread the tuna salad evenly on the bottom portion of each roll. Top the tuna salad with tomatoes, salt, pepper, and sprouts.
3. Spread a tablespoon or more of mayonnaise to coat the inside of the top half of each roll, and place atop the bottom. Holding the palm of one hand over the sandwich to prevent the insides from spilling out, use a serrated knife to carve each sandwich gently in half. *Voilà.*

2 6-ounce cans solid white tuna packed in water or oil, drained

Juice of 1 lemon

½ cup mayonnaise (Jerome's Homemade Mayonnaise, page 177, or from a jar), plus ¼ cup or more for spreading on bread

2 tablespoons chopped fresh dill (page 162)

1 small red onion, diced fine

4 sesame-seed rolls

4 plum tomatoes or 2 beefsteak tomatoes, cored, cut into ½-inch-thick rounds

A sprinkling of salt

½ teaspoon freshly ground black pepper

½ cup alfalfa or radish sprouts

Hummus Sandwich with Crunchy Vegetables, Sprouts, and Ginger-Curry Vinaigrette on Semolina Roll

MAKES 4 SANDWICHES

4 semolina rolls (or any soft white rolls)

1¾ cups (1 recipe) Traditional Hummus (page 181)

2 cucumbers, peeled, halved, seeds removed, and cut on the diagonal into ¼-inch slices (page 117)

2 large carrots, peeled and cut on the diagonal into ¼-inch slices

2 red bell peppers, sliced into ¼ inch rings, seeded and cored (page 117)

2 celery stalks, diced fine

1 medium red onion, quartered and sliced thin

1 cup alfalfa or radish sprouts

1 recipe Ginger-Curry Vinaigrette (page 167)

This is one of our original sandwiches, back from the days when we were a vegetarian café. It's a great warm-weather sandwich—what with all the cool, crunchy vegetables.

1. Slice the rolls in half like a hamburger bun, leaving one side "hinged" to help contain the ingredients. Lay the open rolls on your work surface.
2. Spread the hummus in equal portions over each roll's bottom with a rubber spatula or the back of a spoon. Lay the cucumber slices on top of the hummus in neat rows so that they don't fall off. Then, in this order, lay the carrots, peppers, celery, onion, and sprouts on top of the cucumbers. Using a pastry brush or the back of a spoon, coat the inside of the top of each roll with 2 tablespoons or more of the vinaigrette.
3. Close the sandwiches, pressing the tops down firmly. Hold each sandwich with the palm of one hand, and use a serrated knife with the other to carve gently through the bread without letting the hummus spill out the sides.

"Don't make the process of preparing your own food more difficult than it needs to be. If you don't want to bother to make your own hummus, buy it. As long as you've got good bread and fresh greens, your sandwich will be better than any sandwich for sale out in the world."

—Frank

Goat Cheese Sandwich with Marinated Artichoke Hearts and Black Olive Vinaigrette on a Seeded Sourdough Baguette

MAKES 3 SANDWICHES

A favorite. We have one customer who buys six of these—one for her husband and four for her colleagues at work—every time she comes in. We assume the sixth is for her.

1. Blend the cheese, herbs, and oil in the bowl of a food processor (or a blender) fitted with a metal blade until it is smooth and spreadable, or mix with a sturdy wire whisk or spoon. Goat cheese varies in consistency, so the amount of oil you need may vary slightly.
2. Slice the baguette in half, and lay it, cut side up, with the bottom closer to you and the top directly behind it. Spread the goat-cheese mixture evenly over the bottom half of the baguette, using a rubber spatula or the back of a spoon. Make sure to spread the cheese all the way to the edges of the baguette, so there's good stuff in every bite. Lay the artichokes over the cheese, fitting as many as you can in one layer. Top with the greens.
3. Using a pastry brush, coat the inside of the top half of the baguette with the vinaigrette or drizzle the vinaigrette evenly over the bread.
4. Close the sandwich. Hold the sandwich closed with one hand as you saw through the bread with a serrated knife. We cut this sandwich into thirds on the diagonal. You can cut it into as many pieces as you like.

1 cup (8 ounces) goat cheese

1 teaspoon *herbes de Provence* (page 19)

2 tablespoons olive oil

1 seeded sourdough baguette (or any fresh baguette)

1 cup Marinated Artichoke Hearts with Herbes de Provence (page 184), or 1 11½-ounce jar

2 cups prerinsed mixed baby greens or mesclun

⅓ cup or more Black Olive Vinaigrette (page 170)

Variations on a Goat Cheese Sandwich Theme

Goat cheese is one of our kitchen staples. There are so many things that taste great with goat cheese, some of which you're bound to have in your cupboard or refrigerator. When deciding what to put on goat cheese sandwiches, think: If this were a goat cheese *salad,* what would I put on it? Some things we've come to like a lot with goat cheese:

Marinated Roasted Peppers (page 109), Marinated Artichoke Hearts (page 184), or Marinated Sun-Dried Tomatoes (page 165)

Roasted eggplant, asparagus, zucchini or yellow squash, or yellow onions

Sliced cucumber and celery with salt

Ratatouille (page 37)

Eggplant Caponata (page 172)

Sweet or spicy Italian sausage

Leftover chicken or steak, sliced thin

Avocado and ripe summer tomatoes

Arugula, arugula, arugula

A drizzle of olive oil

Fresh Mozzarella Sandwich with Oven-Roasted Tomatoes and Pesto on Onion Focaccia

Right across the street from Once Upon a Tart is a little Italian cheese shop called Joe's Dairy. It's one of the few shops left from the days when Sullivan Street was an extension of Little Italy, located about half a mile east of us. Frank often walks in to find Anthony (there is no longer a Joe) with his hands in pots of hot water, making fresh cow's-milk mozzarella. (In the olden days, mozzarella was made exclusively from buffalo's milk.) You can use fresh and smoked mozzarella interchangeably in our recipes. What's important is that you not confuse this creamy, sweet, handmade specialty with the rubbery, tasteless lumps you find under the same name in the refrigerator section of the supermarket.

4 4-inch squares onion focaccia

1 pound fresh mozzarella, sliced into ¼-inch rounds

A sprinkling of salt

½ teaspoon freshly ground black pepper

1 recipe Oven-Roasted Tomatoes (page 185); or, in the height of summer, 2 big ripe beefsteak or heirloom tomatoes, sliced ¼ inch thick and sprinkled with salt and pepper

½ cup fresh basil (24 whole leaves)

½ cup Classic Basil Pesto (page 164)

1. Cut the focaccia in half like a hamburger bun and lay it on your work surface with the bottoms closer to you and the matching tops directly behind them. Lay the mozzarella slices so they cover the bottom halves of the focaccia, and sprinkle the mozzarella with salt and pepper.
2. Place a layer of roasted tomatoes over the cheese, and lay the basil leaves over the tomatoes.
3. Using a rubber spatula or the back of a spoon, spread the pesto on the inside of the top half of the bread, making sure to coat the edges.
4. Place the top halves on the respective bottoms. Rest one hand firmly on each sandwich. Use a serrated knife to gently saw the sandwich in half.

Variation: Toasted Melted Fresh Mozzarella Sandwich

This sandwich is delicious served warm with either raw or Oven-Roasted Tomatoes (page 185). Preheat your oven to 400 degrees. Place the assembled sandwiches on a sheet pan lined with parchment paper or aluminum foil, and bake for 5–10 minutes, until the mozzarella is melted and the underside of the bread is crisp. Sprinkle with thin strips of basil.

White-Bean Spread Sandwich with Sautéed Broccoli Rabe and Sun-Dried Tomatoes on Ciabatta

MAKES 4 SANDWICHES

8 cups (2 quarts) cold salted water (for the broccoli rabe)
2 bunches broccoli rabe, rinsed and trimmed of tough ends
¼ cup olive oil
1 garlic clove, smashed and peeled (page 23)
4 ciabatta rolls, or 1 long ciabatta loaf   *continued*

Tomatoes, white beans, and broccoli rabe is a combination handed down from Frank's mother's kitchen. In the winter, she adds sausage and chicken stock to the mix, turning it into a soup, the memory of which still makes Frank swoon. For a hearty winter sandwich, add the crumbled meat of two or three links of sweet or spicy Italian sausage to the garlic and oil. Cook until the sausage is no longer pink, then add the broccoli rabe.

1. Bring the water to a boil in a big pot and add the broccoli rabe. Cook for 5 minutes, or until the thickest stems are tender. Drain well in a colander.

2. Warm the oil and garlic in a large sauté pan over medium heat, and sauté for a few minutes to let the garlic flavor the oil. Add the broccoli rabe and sauté for 5–7 minutes, until the rabe is wilted. Stop cooking before the florets fall apart. Remove the pan from the heat, and allow the broccoli rabe to cool slightly.

3. Dump the broccoli rabe and the garlic onto a cutting board, and chop coarsely. Set the chopped broccoli rabe in a colander to drain off any excess liquid.

4. To assemble the sandwiches, slice the ciabatta rolls in half like a hamburger bun and place them, cut side up, on your work surface with the bottom halves closer to you and the respective tops directly behind them. Using a rubber spatula or the back of a spoon, spread the white beans evenly over each sandwich bottom. Top the spread with a layer of broccoli rabe, then a layer of sun-dried tomatoes. Spread the vinaigrette with a spatula or the back of a spoon on the inside of each sandwich top.

5. Place the top on its respective bottom. Holding the sandwich with one hand, use a serrated knife to saw it gently in half with the other.

2 cups (1 recipe) White-Bean
    Spread (page 180)
12 Marinated Sun-Dried Tomatoes
    (page 165 or from a jar)
½ cup Sun-Dried Tomato Vinai-
    grette (page 166)

What Is Broccoli Rabe?

Despite its clever name, broccoli rabe, also called rape or rapini, isn't a close relative of broccoli at all. It is in the cabbage family (as is broccoli), and is what's known loosely as a "leafy green." A lot of people don't like broccoli rabe because it's very bitter. That's what we love about it. We prepare it only one way—boiled to tender and then sautéed in garlic and olive oil. Once it's sautéed, do with it as you might do with spinach: toss it in a pasta dish with sausage, in a frittata with sun-dried tomatoes, or, along with roasted potatoes, as a side dish to a roasted loin of pork (page 111) or Frank's Roasted Chicken (page 52).

Vermont-Cheddar-and-Cucumber Sandwich with Mango Chutney Mustard on Sliced Seven-Grain Bread

MAKES 4 SANDWICHES

In a sandwich where cheese is the main event, the quality of the cheese you use makes a big difference. We use Vermont cheddar at the store, but you may want to use this sandwich as an excuse to try some of the delicious farmhouse cheeses—Dutch and English—that you will find at specialty-food stores. If you don't have or want to make Mango Chutney Mustard, store-bought Major Grey's mango chutney works fine.

8 slices seven-grain bread (or other sliced grainy, seedy bread)

¾–1 pound sharp cheddar cheese, cut into ¼-inch-thick slices

2 cucumbers, sliced into ½-inch rounds

1 bunch watercress (1 cup), rinsed, dried well, and trimmed of tough ends

½ cup or more Mango Chutney Mustard (page 161) or Major Grey's mango chutney from a jar

1. Set the bread slices on your work surface with four slices in one row and four slices behind them. Arrange the cheddar cheese in an even layer on the first row of bread slices. Add a layer of cucumber slices on top of the cheese, then watercress.
2. Using a spatula or the back of a spoon, spread at least 2 tablespoons of chutney on the remaining slices of bread (the sandwich tops). Close the sandwiches and, using a serrated knife, slice them in half on the diagonal.

"There's this trick with cucumbers that I learned from my father, where you cut off the ends of a cucumber and rub the stump that you cut off with the end that you cut it from until the cucumber begins to foam. Supposedly this takes out any bitterness. I have no idea if it's true, but I do it every time I cut a cucumber."
—Frank

Grilled Chicken Sandwich with Roasted Artichoke Hearts and Fresh Tarragon–Lemon Vinaigrette on Rosemary Focaccia

MAKES 4 SANDWICHES

1 15-ounce can water-packed
   artichoke hearts, drained

2 tablespoons olive oil

2 garlic cloves, peeled and minced
   (page 23)

A sprinkling of salt

½ teaspoon freshly ground black
   pepper

2 cups prerinsed mixed baby greens
   or mesclun

½ cup Fresh Tarragon–Lemon
   Vinaigrette (page 182)

4 4-inch squares rosemary focaccia

2 pounds boneless, skinless
   chicken breasts (about 4 halved
   breasts), grilled (page 97), cut
   into ½-inch slices

This healthy chicken sandwich started out on our "Specials" menu. But every time we didn't have it, we got requests for it, so now we just leave it there. The combination of artichokes with tarragon is very French—and very delicious.

1. Preheat oven to 450 degrees.
2. Cut the artichokes into quarters, and toss in a small bowl with the olive oil, garlic, salt, and pepper. Spread them out on a sheet pan, and place the sheet pan in the oven. Roast the artichokes for 20–25 minutes, until they begin to char at the edges. Remove the sheet pan from the oven, and set it on a wire rack to cool. You can put the artichokes on the sandwiches warm or at room temperature.
3. Just before you're ready to make your sandwiches, toss the greens and vinaigrette in the bowl you used to toss the artichokes.
4. To assemble the sandwiches, cut the focaccia in half like a hamburger bun and lay the slices on your work surface with the bottom halves closer to you and the matching tops directly behind them. Lay the chicken slices on the bottom halves of the focaccia. Lay as many artichoke pieces as you can fit in one layer on top of the chicken, and top the artichokes with a handful of the dressed greens.
5. Place the focaccia tops on their respective bottoms, and use a serrated knife to saw the sandwiches gently in half.

Jerome on Free-Range Chickens

Frank and I have differing opinions about free-range chickens. Frank doesn't like them. He says free-range chicken tastes too gamey. And I tell him: That's what chicken is supposed to taste like. In the village where my mom lives in the south of France, people don't talk about free-range or not free-range. My mother goes down the street to a woman's house to buy eggs, and to another woman to buy chickens. Yes, these chickens run around. And they taste so much better, more tender and more flavorful, than chickens you buy here—unless you're buying free-range chickens, that is.

Grilled Chicken Breasts

Marinate 2 pounds boneless, skinless chicken breasts for at least 2 hours and as long as overnight in ¼ cup olive oil, ¼ cup lemon juice, two or three minced garlic cloves, and a teaspoon each of salt and freshly ground black pepper. You can also add herbs—fresh or dried thyme, fresh or dried rosemary, and fresh tarragon are some we use. Prepare your outdoor grill, or heat a grill pan over high heat. Grill the chicken breasts about 6–8 minutes per side, or until no liquids are released when the center of each breast is pierced with small sharp knife. Your goal is to turn the chicken only once. Turning the pieces more not only disrupts the pretty grill-marks, it can also cause you to cook the chicken unevenly.

Poached Chicken Breasts

Poached chicken breasts are a low-fat-lover's dream. After all, you're cooking white meat chicken in water. Because of the bland flavor of poached chicken, we prefer it for our curried chicken salad. The bland chicken lets the curry stand out. And the curry gives the chicken a reason for being there.

To get two boneless, skinless chicken breasts, start with two bone-in, skin-on chicken breasts (1½–2 pounds). Place them in a pot with enough well-salted water to cover. Add a yellow onion, quartered, a few sprigs of parsley, one bay leaf, two celery stalks including the leaves, and a few peppercorns. Bring the water to a boil, and cook for 15 minutes. Reduce the heat, and continue to simmer the chicken for 30–45 minutes, or until no liquid is released when the center is pierced with a small, sharp knife. (The chicken is cooked in the first 15 minutes. The extra cooking time tenderizes it.) Remove the chicken from the water with a slotted spoon or a pair of tongs, and set it on a plate to cool. When the chicken is cool enough to handle, slide the skin off the breast, then slide the breast off the bone.

Brie Cheese Sandwich on a Baguette with Sliced Pears, Fresh Figs, and Watercress

MAKES 3 SANDWICHES

This is basically a French fruit-and-cheese plate between bread. You can really use any cheese you like: blue cheese, Gorgonzola, Gruyère. You can also play with other fruits, such as tart apples, halved grapes, or even *membrillo,* a winy quince paste that is traditionally eaten with Manchego cheese in Spain. We serve this on a French baguette, just to keep with the theme, but it may be even better on sliced raisin-walnut bread.

1 Anjou or Bosc pear, halved, cored, and thinly sliced

Juice of ½ lemon

1 bunch watercress (1 cup), rinsed, dried well, and trimmed of tough ends

⅓ cup or more Honey-Balsamic Vinaigrette (page 170)

1 French baguette

½ pound Brie cheese, cut into ¼ inch-thick slices

6 ripe figs, stems removed, sliced in half lengthwise

1. Toss the pear slices in a small bowl with the lemon juice.
2. Cut the baguette in half like a sandwich and lay it, cut side up, on your work surface with the bottom half closer to you and the top behind it. Lay the cheese slices evenly over the bottom half of the baguette. Lay the pear slices in one layer over the cheese. Place the halved figs on top of the pears.
3. Toss the watercress in a separate small bowl with the vinaigrette and lay the watercress on top of the figs.
4. Place the top of the baguette on the sandwich and, using a serrated knife, cut on the diagonal into however many sandwiches you want. We cut it into thirds.

"We hate to see anyone measuring lemon juice, because it isn't anything we'd ever do at home. The juice of a lemon is roughly 3 tablespoons."
—Frank

Leftover Turkey Sandwich with Gruyère Cheese and Tomato Chutney on Pumpernickel

MAKES 4 SANDWICHES

8 slices pumpernickel bread

1 pound fresh roasted turkey, cut
  into ¼-inch slices

A sprinkling of salt

½ teaspoon freshly ground black
  pepper

½ pound Gruyère cheese (or other
  Swiss cheese), sliced thin

8 leaves romaine or iceberg lettuce,
  rinsed and dried well

½ cup or more Tomato Chutney
  (page 159)

It's too bad that roasted turkey is relegated to Thanksgiving in this country. There are so many great ways to use turkey leftovers, including this sandwich, that it makes sense to roast a turkey at least twice a year. At the store, we serve this sandwich on pumpernickel for its color and unique flavor. But if it was the day after Thanksgiving at Frank's parents' house, this would have to be served on Jewish rye.

1. Lay the bread on your work surface with four slices in a row and four slices directly behind them. Stack the turkey evenly over the four bottoms, and sprinkle it with salt and pepper. Add the cheese and the lettuce.
2. Using a spatula or the back of a spoon, spread at least 2 tablespoons of the tomato chutney on the remaining bread slices (the sandwich tops), and close each sandwich. Use a serrated knife to saw sandwiches in half on the diagonal.

Make a boxed lunch using a bakery box lined with a napkin—cloth or paper. Fill it with a sand-
wich, a Chinese-takeout container of salad, a whole piece of seasonal fruit, and a cookie or
brownie. When we make boxed lunches at the store, we also throw in a little surprise: a bookmark
or jacks or a pair of colorful painted chopsticks, even for grown-ups.

Tuna-and-Eggplant-Caponata Sandwich with Arugula and Black Olive Tapenade on a Semolina Baguette

2 6-ounce cans solid white tuna packed in water or oil, drained; or 1½ pounds fresh tuna steaks, grilled medium-well (Simple Grilled Tuna Steaks, page 109)

1 cup Eggplant Caponata (page 172)

½ teaspoon salt

A few turns of freshly ground black pepper

1 semolina baguette

1 bunch arugula (2 cups), rinsed and dried well

⅓ cup Black Olive Tapenade (page 169) or black olive paste from a jar

A reporter for the *New York Observer* called this sandwich "scrumptious" but ugly. (The same thing might be said about their newspaper.) Eggplant caponata is an Italian vegetable stew that Frank's Aunt Pina made every time she came from Sicily to visit. What they say is true: this isn't our most beautiful sandwich, but it is delicious.

1. Dump the tuna into a medium-size bowl, and use a fork to crumble it into very small pieces. Add the caponata, salt, and pepper, and work it all together with your fork.

2. Cut the baguette in half like a sandwich and place it, cut side up, on your work surface with the bottom half closer to you and the top directly behind it. Spoon the tuna-caponata mixture onto the bottom half of the baguette, and use the back of the spoon to spread it in one even layer over the bread. Top with the arugula.

3. Using a rubber spatula or the back of a spoon, coat the top half of the baguette with the olive tapenade, taking care to spread it all the way to the edges. Close the sandwich and, using a serrated knife, saw sandwich on the diagonal into thirds (or however many pieces you want).

"It's important to dry your greens before putting them on a sandwich. Wet lettuce makes wet bread."
—Frank

How to Rinse and Dry Arugula (and Other Leafy Greens)

Arugula has a peppery taste that's great on sandwiches. It's often sold with the roots on, and in those roots, lots of dirt. If arugula is not rinsed well, you'll end up with grit in your sandwich. The first thing to do, if your arugula has roots on it, is to cut them off. Next fill a sink or a big bowl with water, and dunk the arugula underwater. Let it sit underwater for about 5–10 minutes so the dirt will fall to the bottom. It's a good idea to do this twice. There's nothing worse than biting into sand. Put the rinsed arugula in a salad spinner, and spin it until all the water is removed. If you don't have a salad spinner, rest a layer of arugula on a paper towel, cover with another paper towel, another layer of arugula, etc. Roll it all up fairly tight, and let it sit until you're ready to use the arugula. Arugula should be bought when you need it and rinsed only as you're going to use it; it tends to wilt pretty quickly.

Some Packaged Breads We Like a Lot

Pita bread: It's thin, so you get a high filling-to-bread ratio, which a lot of people like. We like the way it keeps messy ingredients contained.

English Muffins: You have to toast them. Open-faced, they make a great platform for the Fresh Dill–Tuna (page 87) or the Curried Chicken Salad (page 104) sandwiches.

Seedy Whole-Grain Breads: Those with sunflower seeds and whole-wheat berries are often sweetened with honey, and they're really good, especially toasted.

Jerome on Bread

At Once Upon a Tart we don't bake our own bread and never would. Making bread is a very specific thing; it's very complicated in terms of working with yeast. And it's very hard to get right. That's why real bread-bakers, that's all they do: they bake bread. They have these big expensive ovens. They have the right yeast. In France, it's very rare that someone would bake his own bread at home. You can get really good bread in even the tiniest town. Going to the bread-baker is part of daily life. These days, good bread-bakers who make crusty, European-style breads are popping up all over America. You can get a decent baguette in most grocery stores. Which means you can make a good sandwich at home.

Curried Chicken Salad Wrapped in a Flour Tortilla

MAKES 8 SANDWICHES

¼ cup walnuts, toasted (page 76)

1 pound boneless, skinless chicken breasts (1 whole breast), poached and cut into ½-inch cubes (page 97)

3 celery stalks, diced fine

¼ cup dried currants

1 small red onion, diced fine

½ cup sour cream

½ cup mayonnaise

¼ cup Madras curry powder

2 tablespoons honey

1 teaspoon salt

½ teaspoon fresly ground black pepper

8 large flour tortillas

1 bunch watercress (1 cup), rinsed, dried well, and trimmed of tough ends

Curry means "spice" in India, but in this country it refers to the yellow powder that includes a mix of roasted turmeric, coriander, and cumin. We like the hot Madras curry powder, and we recommend you buy it in small quantities, because it loses its flavor after a few months.

1. Preheat oven to 350 degrees.
2. Break up the walnuts with your fingers, letting them drop into a big bowl. Add the chicken, celery, currants, and onion to the bowl as you cut them.
3. Stir the sour cream, mayonnaise, curry powder, honey, salt, and pepper together in a small bowl. Pour this curry sauce into the bowl with the chicken mixture and toss with a wooden spoon until the chicken and vegetables are coated.
4. Lay the tortillas on a sheet pan, and warm in the oven for about 5 minutes to soften and warm the tortillas slightly. Remove the sheet pan from the oven, and lay the tortillas on your work surface. Spoon the curried chicken in the center of each tortilla, and top the chicken with the watercress.
5. To make the sandwich, fold the left and right sides toward the center. Holding the sides together with one hand, roll the still-open portion of the tortilla from the bottom up, until it is rolled shut. Slice it in half with a serrated knife.

"Once Upon a Tart is definitely not a 'wrap' kind of place. But I will admit tortillas make good sandwiches. We started using them years ago, on weekends when we got really busy and ran out of bread."
—Jerome

Chicken-and-Mashed-Avocado Sandwich Stuffed in Whole-Wheat Pitas with Radish Sprouts and Soy-Ginger Vinaigrette

MAKES 4 SANDWICHES

This sandwich is a mainstay of Frank's when he visits his brother in sunny southern California, where the backyard avocado trees are always bearing fruit. Assembling it may sound more complicated than it is. Basically, you want to resist the temptation to stuff the pita from bottom to top. If you stuff, instead of spreading and layering the ingredients, your first few bites will be all sprouts, and your last will be all chicken and bread. Spreading and layering ensures you get a little bit of everything in every bite, a key characteristic in a good sandwich.

2 pounds boneless, skinless chicken breasts, grilled (page 97), or any leftover chicken without bones (2 whole breasts)

½ cup Soy-Ginger Vinaigrette (page 183)

4 whole-wheat pitas

2 ripe avocados, halved, pits removed (page 63)

1 cucumber, peeled, halved, seeded, and cut into ¼-inch slices (page 117)

1 10-ounce box radish sprouts

1. Cut the chicken into ½-inch slices, and toss in a medium-size bowl with all but a few teaspoons of the vinaigrette.
2. Cut the tops off the pitas in a wedge (from ten o'clock to two o'clock) to create a 3–4-inch opening. Lay the pita pockets down on your work surface with the openings facing you.
3. Scoop half of the meat out of each avocado half with a regular spoon, and plop it onto the bottom of each pita. Using the back of a fork, mash and spread the avocado over the inside surface of the bread. If you're working with a nice ripe avocado, it'll be like spreading soft butter inside the pita. If you're not working with a nice ripe avocado, find one! In addition to being impossible to spread, unripe avocados lack flavor.
4. Slide the chicken slices through the opening and place them in one layer on top

of the avocado. Next, place a layer of cucumbers over the chicken. Lay the sprouts over the cucumbers, using your fingers to break them apart as you would a cotton ball. Drizzle the leftover vinaigrette evenly over the sprouts by placing a spoonful through the opening in the pita.

"Toasting does wonders for bread. For any sandwich, if you're working with either substandard bread or bread that's going stale, toast it, either dry or with a drizzle of olive oil."
—Frank

Chicken Caesar-ish Salad Sandwich on Toasted Country Italian Bread

MAKES 4 SANDWICHES

Toast takes the place of croutons in what amounts to a Caesar salad between slices of bread. We added the "-ish" to the name when we added sliced fennel, a radical departure from the classic Caesar, to our salad.

1. Cut the dark, leafy ends off the romaine leaves. Chop the leaves into 1-inch pieces, and toss them into a big bowl.
2. Cut off the leafy tops and the stalks of the fennel bulb and discard. Cut the fennel bulb in half lengthwise, and use a paring knife to cut out the core. Cut the halves lengthwise into ¼-inch slices, and toss them in with the romaine. Add the chicken cubes.
3. Just before you're ready to serve the sandwiches, add the dressing to the chicken cubes, salt, and pepper, and toss everything with a big spoon or your hands. The lettuce and the chicken should be well coated with the dressing. It's the dressing that makes this sandwich, so add more if necessary.
4. Toast the bread to golden brown. Arrange the toast on the countertop, four slices in a row and four slices behind them. Spoon the chicken salad onto the front slices of bread (the bottoms). Give the chicken salad a few more turns of fresh pepper. Close the sandwiches. Place one hand on each sandwich and, using a serrated knife, gently saw the toasted bread in half without letting the insides fall out.

5 or 6 leaves romaine lettuce, rinsed and dried well

1 medium fennel bulb

1 lb. boneless, skinless chicken breast (1 whole breast), grilled (page 97), cut into ½-inch cubes

½ cup or more Our Own Caesar-ish Dressing (page 179)

½ teaspoon salt

A few twists of freshly ground black pepper

8 slices country Italian bread or other good white bread

Tuna Sandwich with Mascarpone Cheese, Marinated Roasted Peppers, and Arugula on Crusty Italian Rolls

MAKES 4 SANDWICHES

2 6-ounce cans solid white tuna
packed in water or oil, drained;
or 1½ pounds fresh tuna steaks
sliced 1½ inches thick, grilled
(below)

Juice of ½ lemon

½ teaspoon salt

A few turns of freshly ground black
pepper

4 ciabatta rolls or other crusty
Italian rolls

1 cup sliced Marinated Roasted
Peppers (below, or from a jar)

2 bunches arugula, rinsed and
dried well (page 103)

¼ cup mascarpone cheese

Every day, customers come into Once Upon a Tart, take one glance at our Fresh Dill–Tuna Salad Sandwiches (page 87), scrunch up their low-fat noses, and ask: "Does this have mayonnaise in it?" Finally, we decided to placate them by creating an Italian-style tuna salad, one made with olive oil and lemon juice. We spread the bread with mascarpone, a sweet Italian double-cream cheese that goes well with the marinated peppers. We sometimes use smoked mozzarella or Bel Paese, another soft Italian cheese that is not quite as sweet as mascarpone. Of course, the presence of any cheese more than makes up for the absence of mayonnaise, but this is not something we publicize.

1. Dump the tuna into a medium-size bowl and mash it with a fork. Add the lemon juice, salt, and pepper, and work it all together with your fork. If you're using grilled tuna steaks, skip this step, and instead cut the steaks into ½-inch-thick slices.

2. Slice the rolls in half lengthwise like a hamburger bun and lay them, cut side up, on your work surface with the bottom halves closer to you and their respective tops behind them.

3. Spread the mashed tuna in even portions over the four bottom halves, or lay the grilled tuna slices on top. Lay the peppers over the tuna, and top with a heap of arugula.

4. Spread a tablespoon or more of mascarpone on the top half of each roll with the

back of a spoon or a rubber spatula. Place the tops on the sandwich bottoms. Hold the sandwich down with one hand and, using a serrated knife, gently saw each sandwich in half.

Frank's Marinated Roasted Peppers

You can roast peppers on a sheet pan in the oven, but I think the best way is the old-fashioned Italian way: directly on the fire. It gives the peppers a nice smoky flavor.

Place four red or yellow peppers directly on a very hot grill or on the grate of your gas stovetop over a high flame. You want to char the peppers completely on all sides, so, as one side blackens, use a pair of tongs to turn the peppers, exposing a raw side to the fire. When the peppers are black all around, place them in a paper bag for 10–15 minutes so that the steam will loosen up the skins. Hold each pepper in your hands and pull off the skin, rinsing your hands underwater if they're covered with bits of the charred pepper. Don't clean the peppers by running them underwater; you'll be pouring the smoky flavor down the drain.

Pull the stems off the tops of the peppers. Break the peppers apart with your fingers and pull out the seeds. Cut each pepper lengthwise into 8 strips, and toss them with ½ cup or more olive oil, ¼ cup balsamic vinegar, two crushed garlic cloves, a teaspoon salt, and ½ teaspoon freshly ground black pepper. These peppers will last refrigerated in an airtight container for 10 days.

Simple Grilled Tuna Steaks

Fresh tuna is a great fish for grilling. Its beeflike texture prevents it from crumbling on the grill or under the broiler, as so many fish do. We generally like our tuna rare to medium-rare, but crumbled up for tuna salad, we think medium-well works better. There's no reason to cook a tuna steak well. Any cooking past medium-well will just dry the tuna

out. This marinade is subtle, and perfect for sandwiches made of either sliced tuna or tuna salad. If you're going for an Asian flavor, try the Soy-Ginger Vinaigrette (page 183).

To make the marinade, whisk 2 ounces oil with the juice of 1 lemon, 1 tablespoon fresh thyme, 1 clove of garlic, finely chopped, 1 teaspoon salt, and ¼ teaspoon red-pepper flakes in a medium-size bowl or baking dish. Place 1½–2 pounds of tuna steaks in the marinade, and let the tuna marinate from 15 minutes to 3 hours. Preheat your broiler, or fire up your grill with a hot flame. Take the tuna steaks out of the marinade and sprinkle them with salt and pepper. If you like a lot of pepper, pat the tuna steaks with the pepper so that it forms a crust. Place the tuna steaks on the broiler pan or grill and, for rare steaks, cook for about 2–2½ minutes per side; for medium-well steaks, 4 minutes per side.

Pork Loin Sandwich with Frisée and Rosemary-Garlic Aïoli on a Baguette

MAKES 4 SANDWICHES

Jerome's Paris-bistro favorite, a frisée salad with *lardons* (French for chunks of fried bacon), was the inspiration for this sandwich.

1. Use a paring knife to carve the core out of the frisée. Tear the leaves apart with your fingers.
2. Slice the baguette in half lengthwise, like a sandwich, and lay the baguette on your work surface with the bottom closer to you and the top directly behind it.
3. Layer the pork slices to cover the baguette bottom. Top with frisée. Spread the aïoli on the inside of the top half of the baguette, and place the top on the bottom. Holding the sandwich down with one hand, use a serrated knife to carve it into four sandwiches.

1 bunch frisée, rinsed and dried well

1 regular or sourdough baguette

1 pound roasted boneless pork loin (below), cut into ¼-inch slices

½ cup or more Rosemary-Garlic Aïoli (page 178)

Roasted Pork Loin

Roasting a pork loin is so easy. Once it's in the oven, it doesn't require any attention at all, other than to be taken out when it's done. We'd be willing to bet you end up with tender, juicy pork the first time you try this recipe. At the store, we use only Smithfield pork, which means that it is farmed in Smithfield, Virginia, home of the famous eponymous ham. At home, Jerome serves it with roasted potatoes and a green vegetable like broccoli rabe or haricots verts or asparagus.

Preheat oven to 350 degrees. Use a paring knife to slice small slits all over a 2-pound boneless pork loin. Thinly slice 2 cloves garlic, and insert the slivers into the holes. Spread 1 cup Dijon mustard evenly over the entire loin, using your fingers or a small spatula, and sprinkle the loin with 3 tablespoons *herbes de Provence,* 2 teaspoons salt, and a teaspoon of freshly ground black pepper. Place the pork loin on a roasting rack set in a roasting pan and bake for 1 hour at 350 degrees or until a meat thermometer inserted into the center reads 150 degrees. Remove from the oven, and let sit for 5 minutes before slicing.

Once Upon a ...
SALAD

Crunchy Cucumber, Celery, and Red Bell Pepper Salad with Cumin and Fresh Mint
Chickpea-and-Lentil Salad with Sun-Dried Tomato Vinaigrette
Jicama Slaw with Three-Seed Dressing
Roasted Fingerling Potato, Beet, and Corn Salad with Lemon and Chives
Lentil-and-Bulgur Salad with Curried Frizzled Onions
Barley, Wild Rice, and Asparagus Salad with Soy-Ginger Vinaigrette
Wheat-Berry-and-Roasted-Beet Salad with Ginger-Curry Vinaigrette
Couscous Salad with Roasted Vegetables and Sun-Dried Tomatoes
Variation: Roasted Vegetable Platter with Capers and Balsamic Vinegar
Corn-and-Bulgur Salad with Cucumber, Tomato, Lemon, and Parsley
Black-Bean Salad with Avocado, Cilantro, and Jalapeño Pepper
Chickpea-and-Carrot Salad with Cumin and Black Olives
Country Potato Salad with Scarlet Runner Beans and Fresh Herbs
Crudités
Haricot-Vert-and-Corn Salad with Artichoke Hearts and Fresh Tarragon–Lemon Vinaigrette
Lentil-and-Quinoa Salad with Shredded Carrots and Ginger-Curry Vinaigrette
Chunky-Cucumber-and-Watercress Salad with Crumbled Feta Cheese
Penne Pasta Salad with Grilled Fennel, Roasted Eggplant, Black Olives, and Fresh Dill
Gazpacho Salad
Variation: Turning Gazpacho Salad into Bread Salad
Three-Bean Salad with Honey-Balsamic Vinaigrette
Cold Spinach Noodles with Spicy Peanut-Sesame Sauce

When we first started serving savory foods at Once Upon a Tart, we tried to keep the menu all vegetarian, for a couple of reasons. On a very practical level, we didn't have space for storing meats. Also, at about that time we visited a vegetarian restaurant in California Frank had read about. The food we had was nothing like the vegetarian or health food we were used to, where every bite feels like the cook made a compromise. The flavors were so vibrant and the meal was so satisfying, it was incidental that there was no chicken breast lying on the plate. And that was our inspiration.

Neither of us is a vegetarian. And neither of us knew beans about beans—or grains. Quinoa. Who knew what quinoa was? (See page 145.) Back then, the only place we could find recipes for beans and grains was in vegetarian cookbooks. Since we didn't want our food to have that vegetarian, health-food taste, we decided to start from the ground—or the grain—up. We took flavors from all around the world, vegetables and vinaigrettes that we liked, and applied them to what we were doing.

In the process of inventing these salads, we didn't make any fatal errors, like when we baked muffins that didn't rise or scones that had the texture of sod. We were able to sell most of the salads we created, because, unlike baking, salad-making requires no leap of faith. We could taste the salads and decide as we went along if they needed more crunch or more sweetness, more vinegar or salt or oil—whatever. Which is the best thing about salads: you really can't screw them up.

In this chapter, we give you our favorite salad recipes. But we also give you a lot of information about different ingredients and why and how we use them. Because our hope is that eventually you'll simply be boiling up a bunch of beans or rice or potatoes, rummaging through your fridge, raiding your neighbor's garden, peeking into containers of leftovers, and making something really tasty out of what you once might have called, staring into the refrigerator in frustration, "nothing to eat."

THINGS TO KNOW

Making salads might seem intimidating, what with all those ingredients mysteriously composed into one dish. But there are really only a few skills you need to know: chopping vegetables (or it wouldn't be salad, right?), whisking oil and vinegar together, and boiling water.

The first thing we recommend you do is read a recipe all the way through before getting started. Salads are multitask ventures, and having a clear idea of what you'll need and the steps involved will help you organize yourself most efficiently. Maybe you can whisk together a vinaigrette (or throw your laundry in for that matter) while your wheat berries are cooking—that kind of thing.

In our recipes, we specify a medium carrot or a medium red onion, but that's just because we're trying to answer any questions that you might have. But the great thing about salads is their flexibility. You could use twice as many carrots, and nothing bad would happen to any of these salads. "The other night, I took a heaping of the lentil-and-quinoa salad from the store," Frank says. "When I got home, I realized I had to stretch it, so I just mixed it with some brown rice. Since I didn't add more vinaigrette, the curry flavor was more subtle. And it was perfect in its new incarnation."

Chopping vegetables is a major and unavoidable part of salad-making. We've picked up some tricks along the way that make things like mincing a clove of garlic or cutting a carrot into matchsticks less daunting. In this chapter, we'll share these tricks and other methods we've found to make quick work of various vegetables.

In order to keep salad-making from being mess-making, whenever possible we cut each vegetable and then throw it directly into the bowl we're going to toss the salad in. That way, we're not dirtying up a whole pile of bowls unnecessarily. So start with a big bowl—something big enough to hold all your ingredients and with enough room to spare so that you can get a spoon or your hands in there to toss it without worrying about bits of vegetables or quinoa flying out onto the kitchen floor. When you're ready to serve the salad, spoon it onto a platter or into a smaller, prettier bowl. That way the edges of the bowl or platter are nice and clean.

Cooking the beans and grains is the easiest part of salad-making—though, if you've never cooked or even heard of these things before, you might not believe us. Look at it this way: if you can boil a pot of water, you can boil a pot of water with some lentils floating around in it. But before you do any-thing with beans and grains, pour them into a bowl or onto a countertop and run your fingers through them, looking for any unappealing grains or small stones that may have gotten in there. Then rinse the beans or grains in a colander.

Finally, as far as dressing the salad, you can do it one of two ways. Either make a separate vinaigrette and pour it over the salad. Or do what we often do: simply throw all the vinaigrette ingredients on top of the salad and toss them together. The only disadvantage to this shortcut is that you have to toss the salad more, because you're also mixing up the dressing. If you're working with soft ingredients, like crumbled cheese or avocados, you'll want to make the vinaigrette in advance to avoid ending up with a smushed-up salad. Don't just follow our instructions and then put the salad on the table. Taste it to see if it needs more of anything, particularly salt.

A serving in these recipes is roughly 1 cup of salad. But a serving really depends on whether you're serving it as an appetizer, or as a side dish, or making a meal of the salad. When you're thinking quantities, think how much of each ingredient one person would eat. One potato. Maybe half a cucumber. A cup of grain. Let your stomach be your guide.

Frank on Olive Oil

Olive oil extremists will go on about "peppery" or "fruity" when it comes to the subtle differences in olive oils. For me, it's like when people describe wine as having a nose of blackberries or dirty socks. These are not descriptions that mean a lot to me. What I do know, though—in the case of both wine and olive oil—is that when I like it I know it. I also know that it really doesn't need to be expensive to be good. For cooking and salads, any average olive oil will work. I don't even think it has to be extra-virgin. These salads, for instance, have enough flavors in them that they don't need, or even want, a dominant olive-oil flavor. If I am serving something with just olive oil, like heirloom tomatoes in the summer, or a bowl of salted and peppered oil with Italian bread with dinner, then I use the best olive oil I have in the cupboard. You can buy the expensive stuff at stores that provide little cubes of bread and ramekins of oil so you can taste the oils and see what you like. That's all that matters.

Crunchy Cucumber, Celery, and Red Bell Pepper Salad with Cumin and Fresh Mint

6 celery stalks, cut into ¼-inch
    slices

3 cucumbers, peeled, halved,
    seeded, and cut on the diagonal
    into ¼-inch slices

3 scallions, both the white and
    green parts, cut into ¼-inch
    slices (page 117)

½ red onion, halved again and
    sliced thin

1 red bell pepper, julienned

FOR THE VINAIGRETTE

1 tablespoon Dijon mustard

1 garlic clove, peeled and minced
    (page 23)

¼ cup white-wine vinegar

1 teaspoon ground cumin

1 teaspoon salt

A few turns of freshly ground black
    pepper   *continued*

This is a very colorful salad. At home, Frank puts mushrooms in, too—because he likes mushrooms with cumin. Radishes would be another good addition, or even daikon radishes or jicama, cut into sticks.

1. Throw the vegetables into a big bowl as you cut them.
2. To make the vinaigrette, whisk the mustard, garlic, vinegar, cumin, salt, and pepper together in a small bowl. Add the olive oil in a slow, thin, steady stream, whisking as you go to form an emulsion (page 171). Stir in the parsley and the mint.
3. Just before you're ready to serve the salad, pour the vinaigrette over your vegeta-

bles and, using a large metal spoon or your own two hands, toss it up until the vegetables are evenly coated. Taste the salad to see if it needs more of anything, particularly salt.

¼ cup olive oil

2 tablespoons finely chopped fresh
   Italian parsley (page 162)

2 tablespoons finely chopped fresh
   mint (page 162)

How to Deal with a Bell Pepper

Bell peppers are pretty easy to cut up once you get rid of all that air in the middle. First, cut the pepper in half, right down the middle, from top to bottom. Then pull out the core and seeds with your hands. Use a paring knife to carve out the remaining membrane (the part that holds the seeds in). With two halves to work with, you can now dice it or cut it into thin strips, the fancy name for which is "julienne." If the rounded top and bottom are making the pepper difficult to work with, chop those off so you've got a nice flat square. Go back and cut those pieces when you're done cutting the nice flat square. When we're adding raw pepper to a sandwich, like the Hummus Sandwich with Crunchy Vegetables (page 88), we like to cut them into rings. Carve the stem out with a paring knife. Knock the pepper on the counter to spill out the seeds. Slice the pepper crosswise into ¼-inch rings. For recipes for which you want to peel the peppers, leave them whole.

How to Deal with a Cucumber

The first thing to do with a cucumber is cut off each end so that you're dealing with a straight-edged cylindrical thing. Then peel it—either peel the whole thing clean, or leave strips of peel on, for no other reason than that the little strips of green look nice. Once it's peeled, you want to seed it. So cut your cucumber in half lengthwise, and then take a small spoon—a round measuring spoon works well—and run it down the length of the cucumber, scooping out the seeds as you go. Now, unless you specifically want the cucumbers to wilt, it's important not to chop cukes too thin. If you cut them too thin, the acid in the lemon or vinegar "cooks" the cuke, breaking down the fibers of the cucumber so you lose the characteristic cucumber crunch.

How to Deal with a Scallion

We always use both the white and the green part of scallions. Why wouldn't we? They both have lots of flavor and crunch, and green is a nice enough color. Of course, we cut off the roots and the tough, leafy ends of the greens. (The younger and more tender the scallions are, the more of the green part you can use.) Then we line up a few scallions and cut them all at the same time with a big chef's knife.

Chickpea-and-Lentil Salad
with Sun-Dried Tomato Vinaigrette

4 cups cold unsalted water (for the lentils)

1 cup French green lentils (*lentilles de Puy*), picked through and rinsed (page 119)

1 15-ounce can chickpeas; or 1 cup dried chickpeas, soaked overnight (page 61)

1 small red onion, halved, peeled, and diced fine (page 119)

1 red bell pepper, diced fine (page 117)

1 cucumber, peeled, halved, seeded, and diced fine (page 117)

6 Marinated Sun-Dried Tomatoes, (page 165, or from a jar), julienned (page 152)

1 recipe Sun-Dried Tomato Vinaigrette (page 166)

½ cup fresh basil leaves, cut into thin strips (page 162)

Our most popular salad. We cut the vegetables to match the size of chickpeas, and what we end up with is a salad so small and crunchy at the store we refer to it as "salsa."

1. Place the water and lentils in a big saucepan, and bring them to a boil over high heat. Lower the heat and simmer, uncovered, for 20–25 minutes, until the lentils are tender but not losing their skins. The best way to test a lentil is to bite into one; it should be tender and have lost its chalky, raw-bean taste. Drain the lentils in a colander and dump them into a big bowl.

2. Drain and rinse the canned or soaked chickpeas in a colander. If you are using dry chickpeas, place them in a pot with 4 cups of cold unsalted water, and bring them to a boil over high heat. Lower the heat and simmer, uncovered, for an hour or more, until the beans are tender and have lost their chalky, raw-bean flavor. Drain well in a colander and cool to room temperature, then dump the chickpeas into the bowl with the lentils.

3. Toss the remaining ingredients except the basil on top of the beans. Toss the salad with a big spoon or with your hands until all the beans are evenly coated with the vinaigrette. Sprinkle the basil over the salad and toss again, gently, so you don't bruise the basil. Taste for salt. If the flavors need to be heightened a bit, drizzle a tablespoon or two of balsamic vinegar over the salad.

4. Cover and refrigerate the salad for at least an hour, so the beans can absorb the flavor of the vinaigrette. Serve chilled or at room temperature.

What Are French Green Lentils?

French green lentils, or *lentilles de Puy,* are the only lentils we use, for both salads and soups. They're smaller than the brown lentils you most often encounter in soup, and also greener. We think they have more flavor, but the main thing we like about them is that they still have their seed coat on, so they hold their shape after they're cooked, which brown lentils don't.

How to Dice Cylindrically Shaped Vegetables: Zucchini, Yellow Squash, Cucumbers, Carrots . . .

Until you've done it, it can seem like a real challenge to get something with round sides—like a cucumber, say—into little squares, which is what "dice" means. The first thing to do to make the whole cutting process easier is get yourself a flat side. Cut the cylindrically shaped vegetable in half lengthwise, like you would a banana for a banana split. Then cut each half lengthwise into strips as wide as you want the dice. Keep the strips in a line, and cut across the length of the strips, again making the cuts as far apart as you want the dice to be wide. That's it. Diced it is.

How to Slice and Dice an Onion

Chopping onions is probably the most unpopular cooking task there is, for good reason. It makes your fingers smell like onions, and it makes you cry. Some people say if you put a half an onion on the top of your head, it will prevent you from crying. The only logic we can see for this is that if you have half an onion on your head, you are not hunched over the onion with its tear-inducing juices wafting right up into your eyes. The best way we know to keep from tearing is to get the job done as quickly—and with as few cuts—as possible. To chop an onion quickly and tear-free, first, remove all of the outer "paper" from the outside. Next, cut the onion in half from top to bottom. Lay the cut side down on a cutting board and make lengthwise slices as wide as you want your dice. Keeping the slices in place with your free hand, make perpendicular slices the same thickness as the first set of slices, with your other hand. Lift up your hand and what you've got under there is a diced onion, all held together. To cut an onion into thin slices, cut the onion in half through the middle. Lay the cut side down and halve it again so that you're working with a quarter of an onion. Lay the quarter down and, using your free hand, knuckles tucked under your palm, as a guide for your knife, make thin slices from the cut end of the onion, the top of the semicircle, back toward the bottom of the semicircle so that what you end up with are little half-moon-shaped slices of onion. By holding the onion flat against the cutting board and using your hand as a guide, you can cut them so thin they are almost transparent, which is how we like our onion slices when they're not going to be cooked.

Jicama Slaw with Three-Seed Dressing

1 medium bulb jicama, peeled and
    julienned (page 152)

¼ head red cabbage, sliced thin

3 medium carrots, peeled and
    julienned (page 152)

2 red bell peppers, julienned (page
    152)

½ red onion, halved again and
    sliced thin

FOR THE DRESSING

½ cup red-wine vinegar

1 tablespoon sugar

1 teaspoon salt

1 tablespoon poppy seeds

2 teaspoons mustard seeds

2 teaspoons celery seeds

¼ cup olive oil

We decided to make a mayo-free slaw option for our fat-conscious lunchtime customers.

1. Throw the vegetables into a big bowl as you cut them.
2. Just before you're ready to serve the slaw, pour the dressing ingredients over the vegetables and toss them until they're evenly coated. Taste the slaw to make sure it has enough salt.

"It's really easy to put too much onion in a salad. I don't like to bite into a huge chunk of onion. So I always cut them into a really small dice, or slice them very thin."
—Frank

When you're serving salads family-style or on a buffet, it's all about the bowl. Use a bowl that is almost too small. That makes the salad look big and abundant. We love to shop flea markets for different kinds of bowls. It's nice to have an assortment around.

Roasted Fingerling Potato, Beet, and Corn Salad with Lemon and Chives

MAKES 6 SERVINGS

1 pound fingerling or red-skinned
    potatoes, scrubbed and cut into
    ½-inch cubes (page 119)
Juice of 1 lemon
⅓ cup olive oil
Salt and freshly ground black
    pepper (for roasting the
    vegetables)
1 pound yellow beets (if you can
    find them; if not, any beets),
    scrubbed, stems and roots cut
    off
2 cups frozen or canned corn, or
    2–3 ears, shucked and kernels
    cut off the cob
⅓ cup finely chopped or snipped
    fresh chives (page 162)

We roast the corn for this salad. And we use yellow beets when we can find them—just because we like to see all of these different yellow foods in one place. If you have more than one sheet pan, it's fine to roast more than one sheet pan of different vegetables at the same time.

1. Preheat oven to 450 degrees.
2. Toss the potatoes with a third of the lemon juice, 2 tablespoons of the olive oil, a sprinkling of salt (¼ teaspoon), and a few twists of freshly ground black pepper. Spread potatoes out on a sheet pan, and roast until they are very soft when pierced with a fork, 25–30 minutes. The best way to test potatoes is to taste them. Remove the sheet pan from the oven, and use a metal spatula to scrape the potatoes into a big bowl.
3. Cut the beets in half or quarters, depending on how big they are, so that the pieces are roughly the same size. Toss them with 2 tablespoons of the olive oil, a sprinkling of salt (¼ teaspoon), and a few twists of freshly ground black pepper. Place the beets on a sheet pan, cut side down (we do this to get a nice brown side). Place the sheet pan in the oven, and roast until the beets are soft when pierced with a fork, 20–25 minutes. Remove the sheet pan. When beets are cool enough to touch, with small paring knife peel the skin back and remove. Scrape the beets onto a cutting board, and cut into pieces the same size as the potatoes. If you're using red beets, place them in a separate bowl and toss them with the salad just before you're ready to serve it. This way you avoid staining the whole salad.
4. Toss the corn with the remaining olive oil, a sprinkling of salt (¼ teaspoon), and

a few twists of freshly ground black pepper. Scatter the corn on a sheet pan, and roast for 15–20 minutes, until the corn begins to brown. You'll want to shake the pan at least once during the cooking time so that the corn browns evenly and does not burn. Remove the sheet pan from the oven, and use a metal spatula to scrape the corn on top of the potatoes and beets.

5. Sprinkle the vegetables with chopped chives (or snip the chives directly over the bowl) and add the rest of the lemon juice, and toss the salad with a big spoon or with your hands. Taste for salt. Serve while the salad is still warm or at room temperature.

"Corn is still hard to get in France, and corn on the cob is almost impossible to find. The corn produced in France is for animals. My mother would find frozen or canned corn in the grocery store and use it in her salade niçoise, so I wasn't shocked when I saw corn here. But I was shocked when I tasted it. It was a whole different experience from the frozen and canned corn I was used to."
—Jerome

Lentil-and-Bulgur Salad with Curried Frizzled Onions

MAKES 6 SERVINGS

6 cups cold unsalted water (for the
 lentils)

1½ cup French green lentils
 (*lentilles de Puy*), picked
 through and rinsed (page 119)

1 cup bulgur wheat

¾ cup boiling water (for the bulgur
 wheat)

1 cup or more vegetable oil for
 frying

2 big yellow onions, quartered and
 sliced thin

2 red bell peppers, julienned (page
 152)

2 tablespoons Madras curry powder

1 tablespoon salt

¼ teaspoon freshly ground black
 pepper

One of the best things about learning to cook is that you can take other people's ideas and improve upon them. The idea for this recipe came from a tiny Middle Eastern restaurant around the corner. Frank loved their salad consisting of lentils and bulgur with frizzled (yes, that's a word) onions. His favorite part was the onions, though, and in his opinion the salad never had enough. So he added more, and then got the curry idea from the curried onion rings that are a specialty at the restaurant next door to Once Upon a Tart.

1. Place the 6 cups water and the lentils in a big saucepan, and bring to a boil over high heat. Lower the heat and simmer, uncovered, for 20–25 minutes, until the lentils are tender but not losing their skins. The best way to test lentils is to bite into one. You'll know if it needs more time; it'll be hard, for one thing, and it will taste chalky. Drain the lentils in a colander.

2. Place the bulgur in a bowl big enough to hold the whole salad, and pour the boiling water over it. Cover the bowl tightly with plastic wrap, and let the bulgur rest for 15–20 minutes, until it has completely absorbed all of the water. Remove the plastic wrap and fluff the bulgur with a fork. Toss the drained lentils into the bowl on top of the cooked bulgur.

3. Heat a cup or more of vegetable oil in a high-sided sauté pan over high heat until a single onion piece placed in the oil sizzles (oil should be 1 inch deep). If the oil gets so hot that it's smoking, take the pan off the heat until the oil cools slightly.

4. Place the onions in the oil in one layer, being careful as the oil may splatter. Fry the onions until they are golden brown. Remove the onions with a slotted spat-

ula, hold them over the oil for a few seconds to drain, then toss them directly onto the grains. Don't worry about draining every drop of oil; the oil will add needed moisture to the salad. After you've fried all the onions, drain all but ⅓ cup of the oil from the pan.

5. Add the peppers to the pan with the reserved oil and fry them, stirring them with a metal spatula occasionally, until they begin to blacken around the edges. Leaving the peppers in the pan, add the curry powder, reduce the heat to low, and sauté for a few minutes, until the curry gives off a nice smell. Add the salt and pepper to the oil, and pour the oil and peppers over the grains. Toss with a big spoon.

6. Taste the salad to see if it needs more of anything, particularly salt. Serve no more than a few hours after adding the oil to the grains.

What Is Bulgur Wheat?
Bulgur wheat is wheat kernels that have been steamed, dried, and then crushed. When you work with bulgur, you don't cook it exactly. You rehydrate it.

"Our salads make great side dishes. Instead of standing in the kitchen mashing potatoes while your guests are talking in another room, make a lentil salad the night before and just throw the bowl on the table when you're ready to eat."
—Jerome

Barley, Wild Rice, and Asparagus Salad with Soy-Ginger Vinaigrette

MAKES 6 SERVINGS

We love the combination of the toothsome barley with the crunchy wild rice in this salad. If you like onions, add finely chopped scallions to the stir-fry at the last minute. Another great addition is a nice ripe avocado.

1. Place the 2 cups water and the rice in a big saucepan, and bring to a boil over high heat. Lower the heat, and simmer, uncovered, for 40–45 minutes, until the rice is tender but still chewy. (The best way to test it is to taste it.)
2. While the wild rice is cooking, put the 4 cups cold water and the barley in another saucepan, and bring them to a boil over high heat. Lower the heat, and simmer, uncovered, for 25–30 minutes, until the barley is tender to the bite but not mushy.
3. Remove both pots of grains from the heat, and drain each of them separately in a colander. Dump the rice and the barley into one big bowl.
4. Warm the oil in a large sauté pan or wok over high heat. Add the ginger, and sauté until golden brown. With the flame still high, add the asparagus. Stir frequently until the asparagus is tender—this is essentially a stir-fry. You may want to taste a piece here or there so you don't overcook the asparagus; the difference in taste between perfectly cooked and overcooked asparagus is like the difference between fresh food and that which you may remember eating in the school cafeteria. Once they're done, dump the asparagus, along with the oil and ginger, on top of the grains.
5. Just before you're ready to serve the salad, pour the vinaigrette over the grains

2 cups cold salted water (for the rice)

½ cup wild rice (page 128), picked through and rinsed

4 cups cold salted water (for the barley)

1½ cups barley, picked through and rinsed

2 tablespoons canola or vegetable oil

1 2-inch piece fresh ginger, peeled (page 75) and julienned

1 pound fresh asparagus (page 128), cut diagonally into 2-inch pieces

1 teaspoon salt

1 ripe avocado, halved, pitted, and diced (page 63) (optional)

1 recipe Soy-Ginger Vinaigrette (page 183)

What Is Wild Rice?

Wild rice is not rice at all. It's a marsh grass. It has a nutty flavor and chewy texture that we love. Because it is so expensive, we often use it in combination with another grain. It's important to clean wild rice thoroughly. Put it in a bowl with cold water, stir it around a bit, and let it sit for a few minutes. Then drain.

What Is Canola Oil?

We had to look this up in an encyclopedia. Every other oil comes from something we'd heard of—a peanut or an olive, for instance. But a canola? We found that canola oil is really just a made-up name to replace the unattractive real name "rapeseed" oil. Canola oil reputedly has all kinds of health benefits, like lowering cholesterol. We like it because its mild flavor allows the other flavors we're using to shine through.

and vegetables, add the salt, and toss it all with a large spoon or your hands, until everything is evenly coated with the dressing. If you're adding avocado cubes, throw them in the salad midway through the tossing, to prevent them from getting mushed up. We like this salad served right away, at room temperature.

How to Deal with Asparagus

Some people peel the stems of asparagus with a vegetable peeler. That's much too precious for our tastes, and unnecessary. Asparagus magically knows where its woody boundaries are. Which means that, if you simply grab a spear at both ends and snap it, it automatically breaks off in the right place, sparing you its tough, fibrous ends. So snap asparagus before doing anything else with it. The best way to cut asparagus, as with many straight vegetables, is to line up a few spears together, so you're cutting more than one spear with each cut of the knife. You'd be surprised how much time you save that way, plus, it makes you feel like a pro.

Wheat-Berry-and-Roasted-Beet Salad with Ginger-Curry Vinaigrette

MAKES 6 SERVINGS

Jerome loves pomegranates, which are pretty common in the south of France, where he's from. When he can find them, he substitutes pomegranate seeds for the cranberries in this salad. If you don't like beets, you can leave them out and have a simple wheat-berry salad. But be forewarned: we've converted a lot of anti-beet people with this salad.

1. Preheat oven to 450 degrees.
2. Place the water and wheat berries in a large saucepan, and bring them to a boil over high heat. Lower the heat, and simmer, uncovered, for 30–35 minutes, until the wheat berries are tender but still chewy. The only way to test them is to take one out and bite into it. Drain the wheat berries in a colander, and dump them into a bowl big enough to fit the whole salad. Pour the vinegar over the hot wheat berries and toss. Let them cool to room temperature.
3. Cut the beets in half or quarters depending on their size, roughly into same-size pieces. Toss the beets with the olive oil, a sprinkling of salt (¼ teaspoon), and a few turns of freshly ground black pepper. Place the beets, cut side down (to get a nice brown side), on a sheet pan, and place the sheet pan in the oven. Roast for 25–30 minutes, until the beets are soft when pierced with a fork. Remove the sheet pan from the oven, let the beets rest until they are cool enough to handle, then, using a small paring knife, peel the skin off the beets. Cut the beets into ½-inch cubes, and set aside. (We rarely set things aside. Setting things aside just means dirtying more bowls and taking extra steps. Usually this is unnecessary. But we do set aside the beets in this recipe, because their juice will stain the

8 cups cold unsalted water (for the wheat berries)

1½ cups wheat berries

3 tablespoons red-wine vinegar

1 pound red beets, washed, stems and roots cut off

1 tablespoon olive oil

Salt and freshly ground pepper (for the beets)

½ medium red onion, diced fine

4 celery stalks, cut into ¼-inch-thick slices

½ cup dried cranberries (or pomegranate seeds, if you like and can find them)

½ cup pecans, toasted and coarsely chopped (page 76)

½ teaspoon cinnamon

1 recipe Ginger-Curry Vinaigrette (page 167)

What Is a Wheat Berry?

A wheat berry is the whole wheat kernel—only the outer hull has been removed. Wheat berries are really chewy, which is what we like about them. But this makes it challenging to test for doneness. The best way to test is to bite into one. If it tastes like something you want to eat, it's done. We don't bother to soak wheat berries, since we don't think it makes much difference in cooking time.

wheat berries. We throw them in at the end, so the beets will stain the salad as little as possible.)

4. Toss the onion, celery, and dried cranberries or pomegranate seeds into the bowl with the wheat berries.

5. Pour the vinaigrette and cinnamon over the salad, and toss it with a big spoon or your hands. Add the beets midway through the tossing. This salad can be served cool or at room temperature, but if you're going to wait a long time before serving it, you might also wait to add the beets and pomegranate seeds, since they will stain the wheat berries and turn the whole salad purple.

Jerome on Pomegranate Seeds

Pomegranate seeds are like sunflower seeds—they're so much work to get to, it makes you wonder if it's the work that makes you think they're something special. Some people eat the pulp, but I find it bitter. I eat only the tiny little seeds that you pry out of the pithy pulp. They are as sweet as they are tart, which is what I like about them. That and the fact that they're a beautiful bright ruby-red. In France, the pomegranate is pretty common. Grenadine, which is pomegranate-seed juice, is mixed with soda for a popular café drink. When I can get pomegranate in the fall I like to throw the seeds in salads.

Couscous Salad with Roasted Vegetables and Sun-Dried Tomatoes

MAKES 8 SERVINGS

Jerome first threw this salad together with some leftover roasted vegetables. That's how Jerome cooks—very spontaneously. And whatever he makes turns out delicious. It's in his blood.

1. Preheat oven to 450 degrees.
2. Combine the couscous and the currants in a bowl big enough to hold the whole salad.
3. Pour the boiling water mixed with 1 tablespoon of the olive oil over the couscous. Cover the bowl tightly with plastic wrap, and let the couscous rest until it has absorbed all the water, 15–20 minutes. Remove the plastic wrap, and fluff and separate the couscous with a fork or your fingers.
4. Put the eggplant in a colander placed in the sink. Sprinkle the eggplant with a thin coat of salt, and toss it to distribute the salt to all sides of the eggplant. Let the eggplant rest for at least 20 minutes to "sweat" the bitterness out.
5. Toss the zucchini and yellow squash with 1 tablespoon olive oil, a sprinkling of salt (¼ teaspoon), a few twists of freshly ground black pepper, and one-third of the garlic. Spread the zucchini and squash out on a sheet pan, place the pan in the oven, and roast until the vegetables begin to brown, 8–10 minutes. Be careful not to overcook the zucchini and squash, because you don't want them to fall apart when you toss them with the couscous. Remove the sheet pan from the oven, and use a metal spatula to scrape the zucchini and squash (along with the pan bits and juices) off the pan and into the bowl with the fluffed couscous.
6. While the zucchini and squash are roasting, toss the pepper and onion in

1½ cups (1 12-ounce box) couscous (page 133)

¼ cup dried currants

1½ cups boiling unsalted water (for the couscous)

¼ cup olive oil

1 small or ½ large eggplant, cut into ½-inch cubes (page 38)

Salt (for sweating the eggplant) and freshly ground black pepper (for roasting the vegetables)

1 zucchini, diced fine (page 119)

1 yellow squash, diced fine (page 119)

3 garlic cloves, peeled and minced (page 23)

1 red bell pepper, cut into ½-inch squares (page 117)

1 red onion, diced fine (page 119)

⅓ cup balsamic vinegar

10 Marinated Sun-Dried Tomatoes (page 165), julienned (page 152)

½ cup walnuts, toasted, then coarsely chopped (page 76)

½ cup fresh basil (24 whole leaves), cut into thin strips (page 162)

1 tablespoon of olive oil, a sprinkling of salt (¼ teaspoon), a few turns of freshly ground black pepper, and one-third of the minced garlic. When the squash is done, spread the peppers out on the sheet pan and roast for 10–15 minutes, until the edges start to blacken. Use a metal spatula to scrape the peppers, along with the oil and garlic, off the sheet pan and into the bowl with the couscous.

7. Repeat with the eggplant and remaining oil and garlic, but without any additional salt. Roast for 15–20 minutes, until the undersides of the eggplant brown and the insides feel soft and creamy. Remove the sheet pan from the oven, and use a metal spatula to scrape the eggplant, along with the oil and garlic, straight off the sheet pan into the bowl with the couscous and other vegetables.

8. Add the vinegar, sun-dried tomatoes, walnuts, and basil, and gently toss the couscous with a big spoon or with your hands. Do your best to avoid breaking up the vegetables. Taste salad for salt. You'll probably need at least a sprinkling more, as well as a few more turns of the pepper mill.

Variation: Roasted Vegetable Platter with Capers and Balsamic Vinegar

Frank compares this to Italian antipasto. Jerome says it's like French ratatouille. Both of us make it outside the store often. In the summer, we cut the vegetables larger and grill them on an outdoor grill instead of roasting them on a sheet pan.

Cook the vegetables in the same way as above, and use the same amounts (or more) as you did for the couscous, scraping them into separate bowls. When all the vegetables are cooked, arrange them on a platter. In another small bowl, stir 2 tablespoons balsamic vinegar, a tablespoon of capers (including the vinegar), and a little more salt and pepper together, and drizzle over the vegetables.

What Is Couscous?

Jerome's father's family owned a pasta-and-couscous business in Algeria back when Algeria was a French territory. They left in 1962, when the country gained its independence. So couscous was a part of Jerome's life—and thus became a part of our repertoire at the store. Couscous is not a grain. It is a tiny pasta usually made from semolina. The semolina is processed, dried, and shaped into tiny balls. There is also whole-wheat couscous, as well as Israeli couscous, which is made in larger balls. In addition to steaming couscous as we call for in our recipes, you can also "cook" it with an acid such as vinegar or lemon juice until the liquid is absorbed and the couscous is soft. It's the same concept used to soften bulgur for tabbouleh.

Corn-and-Bulgur Salad with Cucumber, Tomato, Lemon, and Parsley

MAKES 6 SERVINGS

1 cup bulgur wheat

¾ cup boiling unsalted water (for the bulgur wheat)

2 cups frozen or canned corn, or 2–3 ears, shucked and kernels cut off cob

1 tablespoon olive oil

1 cucumber, peeled and diced (page 117)

4 plum tomatoes, cored and diced, seeds and liquids reserved

3 scallions, both white and green parts, sliced very thin and separated with your fingers (page 117)

FOR THE VINAIGRETTE

Juice of 1 lemon

1 teaspoon salt

¼ teaspoon freshly ground black pepper

A pinch of cayenne pepper

2 tablespoons olive oil

¼ cup chopped fresh Italian parsley (page 162)

We make this salad only in the height of summer when fresh corn is in season. Sugars in corn begin turning to starch the minute the cobs are plucked from the stalk. So we're not just talking freshness because it has culinary brio. It makes a difference. If you're using really, really, really fresh corn, you won't need to cook it at all. Bulgur has a nice nutty flavor, so we just use lemon juice and olive oil to dress this salad.

1. Place the bulgur in a bowl big enough to hold the whole salad, and pour the boiling water over the bulgur. Cover the bowl tightly with plastic wrap, and let the bulgur rest for 15–20 minutes, until it has absorbed all the water. Remove the plastic wrap, fluff the bulgur with a fork, and allow it to cool to room temperature.

2. Sauté the corn in the olive oil in a sauté pan over high heat for 2–3 minutes—just to take off the raw edge. Add to the bowl with the bulgur.

3. Toss the cucumber, tomatoes, and scallions, as you cut them, into the bowl with the cooled bulgur and corn.

4. To make the vinaigrette, whisk all the ingredients except the olive oil and parsley together in a small bowl. Add the olive oil in a slow, thin, steady stream, whisking as you go to form an emulsion (page 171). Stir in the parsley.

5. Pour the vinaigrette over the salad and toss it all up with a big spoon or your hands.

6. Cover and refrigerate for at least an hour before serving. Serve chilled.

Black-Bean Salad with Avocado, Cilantro, and Jalapeño Pepper

MAKES 6 SERVINGS

We like to use Hass avocados, because they are less watery and have more flavor than the big Florida avocados. Toss the avocados in at the end, so you don't end up with a big mushy avocado-coated mess. We use lime juice in this, in keeping with the flavors of Mexico. If you can find Key limes (also called Mexican limes), they are even tangier, and we think better.

1. Drain and rinse the soaked beans. Put them in a big soup pot along with the onion and water, and bring to a boil over high heat. Lower the heat and simmer, uncovered, for an hour or more, until the beans are soft to the bite but not falling apart or splitting. Drain the beans in a colander. Remove and discard the chunks of onion, and dump the beans into a bowl big enough to hold and toss the entire salad. Pour the vinegar over the warm beans, and toss. Let the beans cool to room temperature.

2. Dump the remaining ingredients except the avocado cubes in the bowl on top of the cooled beans.

3. To make the vinaigrette, whisk together the lime juice, cumin, and pepper in a small bowl. Add the olive oil in a slow, thin, steady stream, whisking as you go to form an emulsion (page 171). Stir in the jalapeño and cilantro.

4. Pour the vinaigrette over the salad, and toss it with a big spoon or your hands until everything is evenly coated with the vinaigrette. Add the avocado midway through the tossing, being careful not to mash the pieces but just to get them into the mix. Serve at room temperature.

2 cups dried black beans, picked through, rinsed, and soaked overnight (page 61)

1 big yellow onion, coarsely quartered

8 cups cold unsalted water

¼ cup red-wine vinegar

1 red bell pepper, diced fine (page 117)

1 small red onion, diced fine (page 119)

2 celery stalks, diced fine

2 scallions, both white and green parts, thinly sliced (page 117)

1 medium avocado, halved, pit removed, and diced (page 63)

FOR THE VINAIGRETTE

Juice of 2 regular or Key limes

1 teaspoon salt

A few turns of freshly ground black pepper

1 tablespoon ground cumin

⅓ cup olive oil

½ jalapeño, halved, seeds removed, and minced

½ cup chopped fresh cilantro (page 162)

Chinese-takeout containers are a nice way to present salads, and they're really convenient since they come in all different sizes. For aesthetic reasons and also to anchor them, we usually set the containers in something—a platter or bucket of dried black beans, or a bed of wheat grass.

Chickpea-and-Carrot Salad with Cumin and Black Olives

MAKES 4 SERVINGS

Jerome's mom serves a simple chickpea salad—along with a little plate of roasted peppers in olive oil, and another of shredded carrots in lemon dressing—at cocktail hour at her home in Avignon, France. We basically combined her chickpea and carrot salads.

1. Drain and rinse the canned or soaked chickpeas in a colander. For dry chickpeas, place them in a pot with 4 cups of cold unsalted water, and bring them to a boil over high heat. Lower the heat and simmer, uncovered, for an hour or more, until the beans are tender and have lost their chalky, raw-bean flavor. Drain well in a colander and cool to room temperature. Dump into a big bowl.
2. To pit the olives, press one between your fingers. The pit will break right through the olive and pop out. Chop the olives coarsely and add to the bowl with the chickpeas. Add the carrots, cilantro, and scallions.
3. To make the vinaigrette, whisk all the ingredients except the olive oil together in a small bowl. Add the olive oil in a slow, thin, steady stream, whisking as you go to form an emulsion (page 171).
4. Pour the vinaigrette over the salad, and toss it all up with a big spoon or with your hands.
5. Cover and refrigerate for at least an hour, so the beans can absorb the flavor of the vinaigrette. Serve chilled or at room temperature.

"When making salads with boiled ingredients, it is important to drain them well. Otherwise you'll end up with a watery salad."
—Frank

2 15-ounce cans chickpeas; or 2 cups dried chickpeas, picked through, rinsed and soaked overnight (pages 181, 61)

⅔ cup black olives (such as Moroccan oil-cured)

3 medium carrots (preferably those sold with tops), coarsely grated with a handheld grater or a food processor

½ cup chopped fresh cilantro (page 162)

2 scallions, halved crosswise, sliced very thin, and separated with your fingers (page 117)

FOR THE VINAIGRETTE
1 garlic clove, peeled and minced (page 23)

Zest and juice of 1 lemon

2 tablepoons ground cumin

2 teaspoons paprika

A pinch of cayenne pepper

2 teaspoons salt

½ teaspoon freshly ground black pepper

3 tablespoons olive oil

Country Potato Salad with Scarlet Runner Beans and Fresh Herbs

In our opinion, salads beg to be played with. And we play with this salad a lot. We sometimes add chives or thyme. We throw fresh corn in during late summer or, when they're in season, fava beans. We simmer the potatoes for this salad because we want to make sure the skins stay on. The skins will fall off if they are knocked around at a hard boil.

1. Place the 4 cups unsalted water and the runner beans in a large saucepan, and bring to a boil over high heat. Lower the heat and simmer, uncovered, for an hour or more, until the beans are tender but not splitting. The best way to test these is to lift a bean out with a fork and taste one. Remove the beans from the heat, and drain in a colander.
2. Place the sliced onion in a big bowl. Dump the drained beans on top of the onion. Their warmth will soften the onion, which is a good thing in this case.
3. Bring the 4 cups of salted water and the potatoes to a soft boil in a large saucepan over medium heat. Lower the heat and simmer, uncovered, for 30–35 minutes, until the potatoes are very tender when pierced with a fork. Remove the potatoes from the heat, and drain in a colander. Dump the drained potatoes on top of the runner beans.
4. Snap off the stem end of the haricots verts or string beans and pull down to remove the strings. Grabbing a bunch at a time, cut them on the diagonal into 1-inch pieces.

4 cups cold unsalted water (for simmering the runner beans)

¾ cup dry scarlet runner beans, picked through, rinsed, and soaked overnight (page 61)

½ medium red onion, halved again and sliced thin

4 cups cold salted water (for the potatoes)

1¼ pounds red-skinned potatoes (5 medium-size), scrubbed and cut into 1-inch cubes

½ pound haricots verts or string beans (green or yellow or both) (page 143)

4 cups cold salted water (for the haricots verts)

4 or 5 plum tomatoes, cored and diced

1 tablespoon drained capers

¼ cup chopped fresh Italian parsley (page 162)   *continued*

1 tablespoon chopped fresh tarragon leaves (page 162)

FOR THE VINAIGRETTE
¼ cup red-wine vinegar
1 teaspoon salt
A few turns of freshly ground black pepper
¼ cup olive oil

5. Bring another 4 cups of salted water to a boil in a large saucepan over high heat. Add the haricots verts and blanch them for 1 minute, maybe less (below). The haricots verts should still be bright-colored and crunchy. Drain in a colander, and immediately run cold water over them to stop them from cooking further. Drain the haricots verts well before dumping them into the bowl with the beans and potatoes.
6. Toss the tomatoes, capers, parsley, and tarragon into the bowl.
7. To make the vinaigrette, whisk the vinegar, salt, and pepper together in a small bowl. Add the olive oil in a slow, thin, steady stream, whisking as you go to form an emulsion (page 171).
8. Pour the vinaigrette over the salad, and toss, using a big spoon or your hands. Serve still warm or at room temperature.

What Is a Runner Bean?

Runner beans are small beige-colored beans with deep-scarlet streaks of color running through them. We like runner beans for their firm, meaty texture. You don't see them called for very often in recipes, but you can substitute them for another type of bean in any bean salad.

What Is Blanching?

Blanching refers to a two-part process, the first of which involves plunging a bunch of fresh vegetables into a pot of boiling water for almost no time whatsoever: a minute, sometimes less. The second part involves plunging the just-boiled vegetables into a bath of ice water to stop the cooking. This is called "shocking" the vegetables, and for good reason. We think that the ice water is a bit extreme, and that running cold water over the vegetables for a few minutes does a good enough job.

The short cooking time of blanching does a lot of good things to vegetables. It brings out their flavor without changing it in the way that *cooking* changes the flavor of vegetables. Blanching softens vegetables ever so slightly, so that they aren't as hard to bite into or to digest. And it brightens their color. We like blanching. Particularly with really fresh and beautiful green vegetables like green beans and asparagus.

To blanch any vegetable, bring a pot of salted water to a boil. Have your colander ready in the sink and, if you want to do it the extreme way, a big bowl filled with ice water next to that. Dump your vegetables in the boiling water. Don't even think about walking away from them. Forty-five seconds later, take one out and taste it. It should still be crisp, and even more brightly colored than it was when it was raw. Dump your veggies into a colander, and either run cold water on them until they are room temperature or drain and plunge them into the ice bath. If you are going to be blanching many different vegetables in succession, it's much more convenient to use the same water than to keep boiling more. So remove the vegetables with a slotted spoon or spatula or a large strainer. Or dump the whole thing into a colander set over a big pot into which the hot water will drain.

Crudités

Crudités, the ubiquitous raw-vegetable plate that you see served so often at art openings and baby showers, can be a really delicious salad plate if you pay proper attention to it. Our idea of a good crudité platter includes any combination of the following, preferably fresh and in season, blanched:

> green beans
> asparagus
> sugar snap peas
> julienned carrots

And raw vegetables including:

> red and yellow bell peppers
> white mushrooms
> julienned celery
> sliced radishes
> sliced fennel
> cherry tomatoes—the little green part left on as a handle

Dips for crackers or vegetables need to be rich and flavorful. Some we like a lot are:

> sour cream mixed with any vinaigrette
> whole-milk yogurt with fresh dill and salt

or a bowl of olive oil sprinkled with salt and freshly ground black pepper

You can also try these combinations from the book:

- 1 cup sour cream mixed with $\frac{1}{3}$ cup classic Basil Pesto (page 164) or Sun-Dried Tomato Vinaigrette (page 166) and a couple tablespoons finely grated Parmesan cheese

- 1 cup Traditional Hummus (page 181) mixed with $\frac{1}{3}$ cup puréed Marinated Roasted Peppers (page 109, including marinade) or Black Olive Vinaigrette (page 170)
- 1 cup sour cream or yogurt mixed with $\frac{1}{3}$ cup finely chopped scallions (white and green parts) and 2 tablespoons Fresh Tarragon–Lemon Vinaigrette (page 182)

Haricot-Vert-and-Corn Salad with Roasted Artichoke Hearts and Fresh Tarragon–Lemon Vinaigrette

MAKES 4 SERVINGS

½ pound haricots verts or string beans (green or yellow or both) (page 143)

4 cups cold salted water (for the haricots verts)

2 cups frozen or canned corn, or 2–3 ears, shucked and kernels cut off the cob

2 tablespoons olive oil

Salt and freshly ground pepper (for roasting the vegetables)

1 13.5-ounce can artichoke hearts packed in water (not marinated in oil)

1 garlic clove, peeled and minced (page 23)

1 recipe Fresh Tarragon–Lemon Vinaigrette (page 182)

We roast the corn for this salad until it is sticky and sweet. With leftover bits of Frank's Roasted Chicken (page 52) thrown in, it's lunch.

1. Preheat oven to 450 degrees.
2. Snap off the stem end of each haricot vert or string bean, and pull down the string to remove. Grabbing a bunch at a time, cut them on the diagonal into 1-inch pieces.
3. Bring the 4 cups of salted water to a boil over high heat. Add the haricots verts, and blanch them for 1 minute, maybe less (page 140). They should still be bright-colored and crunchy. Drain in a colander, and immediately run cold water over them to stop them from cooking further. Drain them well before tossing them into a bowl big enough to hold the entire salad.
4. Toss the corn with 1 tablespoon of the olive oil, a sprinkling of salt (¼ teaspoon), and a few twists of freshly ground black pepper. Scatter the corn on a sheet pan, place the sheet pan in the oven, and roast the corn for 15–20 minutes, until golden brown. You'll want to shake the pan at least once during the cooking time, so that the corn browns evenly and doesn't burn. Remove the pan from the oven, and use a metal spatula to scrape the corn into the bowl with the haricots verts.
5. Drain and rinse the artichokes in a colander. Cut them into quarters and toss with the remaining tablespoon of olive oil and the garlic. Spread artichokes out

on your sheet pan, place the sheet pan in the oven, and roast for 25 minutes until the artichokes begin to brown and the edges char slightly. When they're done, remove the artichokes from the oven, and use a metal spatula to scrape them off the sheet pan into the bowl with the other vegetables.

6. Just before you're ready to serve, pour the vinaigrette over the salad and, using a large metal spoon or your hands, toss until the vegetables are evenly coated. Taste for salt. Serve this salad still warm or at room temperature.

"I learned to make vinaigrette by watching Jerome. He'd just grab some oil, vinegar, mustard, and he'd whisk it up in less than a minute. He made it look so easy. Now, whenever I go to my friends' houses for dinner, they ask me to make the vinaigrette. I haven't convinced them that they can do it themselves."
—Frank

Jerome on Haricots Verts

"Haricots verts" means "green beans" in French. Here it means "French green beans." Haricots verts are longer, skinnier, and more delicate than American string beans, which is why I prefer them. I still remember my mother sitting at the kitchen table with a big bowl of haricots verts. She would break off the end with the string and then pull it down. One at a time, until she got through a big bowl. Some people want to cut the ends off rather than breaking them off to save time, but if you really want them nice, you have to do it my mother's way.

Lentil-and-Quinoa Salad with Shredded Carrots and Ginger-Curry Vinaigrette

MAKES 8 SERVINGS

6 cups cold unsalted water (for the lentils)

1½ cups French green lentils (*lentilles de Puy*), picked through and rinsed (page 119)

3 cups cold unsalted water (for the quinoa)

1 cup quinoa, picked through and rinsed

3 or 4 medium carrots, peeled and coarsely grated (with a handheld grater or in a food processor)

¼ cup chopped fresh cilantro (page 162)

1 recipe Ginger-Curry Vinaigrette (page 167)

When we first started making salads, we were trying to find some new grains to work with. Colette Rossant, the food columnist for the *New York Daily News,* suggested quinoa. We'd never heard of it. Now we love it, especially with lentils, which have more bite—quinoa can get kind of soft. This salad is delicious. And there's no denying: it's 100 percent healthy.

1. Place the 6 cups unsalted water and the lentils in a big saucepan, and bring to a boil over high heat. Lower the heat and simmer, uncovered, for 20–25 minutes, until the beans are tender but not losing their skins. The best way to test is to bite into one. Drain the lentils well in a colander, and dump them into a big bowl.
2. At the same time you're cooking the lentils, place the 3 cups unsalted water and the quinoa in another big saucepan, and bring them to a boil over high heat. Lower the heat and simmer, uncovered, for 10–15 minutes, until the quinoa looks slightly translucent and as if it has a tail, a spiral separating from the grain. Drain well through a fine sieve or mesh colander (the grains will fall through the holes of a regular colander), and add to the bowl with the lentils.
3. Add the grated carrots and the chopped cilantro to the bowl. Pour the vinaigrette over the salad, and toss with a big spoon or with your hands. This salad is delicious any way you serve it: still warm, at room temperature, or chilled.

What Is Quinoa?

A lot of people ask what quinoa is; half say "kin-OH-ah." We say "KEEN-wah." We don't know which is right. Quinoa is an ancient grain from the Andes. Health-food fanatics are really into quinoa, because it has more protein than any other grain. Quinoa is pretty easy to find these days in health-food stores and even some supermarkets. Neither of us had even heard of quinoa before we opened the store. Jerome has come to love quinoa and uses it all the time. "I love the structure of the grain itself. I love to look at it. It's like transparent, with a little tail or something hanging off it when it's cooked."

It's important not to overcook quinoa, or it becomes one big lump of mush. Quinoa takes a quarter of the time to cook that rice does, and its flavor is neutral enough that it can be used in any of our salads, or as a side dish in place of rice. You should always rinse quinoa in cold water before you cook it, but be careful to drain it through a sieve or a fine-mesh colander, because it is small enough that it will fall through the holes of an ordinary colander. At home, when he has the time, Frank will sauté the quinoa before he cooks it, so it absorbs the flavor of the oil. "It's the same concept you use for rice in risotto to intensify the flavor of the grain."

Chunky-Cucumber-and-Watercress Salad with Crumbled Feta Cheese

2 cucumbers, peeled, halved, and seeded (page 117)

½ cup black olives (such as Moroccan oil-cured), pitted and coarsely chopped

½ bunch watercress, rinsed, dried well, and trimmed of tough ends

½ medium red onion, halved again and sliced thin

1 red bell pepper, cut into 1-inch squares (page 117)

4 plum tomatoes, cored and diced (page 119)

1 recipe Black Olive Vinaigrette (page 170)

4 ounces crumbled feta cheese

This salad has the makings of a classic Greek salad. Feta is one of the lowest-fat cheeses, but that's not why we like it. We like it for its tangy delicious taste.

1. Slice the cucumbers lengthwise in half again. Cut each cucumber quarter into 1-inch pieces, and toss them into a big bowl.
2. To pit the olives, press one between your fingers. The pit will break right through the olive and pop out. Coarsely chop the olives and dump them in the bowl with the cucumbers.
3. Add the watercress, onion, pepper, and tomatoes.
4. Just before you're ready to serve the salad, pour the vinaigrette over the vegetables and toss with a big spoon or your hands until the vegetables are evenly coated with the dressing.
5. Crumble the feta cheese over the salad and toss it again, gently, just enough get the cheese into the mix but not so the cheese gets mushy. Taste to see if the salad needs more of anything, particularly salt.

"When using a free-standing cutting board, place a small damp towel or paper towel underneath it to prevent it from sliding around. You always want to work on a sturdy surface when you're using knives."
—Frank

Penne Pasta Salad with Grilled Fennel, Roasted Eggplant, Black Olives, and Fresh Dill

MAKES 4 SERVINGS

Someone gave us a version of this recipe, but neither of us can remember who it was. We'd love to give you credit, so, if you're reading this, let us know. The fennel is roasted until it is caramelized, so it is sweet—and very good.

1. Preheat oven to 450 degrees.
2. Bring the salted water to a boil in a big pot over high heat. Add the pasta and cook until *al dente*—tender but with a bite. Drain the pasta well in a colander. Dump into a bowl big enough to hold the entire salad, and toss with 1 tablespoon of the olive oil to keep the pasta from sticking together.
3. Put the eggplant in a colander placed in the sink. Sprinkle with a thin coat of salt, and toss to distribute salt to all sides of the eggplant. Let the eggplant rest for at least 20 minutes to sweat out the bitterness (see page 38).
4. To prepare the fennel, cut off the leafy tops and the stalks. Cut the fennel in half lengthwise, and use a paring knife to cut out the core. Cut each fennel half lengthwise into ¼-inch slices, and toss them in a small bowl with a tablespoon of the olive oil, a sprinkling of salt (¼ teaspoon), and a few turns of freshly ground black pepper. Spread the fennel slices on a sheet pan, place the sheet pan in the oven, and roast until edges of fennel begin to brown, 25–30 minutes. (If you find the fennel browning unevenly, use a long fork or tongs to turn the pieces over.) Remove the sheet pan from the oven and use a metal spatula to scrape the fennel and oil into the bowl with the pasta.

8 cups cold salted water (for the pasta)

1 pound penne pasta

¼ cup olive oil, plus more for drizzling over the pasta and the finished salad

1 small or ½ large eggplant, cut into ½-inch-wide sticks

Salt and freshly ground black pepper

3 fennel bulbs

1 cup black olives (such as Moroccan oil-cured)

2 garlic cloves, peeled and minced (page 23)

½ cup chopped fresh dill (page 162)

½ cup coarsely grated Pecorino cheese

5. In the same bowl you used to season the fennel, toss the eggplant and garlic with the remaining olive oil and a few turns of freshly ground black pepper. Spread the eggplant on your sheet pan, and roast for 10–15 minutes, until the sides touching the pan are brown and the insides feel soft and creamy. Remove the sheet pan from the oven, and use a metal spatula to scrape the eggplant and oil off the sheet pan into the bowl with the pasta.

6. Pit olives by pressing one between your fingers until the pit breaks through the olive and pops out. Chop the olives coarsley and toss them in the bowl on top of the eggplant.

7. Add the remaining ingredients to the pasta and vegetables and toss the salad using a big spoon or your hands. Taste for salt. Drizzle with a little bit of olive oil before serving. Serve warm or at room temperature.

"I pour a lot of salt into the water when I'm cooking pasta. I want the salt to get in *the noodle, not just* on *the noodle."*
—Frank

Gazpacho Salad

3 cucumbers, halved, seeded, and
  cut on the diagonal into ½-inch
  slices (page 117)
½ medium red onion, diced fine
  (page 119)
1 red or yellow bell pepper, diced
  fine (page 117)
2–3 ears corn, shucked and kernels
  cut off the cob, about 1 cup
6 plum tomatoes, cored and cut
  into eighths (wedges)
2 tablespoons chopped fresh dill
  (page 162)

FOR THE VINAIGRETTE
¼ cup red-wine vinegar
1 teaspoon salt
A few turns of freshly ground black
  pepper
1 garlic clove, peeled and minced
  (page 23)
¼ cup olive oil

Not soup, but salad. And an excellent salad at that. Save this for the height of summer, when corn is fresh, and good sweet thin-skinned tomatoes are piled high at farmers' markets. If you can't find good tomatoes, forget it. Make something else.

1. As you cut up the vegetables, toss them into a bowl big enough to hold the entire salad.
2. To make the vinaigrette, whisk everything but the olive oil together in a small bowl. Add the olive oil in a slow, thin, steady stream, whisking as you go to form an emulsion (page 171).
3. Pour the vinaigrette over the vegetables, and toss them gently with a big spoon or your hands, being careful not to smash the tomatoes. This salad is best served just after the vegetables are cut.

Variation: Turning Gazpacho Salad into Bread Salad

Italians make what's called panzanella, "bread salad," out of their stale bread. It's a total leftovers dish, nothing they'd even think about consulting a recipe to make. To turn this gazpacho into panzanella, let it rest for at least an hour to allow the vegetables to give off liquids. Cut a baguette into ¼-inch slices. Fry the bread slices quickly in olive oil that has been heated with one or two smashed cloves of garlic. Drain the bread on a paper towel and, once the bread slices are cool, toss them in the salad. Top with chopped fresh herbs, whatever you have: basil, Italian parsley, thyme.

Three-Bean Salad with Honey-Balsamic Vinaigrette

MAKES 4 SERVINGS

Jerome grew up in France, so he just doesn't get this salad (he thinks it's too sweet). The honey-balsamic vinaigrette is Frank's way of updating the bean salad we Americans all grew up eating at picnics. You could really choose any three beans you like for this salad. Heck, you could even put four, five, or six beans in if you wanted.

1. Drain and rinse the canned or soaking chickpeas in a colander. To use dried chickpeas, place them in a pot with 4 cups (1 quart) of cold unsalted water, and bring to a boil over high heat. Lower the heat and simmer, uncovered, for an hour or more, until the beans are tender and have lost their chalky, raw-bean flavor. Drain well in a colander and cool to room temperature, then pour into a big bowl.

2. Place the 8 cups of unsalted water and the kidney beans in a big pot, and bring them to a boil over high heat. Lower the heat and simmer, uncovered, for an hour or more, until beans are tender. Drain the beans well in a colander, and dump them into the bowl with the chickpeas.

3. Snap off the stem ends of the haricots verts or string beans, and pull down to remove the strings. Grabbing a bunch at a time, cut them on the diagonal into 1-inch pieces.

4. Bring the 4 cups of salted water to a boil in a big saucepan over high heat. Add the haricots verts, and blanch them for 1 minute, maybe less (page 140). The haricots verts should still be bright-colored and crunchy. Drain in a colander, and immediately run cold water over them to stop them from cooking further.

2 15-ounce cans chickpeas; or 2 cups dried chickpeas, picked through, rinsed, and soaked overnight (page 61)

2 cups dried red kidney beans, picked through and soaked overnight (page 61)

8 cups cold unsalted water (for simmering the kidney beans)

½ pound haricots verts or string beans (green or yellow or both) (page 143)

4 cups salted water (for the haricots verts)

1 medium red onion, diced fine (page 119)

2 Marinated Roasted Peppers (page 109, or from a jar), diced

1 recipe Honey-Balsamic Vinaigrette (page 170)

Drain the haricots verts well before dumping them into the bowl with the beans. Add the onion and the roasted peppers.

5. Pour the vinaigrette over the beans, and toss the salad using a big spoon or your hands. Serve at room temperature or chilled.

"Beans are hearty, so bean salads make a great one-dish meal, especially to take to work. A cucumber salad is not lunch."
—Frank

What Is Julienne?

"Julienne" is a verb that refers to the process of cutting something into thin strips, or what is often referred to as "matchsticks." It sounds a lot harder than it is. To make matchsticks out of something round or oddly shaped, the first thing you want to do is get whatever you're working with flat. Slice the carrot or the jicama or eggplant, whatever it is, on the diagonal into a slice that's as thin as you want the matchstick. The reason we do it on the diagonal is that we end up with a long oval shape as opposed to a round piece that's no bigger than the circumference of whatever we're working with—and thus with longer matchsticks. From there, if you just make thin slices across the width of the flat, you end up with thin little sticks.

Cold Spinach Noodles with Spicy Peanut-Sesame Sauce

MAKES 6 SERVINGS

When Frank first moved to New York, he had no money. But he would splurge on two things: pints of premium ice cream and takeout Chinese food. This is our updated version of the noodles he ordered, with homemade peanut sauce and fresh crunchy vegetables. These noodles make a great side dish for grilled tuna or steaks marinated in Soy-Ginger Vinaigrette (page 183).

8 cups cold salted water (for the pasta)

1 pound spinach linguine

1 tablespoon toasted sesame oil

1 recipe Spicy Peanut-Sesame Sauce (page 175)

2 or 3 medium carrots, peeled and julienned (page 152)

2 or 3 medium cucumbers, peeled, halved, seeded, and julienned (page 117)

2 or 3 scallions, both white and green parts, cut on the diagonal into ¼-inch slices (page 117)

1. Bring the salted water to a boil in a big pot over high heat. Add the linguine and cook until it is *al dente*—tender but with a bite. Drain well in a colander. Dump the linguine into a big bowl and toss it with the sesame oil to keep the noodles from sticking together. Chill.
2. Just before you're ready to serve the salad, pour the spicy peanut-sesame sauce over the pasta and toss it up with a pair of big spoons. If you toss this salad with the sauce more than an hour before you're ready to serve it, the pasta will absorb the sauce, and the salad will be dry. Sprinkle the vegetables over the top for color and crunch. Serve at room temperature.

"If you see beautiful snow peas at the market and they aren't part of your recipe, just throw them in. Nothing bad can come of a handful of fresh-picked peas."
—Jerome

Once Upon a ...
CONDIMENT

Tomato Chutney with Golden Raisins

French-Style Grainy Mustard · Variations on a Mustard Theme

Classic Basil Pesto

Marinated Sun-Dried Tomatoes

Sun-Dried Tomato Vinaigrette

Ginger-Curry Vinaigrette

Black Olive Tapenade

Black Olive Vinaigrette

Honey-Balsamic Vinaigrette

Eggplant Caponata

Once Upon a Tart's Pizza-Style Bruschetta

Frank's Bruschetta

Spicy Peanut-Sesame Sauce

Dijon Vinaigrette with Worcestershire

Jerome's Homemade Mayonnaise · Variation: Rosemary-Garlic Aïoli

Caesar-ish Salad · Our Own Caesar-ish Dressing

White-Bean Spread

Traditional Hummus

Fresh Tarragon–Lemon Vinaigrette

Soy-Ginger Vinaigrette

Marinated Artichoke Hearts with Herbes de Provence

Oven-Roasted Tomatoes

When we began making salads and sandwiches for the store, we approached it like two guys making stuff for a dinner party—a really big dinner party. We'd put together some beans and herbs for a salad, and then turn to the food processor to whip up whatever flavors we were inspired to dress it with. We'd buy some cheddar cheese to make sandwiches, and then think, Hey, some chutney would taste great on this. We were totally unsystematic about it.

Of course, as we started getting more lunchtime business, we had to find ways to cut out steps—and still turn out the same good food. It didn't take us long to figure out that it took the same amount of time and effort to make enough of that inspired dressing for one salad as it did for twenty. What we had to do, then, was to turn each of those previously spontaneous dressings and sides into something standardized. Something commonly known as a recipe.

We urge you to play with both the recipes themselves and the way you use them. Blend the artichokes with oil to turn the mixture into a pesto. Use the Fresh Tarragon–Lemon Vinaigrette (page 182) as a marinade for chicken, or the Honey-Balsamic Vinaigrette (page 170) as a marinade for flank steak. Dilute the Classic Basil Pesto (page 164) or Sun-Dried Tomato Vinaigrette (page 166) with a little olive oil to make a salad out of leftover cold pasta. The concepts here are so basic, and the flavors—mostly Mediterranean-influenced, since both of us are—so versatile, you really can't mess them up. (And if you do mess up a recipe, it'll probably taste good anyway.)

THINGS TO KNOW

We debated including this chapter at all, because we wondered if anyone would turn to a chapter that wasn't about anything you could eat all by itself. But then we thought: These are the things that we name when customers ask us what gives our Chickpea-and-Lentil Salad its unique flavor. Or why their sandwiches never taste as good as ours. We certainly weren't going to hold out on you. We also didn't want to hide these

within the individual recipes that call for them, because they are so versatile. That would be like reserving hot fudge for only one kind of ice cream. Pretty early in life, we all find our own favorite ways to use hot fudge. And we're hoping that, in the same way, you'll find your own favorite ways to use Black Olive Tapenade (page 169) or Tomato Chutney with Golden Raisins (page 159).

Quite often the difference between ordinary food and really good food is just one thing—one last flavor that pulls the whole dish together. But for most people, the only items in the refrigerator with any potential whatsoever to dress up that turkey sandwich are seven different kinds of mustard. Not that we have anything against mustard—we even give you some mustard recipes in this chapter—but let's say you had a few Marinated Sun-Dried Tomatoes (page 165) and a jar of Classic Basil Pesto (page 164) on hand. Wouldn't they make for a much more interesting sandwich?

A lot of the things that pull a meal together aren't things you want to make on the spot. If you want a sandwich, you're not going to have time to make eggplant caponata in the middle of a busy afternoon. Cook when you feel like cooking. Then keep a batch of your favorite vinaigrette or spread (pesto, tapenade) in the refrigerator. That way, you'll have some options beyond the ubiquitous can of tuna when you need to throw together a good, quick meal.

If you have any hope at all for that turkey sandwich, you might want to have some of these condiments around. When you find a recipe you like, make a big batch—at least double—the next time you make it. The vinaigrettes keep for a few weeks in the refrigerator. Fresh garlic or herbs will limit their shelf life, so leave those out if you're making a big batch. When you see basil in the farmers' market sold in huge bunches at fire sale prices, grab it and make pesto to last you through the winter. (It freezes wonderfully.) If you want a simple task to relax yourself after work, that's the perfect time to make a caponata. Chopping vegetables, in case you didn't already know, is therapeutic.

Jerome on Vinegar vs. Lemon Juice

Frank likes to substitute vinegar for lemon juice in vinaigrette recipes, but I don't. Lemon juice and vinegar are both acidic, but they are very different flavors. There are certain things that need a dressing with vinegar, and other things that need one with lemon juice. On any kind of lettuce, I use vinegar. On vegetables—carrots, artichokes, celery, broccoli, asparagus—the dressing has to be made with lemon juice. It all makes sense. Vegetables are so good with just lemon juice on them. And hollandaise, which is made for asparagus, is made of lemon juice. But who ever heard of pouring vinegar on vegetables? Two exceptions to the vegetable rule: cucumbers and tomatoes must have vinegar on them.

Mason jars are a good way to store ingredients—and they work for condiments as well. You can see what's inside—in the fridge or on the shelf—and they look nice on a table, too.

Tomato Chutney with Golden Raisins

MAKES 2½ CUPS

We came up with this recipe when we left our vegetarian days behind and started making sandwiches with meat. We wanted a fruity chutney with a spicy kick that would be a great contrast to turkey, pork, sausages, even a sharp cheddar cheese. We spread it on sandwiches at the store, but it's also delicious with the couscous salad.

1. Dump everything but the raisins into a heavy-bottomed saucepan and simmer over low heat. Continue cooking, stirring frequently to prevent sticking and burning, until most of the liquid—the vinegar and the juices released from the tomatoes—has evaporated and what's left is thick and syrupy, about 45 minutes.
2. Add the raisins, and continue cooking for another 5–10 minutes to plump them up. Don't worry if the chutney seems too runny while it's warm. It will solidify to the consistency of strawberry jam once it cools.

3 pounds plum tomatoes (about 16), peeled (page 76) and diced

2-inch piece fresh ginger, peeled and finely grated (page 75)

1¼ cups sugar

1 medium red onion, diced fine

10 garlic cloves, peeled and minced (page 23)

1 cup apple-cider vinegar

½ cup balsamic vinegar

A pinch of red-pepper flakes

2 teaspoons salt

⅓ cup golden raisins, dark raisins, dried black currants, or dried apricots

"If it's not tomato season but you're craving tomatoes, use tomatoes where the flavor is concentrated—oven-roasted or sun-dried, or tomato chutney."
—Frank

French-Style Grainy Mustard

MAKES 2½ CUPS

1 cup yellow mustard seeds
4 tablespoons dry mustard
1 cup boiling unsalted water
½ cup white-wine vinegar
½ cup orange juice
1 teaspoon salt

"Growing up in America," Frank says, "you think a lot of things just come out of a jar. Mayonnaise, definitely. Mustard, where else?" Then, one day, he put it together—mustard, the condiment, does not grow. Therefore, it must be made. That was a big day for him. He went straight into the kitchen and taught himself how to make mustard.

1. Grind the mustard seeds coarsely in a coffee or spice grinder or with a mortar and pestle.
2. Stir the ground mustard seeds together with the rest of the ingredients in a small bowl or plastic container. Cover, and let sit at room temperature for at least a couple of hours. As the seeds soften up a bit, the liquid and seeds will come together into a spreadable, mustardy consistency. That simple.

"Think outside the box—or the bowl, rather. I like to serve a pesto or mayonnaise in a mortar. Or mustard in an espresso cup, eggcup, or champagne glass."
—Frank

Variations on a Mustard Theme

With big bowls full of the stuff, we were inspired to mix our mustard with other ingredients, which instantly turned the mustard into something else. We love that. Here are some of our favorite ways to transform mustard. These all work to spice up meat or cheese sandwiches. The mustard butter is also delicious on vegetables such as broccoli, asparagus, and beans.

Mango Chutney Mustard: You can make your own mango chutney, of course, but we say, don't bother. The Major Grey's mango chutney that comes in a jar is a little on the sweet side, but it's perfect for this. In the bowl of a food processor (or a blender) fitted with a metal blade, purée 1 cup mustard with ½ cup chutney. We use this on our Vermont-Cheddar-and-Cucumber Sandwich (page 95).

Honey Mustard: 1 cup mustard plus ¼ cup honey.

Horseradish Mustard: 1 cup mustard plus 2 tablespoons horseradish (from a jar).

Herb Mustard: 1 cup mustard plus 2 tablespoons finely chopped fresh tarragon, dill, or thyme.

Caraway Mustard: 1 cup mustard plus 2 teaspoons caraway seeds.

Mustard Butter: 1 stick softened unsalted butter creamed together with 2 tablespoons mustard and chilled.

"Frank has such a sweet tooth. He puts honey in everything. We make a coconut macaroon, he puts honey in it. He puts honey in vinaigrette, honey in mustard. I'm different. To me, mustard is mustard. You add honey, you just break the mustard. I do not like my savory food sweet."
—Jerome

How to Deal with Fresh Herbs

The first task with herbs is to rinse them well. They grow pretty close to the ground, and they often arrive at stores with dirt intact. The best way is to immerse the bunch of herbs in water. This is especially important with a craggy-leafed herb like parsley.

Fill up your sink or a big bowl with water. Plunge the herbs in the water and swish them around with your hands to get all the dirt out. Let the herbs sit underwater so the dirt can work its way out and settle to the bottom. After 5 or 10 minutes, eat an herb to tell if it has any grit on it. If it does, change the water and dunk the herbs again. Remove clean herbs from the water, give them a good shake with your hand, and place them in a colander to drain. If the herbs are still wet when you go to use them, place them on a towel or paper towel and roll it up tight, so the towel will wring out and absorb the water.

As for chopping herbs, there are different methods for different ones. With leafy herbs like cilantro, parsley, and tarragon, bunch them up as tightly as possible. Use your noncutting hand both to hold the herbs and as a guide for your knife. Chop fine in one direction and then in the other (crosswise) direction.

There is another way to chop leafy herbs—and a method unparalleled for chives and dill. Hold herbs in a bunch, this time directly above the bowl you want them in, and use a pair of kitchen shears (or any clean household scissors) to snip them, letting the snipped herbs fall directly into the bowl. Something

about using scissors in the kitchen and having the herbs fall directly into the bowl is guaranteed to make you feel like a real chef.

We use only fresh herbs. They're not hard to find, and the flavor is so different. Thyme, rosemary, and oregano are the three herbs we sometimes make exceptions for. They taste fine dried—though still not as good as fresh. Use half the quantity of dry herbs that you would of fresh.

Fresh thyme doesn't need to be chopped so much as its almost microscopic leaves need to be plucked from the thin twigs they grow on. Same goes for rosemary. Strip the stems of both herbs by gently pulling the leaves from the tip end downward.

Mint and basil have such neat definitive leaves, we think it's easiest, and prettiest, to cut them into thin strips. The technical (i.e., French) word for cutting a leafy thing into thin strips is *chiffonade,* which translates "made of rags." We like that. And we like the method even more. Take your leaves, separated from their stems, and stack five or ten together, all in the same direction, so they're lined up nicely. Take that stack and roll it up tightly. And then chop across the length of the stack into thin, ¼-inch slices. Or do the same thing with a pair of kitchen shears. What you get when you loosen them up is, as promised, thin strips.

Classic Basil Pesto

MAKES 2 CUPS

2 cups whole fresh basil leaves

3 garlic cloves, smashed and
   peeled (page 23)

½ cup grated Parmesan cheese

2 tablespoons pine nuts (or walnuts
   or almonds)

1 teaspoon salt

½ cup olive oil

This is a great way to use up late summer's glut of basil, that which you've grown, or which you'll inevitably find at the market. We sometimes substitute Italian parsley for half the basil, just to add a different flavor. We don't like to leave pesto for more than a week in the refrigerator, but it freezes just fine. Nuts are optional; in fact, we don't use them at the store, because so many people are allergic to them.

1. Toss everything but the olive oil into the bowl of a food processor (or a blender) fitted with a metal blade, and purée until the ingredients are ground together into a paste.
2. Continuing to run the machine, add the oil slowly through the feed tube or the lid of the blender. Before you pour all the oil in, check the consistency of the pesto. It should resemble a thick vinaigrette or a very loose, liquidy paste. How thick you want your pesto is a matter of taste and depends on how you intend to use it. If you're making pasta, for instance, a thinner pesto will help to coat the pasta, so you may want to add more oil.
3. The saltiness of cheese varies, so taste the pesto to make sure you have enough salt before removing it from the food processor. The pesto should be bold and vibrant for all those fresh basil leaves; if it tastes flat, it may need more salt.

Frank on Making Pesto the Old-Fashioned Way

I almost never use a mortar and pestle at the store or at home, because I am just so in love with my food processor. But in Italy they say there is no better way to make pesto than to grind it up by hand. It has to do with the mortar releasing the oils of the basil leaves to their fullest, basiliest potential. To make pesto with a mortar and pestle, pound and grind the garlic, basil, and nuts (if you are using them) together until they form a paste. Add the salt, pepper, and cheese. And, finally, pour in the olive oil slowly, stirring with the pestle all the while.

Marinated Sun-Dried Tomatoes

MAKES 4 CUPS

We love to use sun-dried tomatoes, especially when the only fresh tomatoes are those mealy ones in the grocery store. Sun-dried tomatoes are so dense with flavor. We buy them dried, then blanch and marinate them ourselves. They're much less expensive this way, and we think they're better.

1. Bring the salted water to a boil in a big saucepan over high heat. Add the sun-dried tomatoes, and boil them for 1 minute, just to soften them up. Drain the tomatoes in a colander and let them cool to room temperature.
2. Whisk the vinegar, red-pepper flakes, salt, and pepper together in a medium-size bowl. Add the oil in a thin, steady stream, whisking all the while to form an emulsion (page 171). Add the tomatoes and garlic clove, and stir so that the tomatoes are coated with the marinade.
3. Transfer the tomatoes to a glass jar or a plastic container. Cover and refrigerate overnight and for up to a week. If you want the tomatoes to last longer, pour enough olive oil over the tomatoes to cover them completely. They'll last a few weeks this way, and the leftover oil is great for drizzling on bread or over pasta or sautéing vegetables.

2 cups cold salted water (for the tomatoes)
1 pound sun-dried tomatoes (dry, not in oil)
¾ cup balsamic vinegar
A pinch of red-pepper flakes
¾ teaspoon salt
A few turns of freshly ground black pepper
1½ cups olive oil
1 garlic clove, smashed and peeled (page 23)

"In Avignon, where my parents live, you can find fifty different kinds of olives in the outdoor market and a dozen kinds of tapenade. But you can't find a sun-dried tomato in that town. My mom discovered them in New York and now buys them up every time she visits."
—Jerome

Sun-Dried Tomato Vinaigrette

12 Marinated Sun-Dried Tomatoes
   (page 165, or from a jar)
1 garlic clove, peeled and minced
   (page 23)
⅓ cup balsamic vinegar
½ teaspoon salt
A few turns of freshly ground black
   pepper
½ cup grated Parmesan cheese
¼ cup olive oil

This vinaigrette is rich and sweet from the sun-dried tomatoes, so you don't need to use much of it. To use it like a pesto and make a pasta dish out of it, omit the vinegar, thin it down with more olive oil, and add pine nuts, sautéed zucchini, and chopped fresh basil.

1. Toss everything but the olive oil into the bowl of a food processor (or a blender) fitted with a metal blade, and purée to a thick paste.
2. Continuing to run the machine, add the oil slowly through the feed tube or the lid of the blender. Taste for salt.

"I love basil. Just the smell of it. And there are so many types of basil. Thai basil. Lemon basil. Opal basil. My favorite is the one from France; the leaves are very, very tiny, but the flavor is much more intense. I like to make pesto with unusual basils, just to be different."
—Jerome

Ginger-Curry Vinaigrette

We can turn just about any grain into a tasty salad with this flavorful dressing.

Whisk all the ingredients except the olive oil together in a small bowl. Add the olive oil in a slow, thin, steady stream, whisking as you go to form an emulsion (page 171).

Juice of 1 lemon

2 tablespoons red wine vinegar

1 tablespoon Madras curry powder

1-inch piece fresh ginger, peeled (page 75) and finely grated

1 garlic clove, minced (page 23)

1 teaspoon salt

A few turns of freshly ground black pepper

½ cup olive oil

Frank on Why He Loves His Food Processor

My food processor is, hands down, my favorite kitchen appliance. Some people think food processors are a pain to clean. But really you take the blade out of the bowl and from there it's a soap and water job. I think it's worth it. I use my food processor all the time, for making vinaigrettes, for cutting butter into flour to make scones or cookies or crusts for pies and tarts. In these recipes, we've given you a method for making vinaigrettes by hand. We did this for a few reasons. First, because it's so easy and we think everyone should, and would be glad to, know how to whisk together a simple vinaigrette. Second, because not everyone has a food processor. And, last, because we've heard that many people who do have food processors store them in hard-to-reach, out-of-the-way places and are therefore reluctant to make something "if it means dragging out the food processor." I'd like to tell you to drag out that food processor for the last time. And leave it out. But I don't think it's my place. So, for now, I'll just tell you how to use it.

To make any of these dressings by machine, take all the ingredients minus the olive oil and purée them in the bowl of a food processor (or a blender) fitted with a metal blade. Keeping the motor running, pour the olive oil—slowly, in a thin stream, and just a little at time—through the feed tube of the food processor. And that's it. Aren't you glad you dragged the food processor out?

Black Olive Tapenade

This is our version of a classic tapenade, made thinner with oil, which makes it easier to spread on bread for sandwiches. Classic tapenade also has anchovies. We chose not to use them, because so many people don't like anchovies. But if you like them, throw some in.

1. Toss all the ingredients except the olive oil into the bowl of a food processor (or a blender) fitted with a metal blade, and blend until they're combined into a paste.
2. With the machine still running, gradually pour the olive oil in through the feed tube or the lid of the blender. Check the tapenade before you pour in all the oil, because you will want to stop adding oil when you have a thick spread.

1½ cups black olive purée (jarred, or puréed from olives)
2 garlic cloves, smashed and peeled (page 23)
4 tablespoons capers, drained
Juice of 1 lemon
1 cup fresh basil leaves
½ cup olive oil

We like to offer a variety of condiments at our table. They add both taste and color.

Black Olive Vinaigrette

MAKES ½ CUP

¼ cup red-wine vinegar

2 tablespoons Black Olive Tapenade
   (page 169) or olive paste (from
   a jar)

½ teaspoon fresh or ¼ teaspoon
   dried oregano

½ teaspoon salt

A few turns of freshly ground black
   pepper

¼ cup olive oil

We use this on our Chunky-Cucumber-and-Watercress Salad with Crumbled Feta (page 146). Use it in combination with anything you'd eat with black olives—on a salade niçoise, or to moisten the bread of a salami, prosciutto, or goat cheese sandwich.

Whisk everything except the olive oil together in a small bowl. Add the olive oil in a slow, thin, steady stream, whisking as you go to form an emulsion (page 171).

Honey-Balsamic Vinaigrette

MAKES 1 CUP

¼ medium red onion, coarsely
   chopped

¼ cup balsamic vinegar

2 tablespoons honey

1 teaspoon Dijon mustard

1 teaspoon salt

A few turns of freshly ground black
   pepper

½ cup olive oil

This is distinct from other balsamic vinaigrettes in that it has puréed onions in it. It's a little on the sweet side, because Frank likes his vinaigrettes sweet. If you think it might be too sweet for your taste, add the honey at the end, a little at a time, tasting it as you go.

Chop the onions fine in the bowl of a food processor (or a blender) fitted with a metal blade. Add everything else but the olive oil, and purée. With the machine running, add the olive oil in a slow, thin, steady stream to form an emulsion (page 171). You can make this dressing without a machine; just be sure to chop the onions as fine as possible—you want the flavor of the onion, not chunks of onion.

What Is an Emulsion?

"Emulsion" refers to the integration of two ingredients that don't want to integrate. Like oil and water. Or oil and vinegar. The two are combined by adding one ingredient to the other slowly and gradually. This process causes the ingredients to be suspended among each other. So they're still not mixed exactly, but commingling in a very micro way. Mayonnaise is an emulsion of eggs, oil, and lemon juice, as is hollandaise sauce. And vinaigrette. When an emulsion forms in a vinaigrette, that means the oil isn't going to sink to the bottom when you turn your back. The oil and vinegar are united. You know you've got an emulsion when you're whisking away adding the oil to the vinegar and the two begin to look like one smooth, creamy mixture. It won't always happen. But it will never happen if you add too much oil at once, or if you aren't whisking furiously. If it doesn't happen, if

you find the oil and vinegar have gone their separate ways, there are two ways you can fix it. The first way: turn on a food processor or blender and, through the feed tube or lid, slowly add the whole unemulsified concoction. Stop the motor once you've poured it all in. What you're now looking at, we hope, is an emulsion.

The other option is to take a quarter of the non-emulsified mixture and pour it in a separate bowl, then, very slowly, whisk three-quarters of the remaining non-emulsified stuff back into the new bowl of non-emulsified mixture. If that doesn't work, settle for a separated vinaigrette and try again next time.

Eggplant Caponata

1–2 large eggplants (1 pound), cut
  into 1-inch cubes (pages 38,
  119)
½ tablespoon salt, plus more for
  "sweating" the eggplant
⅓ cup olive oil
1 big yellow onion, diced (page
  119)
4 celery stalks (¾ pound), diced
½ cup dried currants
¾ pound tomatoes, cored and cut
  ½-inch dice
3 tablespoons capers, drained
½ cup red-wine vinegar
¼ cup sugar
A few turns of freshly ground black
  pepper

Frank's late Auntie Pina, who came from Catania, Sicily, to live in the United States when he was little, used to make this for him. It's like the Italian version of ratatouille. Frank used to go into the refrigerator with a spoon and eat it straight out of the container. He still loves it, for all the sweet, savory, and acidic tastes going on in one dish. You can eat it on toast, or with chicken or pork, or on just about any sandwich. Auntie Pina typically added about ½ cup pitted and chopped green Sicilian olives to her caponata. If you're into olives, you should, too.

1. Put the eggplant in a colander placed in the sink. Sprinkle with a thin coat of salt, and toss to distribute evenly over the eggplant. Let the eggplant rest for at least 20 minutes to "sweat" the bitterness out.
2. Sauté the eggplant cubes with 2–3 tablespoons of the olive oil in a large heavy-bottomed saucepan over high heat, stirring occasionally, until they start to soften, in 5–10 minutes. Lower the heat, and continue to cook for 8–10 minutes, until the eggplant softens. Remove the pan from the heat, and transfer the eggplant to a medium-size bowl.
3. In the same pan, sauté the onion with half of the remaining olive oil over medium heat, until the onion is tender and translucent, 10–15 minutes. Scrape the onion into the bowl on top of the eggplant.
4. Repeat with the celery, using the remaining olive oil and sautéing over high heat until the celery is tender.
5. Lower the flame, and return the eggplant and onions to the pot with the celery. Stir in the currants, tomatoes, capers, vinegar, sugar, ½ tablespoon salt, and pep-

per, and simmer, uncovered, for 45–50 minutes, stirring from time to time. The vegetables will cook down and give off a lot of juices. By the time you're done cooking this dish, the vegetables should have melded into one another and the water should have evaporated, so that you have one thick mélange of vegetables so chunky you could eat it with a fork. Serve at room temperature or chilled. This caponata will keep for a few days, refrigerated in a covered container.

"Next time you're cooking pasta, throw in some extra—and don't toss it with your sauce. Instead, take the extra pasta, toss it with a little olive oil, and refrigerate it. When you need a quick lunch, toss the pasta with our Eggplant Caponata. What you've got there is a tasty pasta salad."
—Frank

Frank's Bruschetta

In my house, bruschetta isn't a fancy appetizer, it's a way to use up stale bread. I slice it about ¼ inch thin, rub it with raw garlic, drizzle the bread with olive oil, and toast it on a sheet pan in a 450-degree oven. I top the toast with just about anything I like to eat: fresh tomatoes in the summer, grilled portobellos, pesto, hummus, scraps of cheese, fresh herbs. Some combinations I like a lot are:

- goat cheese with roasted peppers and chopped oil-cured black olives
- Black Olive Tapenade (page 169) with grilled or marinated artichokes and shaved Parmesan cheese
- Eggplant Caponata (page 172) with grated fresh or smoked mozzarella
- Sun-Dried Tomato Vinaigrette (page 166) with garlic-sautéed broccoli rabe or spinach and smoked mozzarella
- Diced summer tomatoes with fresh mozzarella and thin strips of fresh basil

Once Upon a Tart's Pizza-Style Bruschetta

At the store, we have a bruschetta "special" every day. We take a ciabatta roll, cut it in half, and brush it with a pesto or Black Olive Tapenade (page 169). We then cover the bread with a layer of thinly sliced potatoes roasted in olive oil and garlic. Next we add something rich and flavorful, like sun-dried tomatoes, roasted red peppers, roasted portobello mushrooms, or artichoke hearts on top of the potatoes. We cover the whole thing with fresh or smoked mozzarella, and then throw it into the oven until the cheese is melted and bubbling. It's really more like a grilled open-face sandwich or a pizza than bruschetta. But we haven't heard anyone complaining.

Spicy Peanut-Sesame Sauce

MAKES 2 CUPS

When we use this over pasta (page 153), we add a little water or cooled black tea so that it coats the pasta more smoothly. We also make sandwiches with it: chicken, cucumbers, sprouts, avocado, and some of this sauce inside a whole-wheat pita. Yum.

Toss all the ingredients except the black tea or water into the bowl of a food processor (or a blender) fitted with a metal blade, and blend until you have a smooth paste that is just thin enough to pour. If it's too thick, add a little of the tea or water.

"I often use tamari in lieu of soy. Tamari is a wheat-free soy sauce. It's healthier than soy sauce, and I prefer the taste."
—Frank

3 garlic cloves, peeled and coarsely chopped (page 23)
½ cup chopped cilantro, including the tender part of the stems (page 162)
2-inch piece fresh ginger, peeled and coarsely chopped (page 75)
¼ cup canola or vegetable oil
2 tablespoons toasted sesame oil
2 tablespoons tahini (sesame butter)
⅓ cup smooth peanut butter
¼ cup tamari or soy sauce
1 tablespoon honey
2 tablespoons white-wine vinegar
½ teaspoon red-pepper flakes
¼ cup cold water; or brewed black tea, cooled to room temperature

Dijon Vinaigrette with Worcestershire

MAKES 1½ CUPS

This is our take on the classic French vinaigrette.

Whisk everything except the olive oil together in a small bowl. Add the olive oil in a slow, thin, steady stream, whisking as you go to form an emulsion (page 171).

¼ cup red-wine vinegar
1 teaspoon balsamic vinegar
3 tablespoons Dijon mustard
½ teaspoon Worcestershire sauce
1 teaspoon salt
A few turns of freshly ground black pepper
1 cup olive oil

Jerome's Homemade Mayonnaise

MAKES 1 CUP

Jerome never saw a jar of mayonnaise when he was growing up. "In France, people make their own mayonnaise. It's so easy," he says. Just an emulsion of egg yolks, mustard, and vegetable oil. "And it tastes and looks so different from jarred mayonnaise. Hellmann's is white. Real mayonnaise is yellow—and you can taste the egg." To make mayonnaise, Jerome's mother always told him: Make sure you start with very cold eggs. Otherwise it won't emulsify. He never questioned this. This mayonnaise will keep, refrigerated, for about two weeks.

1 large egg yolk
1½ teaspoons Dijon mustard
1½ teaspoons white-wine vinegar
½ teaspoon salt
A few turns of freshly ground black
   pepper
1 cup vegetable oil

1. Blend everything but the vegetable oil in the bowl of a food processor (or a blender) fitted with a metal blade until they're combined.
2. With the motor running, add a quarter of the oil in a slow, thin, steady stream through the feed tube or lid of the blender until you've got a smooth, creamy consistency. This means that you have formed an emulsion (page 171). Good.
3. Add the rest of the oil, a little faster now, with the motor still running, and— *voilà!*—creamy, delicious yellow mayo.

One cup of Jerome's homemade mayonnaise goes into making Rosemary-Garlic Aïoli, page 178.

Variation: Rosemary-Garlic Aïoli

Technically speaking, aïoli is made with olive oil, not vegetable oil—and also lots of garlic—because it's made in the south of France. We like to tone down the garlic to make room for other flavors, like rosemary. If you feel like experimenting, try substituting Italian parsley, Black Olive Tapenade (page 169, or black olive paste from a jar), Sun-Dried Tomato Vinaigrette (page 166), or French-Style Grainy Mustard (page 161) for the rosemary. We love aïoli as a dip for crudité or spread on bread for sandwiches.

Stir 1 cup Jerome's Homemade Mayonnaise together with 3 cloves of garlic, minced, a teaspoon of finely chopped rosemary needles, ¼ teaspoon freshly grated black pepper, and ½ teaspoon of salt. That's it.

Caesar-ish Salad

Caesar salad is simple, but few people do it well. Ours isn't the most traditional Caesar, but it is delicious. We think the secret lies in discarding way more of the romaine lettuce than you probably feel comfortable doing. The dressing for this salad is so rich and creamy that only the crispest hearts of the romaine can hold their own with it. To make a Caesar salad for four, remove all the outer dark-green leaves from two heads of romaine. Trim the leaves that are left of the last 3 or 4 inches—again, the dark, leafy greens. At this point, you can either leave the hearts of romaine leaves whole, which is how they are in a traditional Caesar, or chop them into roughly 2-inch pieces. Rinse the lettuce, and dry it well, either in a salad spinner or by blotting it with paper or dish towels.

Now the only thing left is the croutons. We use leftover sourdough bread to make ours, but any good white bread will do. Preheat the oven to 400 degrees. Cut a loaf of bread into 1-inch cubes (with or without crusts, depending on what you like), or a baguette into ¼-inch slices, and toss the bread into a bowl. Drizzle enough olive oil to coat the bread lightly (¼ cup or more), and add a clove of minced garlic, a teaspoon of salt, a few turns of pepper, and either dried oregano or thyme. Toss this all together. Spread the croutons out on a sheet pan, and bake for 10–15 minutes, until the croutons are golden brown and crispy. Remove the pan from the oven, and let the croutons cool before tossing them in the salad. The croutons will stay fresh in a sealed plastic bag for up to a week.

Just before you're ready to serve the salad, toss the lettuce with ½ cup or more of the dressing, a handful of croutons, and a few turns of freshly ground pepper.

Our Own Caesar-ish Dressing

MAKES 1½ CUPS

There are people for whom a salad means greens and nothing but—no beets, no potatoes, and certainly no quinoa. For those customers, we offer a Caesar salad. They don't seem to mind the croutons interfering with the purity of the romaine lettuce. The Caesar dressing we make at the store isn't classic (thus the *-ish*), in that we start with homemade mayonnaise rather than a raw egg, which the original recipe calls for. We also add parsley, because we like it. Still, the lemon juice and the Parmesan cheese make it very Caesar-like despite its departure from the original. You can use jarred mayonnaise, but the rich egginess of the homemade mayo makes a big difference in this dressing. We recommend adding the anchovies, even if you think you don't like them. They add a nice salty flavor, and we don't think you'll taste the anchovies themselves. Keeps refrigerated for a couple of weeks.

Toss everything into the bowl of a food processor (or a blender) fitted with a metal blade, and purée. Taste for salt.

1 cup Jerome's Homemade Mayonnaise (page 177) or jarred mayonnaise

2 garlic cloves, smashed and peeled (page 23)

2 small anchovies from a can, drained

2 tablespoons chopped fresh Italian parsley (page 162)

Juice of 1 lemon

1½ teaspoons Worcestershire sauce

1 teaspoon white-wine vinegar

⅓ cup grated Parmesan cheese

½ teaspoon salt

A few turns of freshly ground black pepper

"Anchovies don't last very long once the tin or jar is opened. After I make a Caesar at home, I throw the rest into a Greek salad, or lay them over a plate of grilled vegetable antipasto or on bruschetta."
—Frank

White-Bean Spread

2 15-ounce cans white beans or
1¼ cups dried white cannellini
or Great Northern beans, picked
through, rinsed, and soaked
overnight (page 61)

3 tablespoons or more olive oil

1 garlic clove, peeled and coarsely
chopped (page 23)

¼ cup chopped fresh Italian parsley (page 162)

1 teaspoon salt

½ teaspoon freshly ground black
pepper

This is a classic Italian spread—used on toast for bruschetta, and as a dip for bread and vegetables. We like it in combination with broccoli rabe and with fresh or sun-dried tomatoes.

1. Drain and rinse the canned beans in a colander. For dried beans, rinse the soaked beans and dump them into a big soup pot with 8 cups (2 quarts) unsalted water. Bring to a boil over high heat, lower the heat, and simmer for an hour or more, until the beans are tender to the bite but not falling apart or splitting. Drain and rinse the beans in a colander, and allow them to cool.

2. Place the beans, oil, garlic, parsley, salt, and pepper into the bowl of a food processor (or a blender) fitted with a metal blade, and blend until you have a smooth, spreadable purée. Add a touch more olive oil if the spread is too thick.

Traditional Hummus

MAKES 1¾ CUPS

Hummus is a great standby for the home cook. The ingredients—canned garbanzo beans, tahini (sesame seed butter), lemon juice, and garlic—are things you can keep in your pantry. And it takes about 5 minutes to whip up in a food processor.

Toss everything but the olive oil into the bowl of a food processor (or a blender) fitted with a metal blade, and blend until the chickpeas are puréed. With the motor still running, add the olive oil. The hummus should be the consistency of a smooth, spreadable paste. If it is too thick, blend in a little more olive oil or water.

1 15-ounce can chickpeas, rinsed
   and drained
¼ cup tahini
Juice of 1 lemon
1 tablespoon cumin
1 teaspoon salt
½ teaspoon freshly ground black
   pepper
½ cup olive oil

Frank on Chickpeas

Chickpeas are the same thing as garbanzo beans, or *ceci* beans in Italian. They have a delicious, sweet, nutty flavor. They're what hummus is made of. Jerome and I both grew up with chickpeas, so they naturally made their way into many dishes at the store. Jerome grew up with chickpeas in couscous and in a simple salad his mother made of chickpeas and olive oil. I remember them mostly in minestrone, and also dried and baked with salt until they became a crunchy little snack. Chickpeas are the one bean I will use out of a can. Of course, they're probably slightly better when you cook the dried beans yourself, but the difference isn't so great that I'm convinced it's worth the effort. Like all canned beans, chickpeas come in a sort of viscous salty water, so you need to drain them in a colander and rinse them well before adding them to any recipe.

Fresh Tarragon–Lemon Vinaigrette

MAKES ½ CUP

1 tablespoon finely chopped fresh
   tarragon leaves (page 162)
Juice of 1 lemon
1 tablespoon Dijon mustard
1 teaspoon salt
A few turns of freshly ground
   pepper
⅓ cup olive oil

Jerome made this with lemon rather than vinegar because his mom insists you cannot mix vinegar with tarragon. We use it on chicken sandwiches and in potato salads—tarragon and potatoes being a classic combination. Because of the abundance of tarragon leaves in this vinaigrette, this is best made with a food processor. If you don't have a food processor, chop the leaves very fine, whisk the ingredients together to form an emulsion, and stir the chopped tarragon in at the end.

Whisk everything but the olive oil together in a small bowl. Add the oil in a slow, thin, steady stream, whisking all the while to form an emulsion (page 171).

Soy-Ginger Vinaigrette

MAKES 1½ CUPS

We have very few Asian-inspired foods on our menu, but occasionally one of us will hop on his bicycle and go down to Chinatown to pick up some vegetables. That's how this dressing came to be. "I consider soy and ginger the essential Asian combination," Frank says. Whenever we use what we perceive as an Asian vegetable in a salad—bean sprouts, snow peas, Savoy cabbage—we'll toss it with this vinaigrette. This will keep for several weeks in the refrigerator.

Whisk all the ingredients except the oil together in a small bowl. Add the oil in a slow, thin, steady stream, whisking as you go to form an emulsion (page 171).

Juice of 1 lemon (3 tablespoons)
¼ cup apple-cider vinegar
2 tablespoons honey
1-inch piece fresh ginger, peeled and finely grated (page 75)
¼ cup tamari or soy sauce
1½ teaspoons salt
½ teaspoon freshly ground black pepper
¾ cup canola or vegetable oil

"It's important to taste your vinaigrette not just with your finger but with the greens, or whatever you're eating it with."
—Frank

Marinated Artichoke Hearts with Herbes de Provence

MAKES 2 CUPS

1 15-ounce can water-packed
   artichoke hearts, drained
A pinch of red-pepper flakes
A few turns of freshly ground black
   pepper
1 teaspoon *herbes de Provence*
   (page 19)
1 garlic clove, peeled and minced
   (page 23)
½ cup olive oil

We marinate our own artichoke hearts, because most store-bought varieties are too oily for our taste. We start with canned artichoke hearts, but if you have the inclination and they're in season, you could buy fresh artichokes and whittle them down to hearts, though it's a lot of work. We think that, after they've been marinated, they're good enough this way to justify the shortcut.

1. Cut each artichoke heart into quarters.
2. Whisk the remaining ingredients together in a small bowl. Pour this mixture into a glass jar or plastic container big enough to hold the artichokes. Add the artichokes. Stir or gently shake the container so that the artichokes are covered with the oil. Cover, and refrigerate overnight, or at least a few hours, before using the artichokes. The artichokes will last a couple of weeks in the refrigerator. If you want them to last longer, pour enough olive oil over them to cover completely. You can drizzle the excess oil over salads, pasta, or whatever you're using the artichokes with.

"Normally I wouldn't even think about eating any vegetable that came out of a can. But I make an exception for canned artichokes. Not the oily chokes that come in a bottle. Truly, canned. (You'll find them right next to the canned black olives in your local grocery store.) Roasting cooks out the canned flavor. The artichokes get nice and charred around the edges, and develop a nice smoky note from the roasting."
—Frank

Oven-Roasted Tomatoes

These sweet, juicy tomatoes fall somewhere between the glorious taste of a ripe summer tomato and the richness of a sun-dried. We got the idea from tomatoes Provençal, a dish where the tomatoes are stuffed with a mixture of garlic, parsley, breadcrumbs, and Parmesan cheese, then baked. Oven-roasted tomatoes make a delicious, colorful side dish to fish, pork, or beef, and taste great on sandwiches or tossed with pasta and a soft cheese. If you're making the tomatoes just for pasta, try cutting them into four wedges instead of rounds.

1. Preheat oven to 475 degrees.
2. Toss the tomatoes with the rest of the ingredients in a medium-size bowl.
3. Place the tomatoes, cut side down, on a sheet pan. Place the sheet pan in the oven, and roast the tomatoes until they begin to blacken around the edges, 25–30 minutes. Check the tomatoes occasionally to make sure they're not charring. If they are, lower the oven temperature to 400.
4. Use the tomatoes immediately, or store them, tightly covered, in the refrigerator for up to 3 days.

1 pound plum tomatoes (about 6), cored and cut into 4 rounds
¼ cup olive oil
1 teaspoon salt
A few turns of freshly ground black pepper
2 garlic cloves, peeled and minced (page 23)
¼ cup chopped fresh basil (page 162)

Once Upon a ...
SWEET TART

Flaky Tart Crust

Apricot Glaze

Jerome's Mother's Famous Apricot Tart

Pear-and-Almond Tart

Poached Fruit

Chocolate-Pear Tart

Alsatian Apple Tart

Chocolate-Banana Tart

Baked Lemon Tart

Fresh Fruit Tart with Vanilla Cream

Apple, Walnut, and Raisin Tart with Frangipane

Strawberry-Rhubarb Tart with Shamey's Crisp Topping

Shamey's Crisp Topping

Black-Plum-and-Honey Tart · Variation: Spiced Italian Prune Plum Tart

Peach-and-Blueberry Free-Form Tart

Chocolate-Walnut Tart

Coffee-Pecan Tart

Raspberry-Cranberry Linzer Tart with a Linzer Lattice Crust

Pumpkin Tart with Sugared Pastry Leaves

Frank's Simple Whipped Cream

Cranberry-and-Sour-Apple Tart

Our business in sweet tarts came to us the way so many good things come to be—by accident. We had decided to start a wholesale business selling savory tarts. The reason behind the wholesale business was to test the market for savory tarts. We didn't feel a need to test the market for sweet tarts. Sweet tarts are so much like pies, we figured Americans would understand them, and like them, right away. And we were right.

When we were designing our menu, we needed a few items to "weigh" the bottom. So we threw the names of a few sweet tarts—rice pudding, Key lime, and chocolate fudge—on there. Jerome took that menu, along with samples of savory tarts (since that's all we were actually making), to some upscale grocery stores in New York City. Next thing we knew, our very first client, Grace's Market Place, an exclusive neighborhood market on the Upper East Side of Manhattan, placed a huge order. All of them for sweet tarts. And all of them to be delivered the next day. Meanwhile, we hadn't developed a single recipe for sweet tarts.

Jerome was leaving for France the day of the delivery. But before he left, he opened his book from Tarte Margot. We started there, with the dough recipe for sweet tarts. And Frank knew how to make a pie or two. We stayed up all night trying to fill this order. The Key lime gave us the hardest time. The tarts were too tart, or too Jell-O–like, or too runny. We kept making them and chucking them. Finally, Frank took a crème brulée recipe that he knew worked and added some lime juice and zest, and that became our Key lime tart—for that order, anyway. Jerome caught his plane to France. Grace's was happy. And we were now in the business of sweet tarts, too.

Maybe because Jerome is French and Frank is American,

our sweet tarts turned out to be a hybrid of classic French tart and good old American pie. We took the concept of sweet tarts, or, more specifically, the pan, and made something a little more rustic. The style varies from tart to tart. Some are a little fancier, like the pear tarts, where the fruit is fanned out, or the Alsatian Apple Tart (page 201), where very thinly sliced apples are arranged in concentric circles. The Peach-and-Blueberry, on the other hand, is a free-form tart (page 219); we lay the ingredients on a sheet of dough and then fold up the sides. The Strawberry-Rhubarb Tart (page 213) is a pie with crisp topping that just happened to get thrown in a tart shell. Except for a sprinkling of sugar or a brushing of glaze, none of our tarts are decorated. We don't go for precious. We go for delicious.

THINGS TO KNOW

What with their fluted edges and their Parisian connotation, making a tart from the crust up may seem a bit intimidating to an American. In fact, making tarts is not any more difficult than making pie. It's just in a different pan.

For the tart (or pie) novice, the first hurdle to making a tart is making dough. Dough is one of those things that, had you learned it from your grandmother, would be just another task—like laundry. But learning it late in life is like learni late in life to pronounce "rue du Regard." It feels impo awkward. Really, though, making tart dough is easy. I Lessons (page 6), we tell you all there is to kno through before you start baking. Once you make times, it'll be easy.

In these recipes, we call for tart shells that are either prepared, par-baked, or prebaked. By "prepared," we simply mean that the dough is in the tart pan, ready to be filled and then baked right along with the filling. We use prepared raw tart shells when the filling needs to be baked for a long time. Par-baked shells have been partially baked (thus "par," which may also make it easy for you to remember). We use par-baked shells when the shell needs a little more time to bake than the filling. A prebaked shell is just what it sounds like: the shell is prebaked totally before you put any filling in. We use a prebaked shell only for the Fresh Fruit Tart with Vanilla Cream (page 208), and when we fill a tart shell with Very Lemony Curd (page 252).

Always use the best fruit you can find. That process starts with using fruits that are in season. A bland pear is not going to taste good just because you've put it in a tart shell and surrounded it with chocolate. Speaking of which, we use semisweet chocolate chips in our recipes because they're easy to measure. And that way we only have to keep one chocolate on hand. (We have such a small kitchen that we're forced to keep things simple.) If you wanted to, you could use a high-quality dark chocolate like Valrhona or Scharffen Berger, cut into chunks, in any of our recipes where we call for chocolate chips.

Some of our tarts call for a very specific arrangement of the fruit—pears fanned out or plums arranged in a camellia pattern. Think of this as a goal, but don't get hung up on it. It's going to taste the same no matter what the design.

We give cooking times, but it's important to keep an eye on your tarts while they're baking. Ovens don't always do what they promise. You set yours at 375 degrees, but meanwhile, it's actually revved up to 450 degrees. Even within a single oven, the temperature can be considerably hotter in one spot than in another. If you bake enough, you'll get to know your oven's idiosyncrasies. In the meantime, watch whatever you've got in the oven. And trust your instincts. If the back of the tart is brown and the front looks raw, turn it around. If the tart is charring before the filling is set, open the oven door and turn the temperature down to cool it off.

Removing the tart from the tart pan isn't as difficult as it may sound from our instructions. We call for you to rest it on a big can, but anything will work—a big mug, a saucepan turned upside down. You just want to get the tart *up* on something so that there's room to slide the outer ring *down*. If the tart cools completely before you take it out of the pan, any sugar from the tart that may have dripped onto the pan will have hardened, causing the tart to stick relentlessly to the pan. In this case, place the tart in a 200-degree oven for a few minutes to warm it up and remelt the sugar.

Flaky Tart Crust

MAKES ENOUGH FOR TWO 9-INCH TART CRUSTS,
ONE FOR NOW, AND ONE TO FREEZE FOR LATER

2½ cups unbleached all-purpose
  flour
1 teaspoon sugar
1 teaspoon salt
12 tablespoons (1½ sticks) cold
  unsalted butter, cut into ¼-inch
  cubes
5 tablespoons solid vegetable
  shortening
A small glass of ice water
1 9-inch tart pan (with fluted edges
  and removable bottom)

The fat in our tart dough is mostly butter with a little shortening. Many people think that an all-butter crust is the goal. But even Julia Child, America's foremost champion of butter, recommends making crusts with a combination of butter and shortening. Butter for its inimitable flavor, and shortening because that's what makes a crust flaky.

We call for butter to be cut into ¼-inch cubes to make tart dough. The truth is, you only need to cut it that small if you're making crust by hand. If you're using a food processor, the whirling metal blade works so well to cut up the butter that you can get away with roughly chopping it into slabs.

Once you have the food processor out (if you're using one) and the counters all floured up, we think it's a great idea to make as much dough as you'll use for the next 2 months. But don't make the mistake of doubling the recipe. Make a batch of dough, and then make it again. And again. Making dough in small batches is key. When you make crust dough in bigger batches, you have to work it more, to cut the butter into the flour and then to work the dough into a ball. Working dough is bad. Overworking dough is a crust crime.

1. Dump the flour, sugar, and salt into the bowl of a food processor fitted with a metal blade, and pulse a couple of times to make sure the salt is distributed evenly throughout the flour.
2. Add the butter and the shortening all at once, and pulse five to ten times, until the mixture forms little balls, like moist crumbs, and no chunks of butter or

shortening remain. You must pulse, not run, the food processor. The worst thing that could happen at this stage of the crust-making game would be for the flours and fats to come together completely into a paste.

3. Remove the blade from the food processor, and dump the crumbs into a big bowl. Sprinkle a tablespoon of ice water over the surface of the crumbs. Repeat with 3 more tablespoons of ice water.

4. Use your hands or a wooden spoon to bring the dough together. Add more water if you have to, 1 tablespoon at a time. The dough should be just past crumbly and just barely coming together. You don't want it to be so wet that it *sticks* together or turns sticky-white in color.

5. Cut the dough in half, press each of the halves into a disk, and wrap the disks in plastic wrap. Refrigerate the dough for at least 30 minutes before rolling it out.

6. If you are par-baking or prebaking your crust, position your oven racks so that one is in the center, and preheat the oven to 400 degrees.

7. Roll out one disk of dough to ⅜ inch thick. Fit the dough into your tart pan. (See Dough Lessons, page 10.)

8. For a prepared crust, refrigerate the dough that has been fitted into a tart pan until you're ready to use it.

9. For a par-baked crust, prick holes in the tart dough with the tines of a fork. Line the bed of the tart with parchment paper or aluminum foil, and weigh it down with pie weights or dried beans (page 13). Place the tart shell on the center rack in the oven, and bake for 10 minutes at 400 degrees. Remove the tart shell from the oven, and remove the paper and weights from the pan. Return the tart shell to the oven, and bake it for another 5 minutes, until the bed of the tart shell appears dry. Remove the tart shell from the oven, and set it on a wire rack to cool.

10. For a prebaked crust, follow the instructions for the par-baked crust, but increase the second baking time to 15–18 minutes, or until the tart shell is golden brown all over.

Apricot Glaze

We brush apricot glaze on our fruit tarts after baking them. The glaze brings out the color of the fruit and gives the tart a finished, bakeshop look. You can buy apricot glaze in a jar at specialty stores, or you can make your own: Add 2 tablespoons of warm water to ½ cup of apricot jam. Stir until the jam melts and thins out, then pour the glaze through a strainer. Depending on how much whole fruit is in the jam, you'll end up with ¼–½ cup of glaze. (Our recipes all call for ¼ cup.) With darker fruits like plums or berries, you can use a darker jam, like strawberry, plum, or raspberry, as long as you strain out the seeds. Melt cooled glaze over low heat or in the microwave.

Jerome's Mother's Famous Apricot Tart

MAKES ONE 9-INCH TART

Before we opened Once Upon a Tart, Jerome's mom came from France to help us with our sweet tarts. She started with an apricot tart, since that's what she's famous for at home. She went all over New York to different shops and farmers' markets until she found just the right sweet, ripe apricots that met her standards. When she was cooking the tart, she kept looking inside the oven—to see if the apricots were juicing up, which is how you know when a fruit tart is done, and to sprinkle it with sugar occasionally to give them nice brown caramelized edges. She was so obsessed with these apricots. "That's when I really got it," Frank says. "An apricot tart is just about the apricots. So the apricots better be good, and they better be cooked right." With all due respect to Jerome's mom, we make this tart only in the summer, when apricots are in season.

1 par-baked 9-inch Flaky Tart Crust (page 190)

½ cup applesauce or apple butter

15 medium apricots, halved, pits removed (not peeled)

¼ cup sugar

¼ cup Apricot Glaze, melted (page 192, or from a jar)

1. Position your oven racks so that one is in the center, and preheat oven to 375 degrees.
2. Spread the applesauce or apple butter evenly over your par-baked tart shell with a rubber spatula or the back of a spoon. Arrange the apricot halves in the shell, pitted side up, in a circular pattern, overlapping them so that the bottom apricot cradles the next one, which cradles the next one.
3. Holding your hand about 6 inches over the tart, sprinkle the sugar evenly over the apricots.
4. Place the tart on the center rack in the oven, and bake for 50–55 minutes, or until the apricots are a nice dark brown and even darker around their edges. It's important to give the apricots the time to brown. Your tart will look better and,

more important, taste better. The fruit will caramelize, and when that happens, the taste changes from fruit to fruit dessert.

5. Remove the tart from the oven, and set it on a rack to cool slightly.

6. To remove the tart from the pan, rest it on a big can. Make sure the tart is steady and balanced. Slide the outside ring of the pan down off the tart. Then place the tart on your work surface, and slide the tart off the pan bottom and onto a rimless serving dish or a cutting board.

7. Use a pastry brush or a scrunched-up paper towel to coat the apricots with the glaze. We like this served at room temperature because it's a summer tart. It's certainly good fresh from the oven.

"At home, I can never seem to find a pastry brush when I need one. So I often use a scrunched-up paper towel instead. Not very elegant, but it works just fine. And well it should. I learned the trick from my grandmother."
—Frank

Pear-and-Almond Tart

This tart may seem fancy, what with the fanned-out pears and all. But it isn't hard to make. Really. If you want to get a head start, poach the pears in advance and refrigerate them with the poaching liquid for a few days. Also, if you're looking to save time, start with very ripe, sweet pears and skip the poaching step altogether.

1. Position your oven racks so that one is in the center, and preheat the oven to 375 degrees.
2. Bring the water and 1 cup of the sugar to a boil in a large saucepan over high heat. When the sugar has dissolved completely, carefully place the pears in the water. Bring the water back to a boil, and continue cooking at a low boil for 10–15 minutes, until the pears are tender when pierced with a fork but not mushy; you don't want them to fall apart. Periodically check the pears for doneness, because the cooking time will vary depending on the variety, size, and ripeness of the pears. Better to undercook than to overcook them; they'll cook a little more when you bake the tart. And anyway, there's nothing wrong with a raw pear. Using a slotted spoon, remove the pears from the water and set them in a colander to drain. If you're making the pears ahead of time, let the water and the pears cool separately (so the pears don't continue to cook in the warm water), then return the pears to the cooled water to refrigerate.
3. Whisk the eggs and the remaining sugar together in a small bowl until they are pale yellow. Whisk in the extracts and the cream and, finally, stir in the almonds.
4. Carefully transfer the cooked pears to a cutting board and, holding each pear with one hand to keep it intact as much as possible, cut it horizontally into thin slices (⅛ inch).

4 cups cold unsalted water (for the pears)

1⅓ cups sugar

3 large ripe Anjou or Bosc pears, peeled, halved lengthwise, and cored

2 large eggs

1½ teaspoons vanilla extract

1 teaspoon almond extract

¾ cup light cream

½ cup almonds, finely chopped

1 prepared (unbaked) 9-inch Flaky Tart Crust (page 190)

¼ cup Apricot Glaze, melted (page 192, or from a jar)

Confectioners' sugar for sprinkling

5. Fan out the pear slices, by placing the palm of your hand over the pear half with your fingers pointing toward the narrow end of the pear. Apply light pressure to the pear and draw your hand outward, toward the edge of the cutting board. It's not as complicated as it sounds— think blackjack dealer, with the pear being the deck of cards.

6. Lift up the fanned pears by placing your knife under the concave portion that used to be the core of the pear and holding the slices in place against the knife with your free hand. With the narrower stem ends of the pears pointing toward the center of your tart, rest each pear on top of the tart shell so that the six pear halves form a sort of star or flower over the whole tart.

"For the pear tarts, the pears must be ripe because the tart is all about the pears. But it can be hard to know if a pear is ripe. Pears are hard. The best way to tell if a pear is ripe? It will smell like a pear."
—Jerome

7. Pour the custard into the tart shell. Try to pour it between the pears, rather than just dumping it over the fruit.

8. Place the tart on the center rack in the oven, and bake for 50–55 minutes, or until the crust is brown and the custard is set. When the custard is set, it will be puffed up and slightly browned and it will be firm to the touch.

9. Remove the tart from the oven, and place it on a wire rack to cool slightly.

10. To remove the tart from the pan, rest it on a big can. Make sure that the tart is steady and balanced. Slide the outside ring of the pan down off the tart. Place

the tart on your work surface, and slide the tart off the pan bottom onto a rimless serving dish or a cutting board.

11. Coat the pears with the apricot glaze using a pastry brush or a scrunched-up paper towel. Use a sifter or sieve to sprinkle the custard with confectioners' sugar. Don't worry if sugar gets on the pears: the moisture from the sugar will melt into the glaze. Serve warm or at room temperature.

Poached Fruit

Peaches, pears, plums, apricots, nectarines, even quince—they can all be poached in the same way. Start with fruit that's ripe but not overripe. Also, start with the tastiest fruit you can find. You're not going to get a dry, mealy, unsweet peach to turn delicious after it's poached. To poach your fruit, set the fruit in a pot of boiling water and 1 cup of sugar, and cook at a low boil until the fruit is tender. Carefully lift the poached fruit out of the poaching liquid and set it in a colander to drain and cool. In our homes, we often poach the pears in Muscadet, or red wine, or water with a splash of Marsala and honey. We don't poach in alcohol at the store, because we don't keep any alcohol at the store. Serve poached fruit with vanilla ice cream, fresh berries, crumbled toasted almonds or pecans, or crumbled biscotti.

"I don't like to say never, because I like to think cooking is flexible. But we never use frozen or canned fruits in our tarts."
—Jerome

Chocolate-Pear Tart

MAKES ONE 9-INCH TART

1 prepared (unbaked) 9-inch Flaky
Tart Crust (page 190)

4 cups (1 quart) cold unsalted
water (for the pears)

1¼ cups sugar

2 large ripe Anjou or Bosc pears,
peeled, halved lengthwise, and
cored

1 large egg

1 large egg yolk

1 teaspoon vanilla extract

1 cup semisweet chocolate chips;
or 6 ounces good-quality dark
chocolate, broken into pieces

¾ cup heavy cream

¼ cup Apricot Glaze, melted (page
192, or from a jar)

We made this variation on our pear tart for those who don't like nuts or who absolutely have to have chocolate in their desserts. We try to satisfy a lot of different people. We're feeding the public, so that's our thing.

1. Position your oven racks so that one is in the center, and preheat the oven to 375 degrees.

2. Bring the water and 1 cup of the sugar to a boil in a large saucepan over high heat. When the sugar has dissolved completely, carefully place the pears in the water. Bring the water back to a boil, and continue cooking at a low boil for 10–15 minutes, until the pears are tender when pierced with a fork but not mushy—you don't want them to fall apart. Periodically check the pears for doneness: the cooking time will vary depending on the variety, size, and ripeness of the pears. Using a slotted spoon, remove the pears from the water and set in a colander to drain.

3. Whisk the egg and egg yolk in a medium-size bowl to break up the yolks. Whisk in the vanilla. Melt the chocolate chips with the cream in a double boiler (or a metal bowl placed over a pot of boiling water) over high heat, stirring in a figure-eight motion with a wooden spoon or heatproof rubber spatula to prevent the chocolate from burning around the edges of the pot. Stir in the remaining sugar, and cook for a few more minutes. Remove the pot from the heat, and allow the chocolate mixture to cool while you slice the pears.

4. Carefully transfer your poached pears to a cutting board and, holding the pear with one hand to keep it intact as much as possible, cut the pear horizontally into thin slices (⅛ inch).

5. To fan out the pear slices, place the palm of your hand over the pear half with

your fingers pointing toward the narrow end of the pear. Apply light pressure to the pear and draw your hand outward, toward the edge of the board.

6. Lift up the fanned pears by placing your knife under the concave portion that used to be the core of the pear and holding the slices in place against the knife with your free hand. With the narrower stem ends of the pears pointing toward the center of your tart, rest each pear on top of the tart shell so that the four pear halves form a sort of star or flower over the whole tart.

7. Very slowly and gradually whisk the chocolate into the bowl with the eggs. (Any time that you're combining eggs with warm ingredients, you need to add the hot mixture slowly—and a little bit at a time. This allows the heat to warm rather than cook the eggs. You don't want scrambled eggs floating in an otherwise smooth custard.) Once you've added about half of the chocolate, you can dump the rest in all at once—because the eggs are already warmed up.

8. Pour the chocolate custard into the tart shell. Try to pour it between the pears, rather than just dumping it over the fruit. It'll look nicer that way.

9. Place the tart on the center rack in the oven, and bake for 50–55 minutes, or until the crust is brown and the chocolate custard is set. When the custard is set, it will be firm to the touch and slightly cracked around the edges.

10. Remove the tart from the oven, and place it on a wire rack to cool slightly.

11. To remove the tart from the pan, rest it on a big can. Make sure that the tart is steady and balanced. Slide the outside ring of the pan down off the tart. Place the tart on your work surface, and slide the tart off the pan bottom onto a rimless serving dish or a cutting board.

12. Use a pastry brush or a scrunched-up paper towel to coat the pears with the apricot glaze. Serve warm or at room temperature.

"Our tarts are beautiful, but they're simple. They are not architectural or graphic. They're also not as delicate-looking or fancy as they are in France. That's what I like about them."
—Jerome

Alsatian Apple Tart

We wanted to offer an apple pie, but, being a tart shop, we didn't think it was right to make apple pie—exactly. So this is what we came up with. Here the apples are sliced very thin and then artfully arranged. We keep this on the menu year-round, because we can always get good Granny Smith apples. Like apple pie, this tart is good fresh from the oven or warmed up, and great with ice cream or, since it is French, crème fraîche.

3–4 big tart apples (1½ pounds), such as Granny Smith, peeled, cored, and halved from top to bottom

1 prepared (unbaked) 9-inch Flaky Tart Crust (page 190)

2 large eggs

⅓ cup sugar

½ cup light cream

½ cup milk

1 teaspoon vanilla extract

¼ cup Apricot Glaze, melted (page 192, or from a jar)

1. Position your oven racks so that one is in the center, and preheat the oven to 375 degrees.

2. Using either a knife or a mandoline, slice the apples thin (⅛ inch) lengthwise (page 203).

3. Arrange the apple slices in your tart shell, starting from the top tart edge and working all the way around the perimeter of the pan. Repeat, laying the apples in rows of overlapping concentric circles, until the tart shell is full. Use small pieces of apple to fill any gaps.

4. Whisk the eggs and sugar together in a small bowl until they are pale yellow. Whisk in the cream, milk, and vanilla. Pour this custard over the apple slices.

5. The custard comes very near to the top of the tart pan, so you must be careful when you move it to the oven. You can also set the tart pan with the apples on the oven rack with the oven door open and the rack slid out about halfway, and *then* pour the custard in the tart shell; this way you don't have to move the custard-filled tart pan. Either way, with the tart on the center rack in the oven, bake the tart for 1 hour and 15 minutes, until the apples are golden brown and the custard is set. It will feel firm to the touch and won't jiggle in the middle when you shake the pan.

6. Remove the tart from the oven, and set it on a wire rack to cool slightly.

7. To remove the tart from the pan, rest it on a big can. Make sure the tart is steady and balanced. Slide the outside ring of the pan down off the tart. Place the tart on your work surface, and slide the tart off the pan bottom onto a rimless serving dish or a cutting board.

8. Use a pastry brush or a scrunched-up paper towel to coat the apples with the apricot glaze. Serve warm or at room temperature.

"We say 'large' eggs. Do we mean it? If we said 'extra large' and you used small eggs, it might make a difference. For the sake of consistency, we always say—and we always use—large eggs."

—Frank

Frank on Apples

If you grow up anywhere near apple country, you may know that a just-picked, early-season McIntosh is a whole different thing than those soft smushy Macs you see in the store. Still, apples hold up pretty well. That's why the apple guys are at the farmers' market all year round. When everyone else has gone home for the winter, there they are, selling their hot cider and a diminishing selection of apples, picked in September and October and stored in big, house-size coolers on the farm throughout the year. They're surprisingly good, these refrigerated apples, considering they could be nearly a year old. We call for Granny Smiths because, no matter what the season, you can always find them. But if you're making a recipe that calls for apples during apple season, try using a more unusual hard, tart apple: Northern Spies, Golden Russets, Romes, or Opalescents.

How to Slice an Apple

You want the apples in this tart to be sliced very thin and to be even in width. The best way to do this is: Cut the apples in half, carve out the core with a paring knife, and set the apple cored side down. Hold the knife in your right hand (if you're right-handed), and place the palm of your left over the apple, with your fingers curled underneath as if you were making a fist. Start at the right side of the apple (if you're right-handed) and move your left hand leftward, using your left knuckles to guide the knife, until you have thinly sliced the entire apple half. Same goes for pears.

203

Chocolate-Banana Tart

½ cup semisweet chocolate chips;
   or 3 ounces good-quality dark
   chocolate, broken into pieces
2 tablespoons (¼ stick) unsalted
   butter
⅓ cup light corn syrup
¼ cup sugar
3–5 ripe bananas
1 prepared (unbaked) 9-inch Flaky
   Tart Crust (page 190)
1 large egg
1 large egg yolk
½ teaspoon vanilla extract

This is our richest, sweetest tart. The filling is dense, somewhere between chocolate pudding and ganache.

1. Position your oven racks so that one is in the center, and preheat the oven to 375 degrees.
2. Melt the chocolate and the butter together in a double boiler (or a metal bowl placed over a pot of boiling water) over medium heat, stirring occasionally with a wooden spoon or a heatproof spatula.
3. Bring the corn syrup and sugar to a boil in a heavy-bottomed saucepan. Lower the heat to prevent them from burning, and cook, stirring constantly with a wooden spoon or heatproof rubber spatula, for 2–3 minutes, until the sugar is dissolved into the syrup. Remove the pot from the heat, and allow to cool slightly.
4. Slice the bananas into ¾-inch disks, and place as many slices as you can in one layer in the tart shell so that the bottom of the crust is completely covered. We arrange the bananas in concentric circles, but don't get bogged down with this; the arrangement of bananas is covered with chocolate in the end.
5. Whisk the egg and the egg yolk together. Slowly whisk about a third of the chocolate-butter mixture into the eggs. You do this to warm up the eggs. Otherwise the heat of the chocolate will actually cook the eggs, leaving you with bits of scrambled egg in your custard. Use the whisk to stir in the corn syrup mixture until you have a smooth and shiny custard. Stir in the vanilla, and pour this chocolate custard over the bananas.
6. Place the tart on the center rack in the oven, balancing it carefully as you move it, so the custard doesn't spill out over the edges.

7. Bake the tart until the custard is firm to the touch and doesn't jiggle when you shake the pan, 40–45 minutes.
8. Remove the tart from the oven, and set it on a wire rack to cool slightly.
9. To remove the tart from the pan, rest it on a big can. Make sure the tart is steady and balanced. Slide the outside ring of the pan down off the tart. Move the tart to your work surface, and slide the tart off the pan bottom onto a rimless serving dish or a cutting board. Serve at room temperature or chilled.

"There's no reason you couldn't glaze a fruit tart straight from the oven, but I always do it after it's out of the tart pan. It's just one more sticky thing that might make the tart stick to the pan."
—Frank

Baked Lemon Tart

One of our most popular tarts, and also one of the easiest to make, this tart is all and only about the lemons.

1. Position your oven racks so that one is in the center, and preheat the oven to 350 degrees.
2. Whisk the eggs and yolks together in a medium-size bowl. Add the sugar with one hand while continuing to whisk with the other. Still whisking, pour in the lemon zest and juice, then the cream. Pour this lemon custard into your par-baked tart shell. It should come to ⅛ inch from the top edge of the tart. You may have leftover custard, which you can bake in a small ramekin—a little treat for yourself.
3. Place the tart on the center rack in the oven, taking care not to spill the custard, and bake the tart for 25–30 minutes, or until filling is firm to the touch and doesn't jiggle when you shake the pan.
4. Remove the tart from the oven, and set it on a wire rack to cool slightly.
5. To remove the tart from the pan, rest it on a big can. Make sure the tart is steady and balanced. Slide the outside ring of the pan down off the tart. Move the tart to your work surface, and slide the tart off the pan bottom onto a rimless serving dish or a cutting board. Serve at room temperature or chilled.

3 large eggs
3 large egg yolks (save the whites for Hazelnut Meringues, page 324)
½ cup sugar
Zest of 1 lemon
¾ cup lemon juice (juice of 4 lemons)
¾ cup heavy cream
1 par-baked 9-inch Flaky Tart Crust (page 190)

Fresh Fruit Tart with Vanilla Cream

MAKES ONE 9-INCH TART

⅔ cup sugar

¼ cup cornstarch

2½ cups light cream

1 teaspoon vanilla extract

2 large egg yolks (use the whites to
make Pine Nut Cookies, page
343)

1 prebaked 9-inch Flaky Tart Crust
(page 190)

Fresh fruit (enough to cover the
tart, about 2 pounds), rinsed,
stone fruits pitted, cut into
¼ inch slices (not peeled)

¼ cup Apricot Glaze, melted (page
192, or from a jar)

For this tart, you must use good, ripe fruit because you're not adding spice or sugar to the fruit, nor are you cooking it. We use any fruit that's ripe and soft to the bite: peaches, nectarines, plums, berries. We wouldn't use apples or pears, because they're just not the right texture for this. And we don't use tropical fruits, but that's just because we don't care for them. The French arrange the fruit in one neat layer, but who's to say you can't pile the fruit on? If you want to get a head start, make the vanilla cream in advance and refrigerate it for up to 3 days. But you want to serve this tart the same day you make it; otherwise the vanilla cream will make the crust soggy.

1. Whisk the sugar and the cornstarch together in a heavy-bottomed saucepan. Place the pan over medium heat, whisk in the cream and the vanilla, and cook, stirring constantly with a wooden spoon or a heatproof spatula in a figure-eight motion making sure to touch all edges of the pot. Continue cooking until the custard thickens and begins to bubble. Remove the pot from the heat.

2. Whisk the egg yolks in a medium-size bowl. Slowly pour half of the warm cream mixture into the bowl with the eggs, whisking all the while. This warms the eggs slowly, so that the warm cream doesn't cook the eggs.

3. Pour the custard back in the pot, return the pot to the heat, and cook for another 2–3 minutes, until the vanilla cream is almost as thick as pudding. It may look a little lumpy at first, but it will smooth out as you cook it.

4. Pour the vanilla cream into a bowl, cover it with plastic wrap to prevent a "skin" from forming over it, and refrigerate until it is chilled, at least 1 hour or until you're ready to assemble the tart. If you need to cool the vanilla cream quickly, pour it onto a chilled sheet pan instead of into a bowl, then place the sheet pan,

uncovered, in the refrigerator for 10–15 minutes.

5. No more than a few hours before you're ready to serve the tart, fill the tart shell three-quarters of the way to the top with the vanilla cream. Place the fruit on top in whatever pattern or combination you like.

6. To remove the tart from the pan, rest it on a big can. Make sure the tart is steady and balanced. Slide the outside ring of the pan down off the tart. Move the tart to your work surface, and slide the tart off the pan bottom onto a rimless serving dish or a cutting board.

7. Use a pastry brush or a scrunched-up paper towel to coat the fruit with the apricot glaze. Refrigerate until you're ready to serve the tart. Serve this tart chilled, within hours of making it.

Apple, Walnut, and Raisin Tart with Frangipane

MAKES ONE 9-INCH TART

8 medium-size tart apples (such as
    Granny Smith), peeled and cored

⅓ cup plus 2 tablespoons sugar

1 teaspoon cinnamon

½ cup dark raisins

⅓ cup walnuts, coarsely chopped

1 prepared (unbaked) 9-inch Flaky
    Tart Crust (page 190)

¼ cup Apricot Glaze, melted (page
    192, or from a jar)

FOR THE FRANGIPANE

4 tablespoons (½ stick) unsalted
    butter, softened at room
    temperature

¼ cup sugar

¼ cup almond paste (page 211)

1 large egg, slightly beaten

½ teaspoon vanilla extract

2 tablespoons (⅛ cup) unbleached
    all-purpose flour

⅛ teaspoon salt

Frangipane is an almond-based pastry filling that's moist, like marzipan, but not as dense. It puffs up when it cooks. Frank loves the combination of nuts and raisins, so he decided to pair the frangipane with raisins and apples that have been marinated in sugar and cinnamon.

1. Position your oven racks so that one is in the center, and preheat oven to 375 degrees.

2. Cut four of the apples into ½-inch dice, and toss them in a medium-size bowl with ⅓ cup of the sugar, the cinnamon, raisins, and walnuts.

3. Thinly slice the remaining apples (⅛ inch) lengthwise with a knife or a mandoline. Toss them in a small bowl with the remaining 2 tablespoons of sugar. Let both bowls of apples rest for 30 minutes to 1 hour; the sugar "marinates" the apples, softening them and making them easier to arrange on top of the tart.

4. To make the frangipane, cream the butter and the sugar together in a separate, medium-size mixing bowl, using the whisk attachment of an electric mixer (or a sturdy wire whisk) until they are fluffy and light lemon-yellow in color, about 5 minutes. Add the almond paste, and continue to beat until it is fully integrated with the butter. Beat in the egg and the vanilla.

5. Stir the flour and salt together in a small bowl to distribute the salt. Using the paddle attachment of your mixer (or a wooden spoon), stir this into the bowl with the butter and sugar until no flour is visible.

6. Using a rubber spatula, scrape the frangipane out of the bowl and spread it evenly in your tart crust. Dump the chopped apple mixture over the frangipane, and use your hands to spread them out in an even mound.

7. Arrange a ring of overlapping apple slices around the outside of the tart pan. Working from the outside in, continue to arrange the apples in overlapping concentric circles. Using a small knife or your fingers, lift the first apple slice in each circle and tuck the last apple slice underneath it, to create a continuous circle. The apple slices should hang over the outside rim of the tart pan slightly, and the circles should also overlap one another, so that the apple slices form a blanket that seals in the chopped apples and frangipane.

8. Place the tart on the center rack in the oven, and bake for 1 hour and 10–15 minutes, or until apples turn golden brown and the edges darker brown and sweet apple smells have begun to come from your oven.

9. Remove the tart from the oven, and place it on a wire rack. Allow the tart to cool for just a few minutes. It's important to remove this tart from the pan while it's still warm—before the apples overlapping the tart pan harden onto the pan.

10. To remove the tart from the pan, rest it on a big can. Make sure the tart is steady and balanced. Slide the outside ring of the pan down off the tart. Move the tart to your work surface, and slide the tart off the pan bottom onto a rimless serving dish or a cutting board.

11. Use a pastry brush or a scrunched-up paper towel to coat the apples with the apricot glaze. This tart is delicious served warm, but it's easier to slice after it's cooled slightly.

"I like to measure nuts and then chop them. It's easier than chopping, then measuring, then going back to chop more because you didn't chop enough the first time."
—Jerome

What Is Almond Paste?

Almond paste is a mixture of very finely ground blanched almonds and sugar. It's used often in baking—particularly in Italian and French baking. You can find it in the baking section of grocery stores. If you buy some and find it's hard, or if it has hardened in your cupboard since the last time you used it, a few seconds in the microwave will soften it right up.

Strawberry-Rhubarb Tart with Shamey's Crisp Topping

MAKES ONE 9-INCH TART

When Frank was growing up, there was an annual backyard party given by his neighbors. "It was the kind of event where you were sure to see people you hadn't seen since the same party the year before. And that you wouldn't see again until next year's party." Frank particularly looked forward to the strawberry-rhubarb crisp brought every year by a woman named Shamey. Well, Shamey gave Frank the recipe. And Frank made it into a tart. At home, he still makes it as a crisp—because it's easier, and because he likes the higher fruit-to-crust ratio. Theoretically, rhubarb is harvested in the earliest days of summer, at the same time strawberries come into their own sweet selves. If for some reason you find strawberries but no rhubarb, you can substitute sliced tart apples for the rhubarb in this recipe.

1. Position your oven racks so that one is in the center, and preheat the oven to 375 degrees.
2. Toss the strawberries, rhubarb, flour, sugar, and cinnamon together in a big bowl. Dump this mixture into your par-baked tart shell and spread it out evenly. Using your fingers, sprinkle Shamey's topping over the fruit, taking care to cover its entire surface area, especially around the edges.
3. Place the tart on the center rack in the oven, and bake for 35–40 minutes, or until you see fruit juices bubbling up through the topping and down around the sides of the tart. You may want to place a baking sheet under the tart before you bake it to catch the spilled juices.

1 pint strawberries, stems cut out and berries cut in quarters

1½ pounds rhubarb, rinsed, leafy ends removed, and cut into ½ inch slices; or tart apples, cut into ½-inch wedges

3 tablespoons unbleached all-purpose flour

⅔ cup sugar

½ teaspoon cinnamon

1 par-baked Flaky Tart Crust (page 190)

1 recipe Shamey's Crisp Topping (page 215)

4. Remove the tart from the oven, and set it on a wire rack to cool slightly.
5. To remove the tart from the pan, rest it on a big can. Make sure the tart is steady and balanced, then slide the outside ring of pan down off the tart. Move the tart to your work surface, and slide the tart off the pan bottom onto a rimless serving dish or a cutting board. We love this tart fresh from the oven, with a scoop of vanilla ice cream.

What Is Rhubarb?

We like rhubarb because it seems so old-fashioned. Rhubarb's problem (besides its name) is that people don't know what it is. And if they know what it is, they don't know what to do with it. Rhubarb is most commonly known for its relationship to strawberries in pie. They're about the only two things harvested in the last weeks of spring or first weeks of summer in New England, which is likely how they got stuck together. Lucky for everyone, the two work perfectly together. (That's nature for you.) Whereas strawberries turn to juice when they're cooked, rhubarb, which is actually a vegetable that looks like red celery (its giant green-and-red leaves are usually cut off before they hit the stores), holds its shape. And it's high in pectin (nature's thickener), which thickens the juice given off by the strawberries. Rhubarb is also extremely tart, which is delicious as long as it's offset by the sweetness of the berries—and, of course, sugar. It has a short season, but when you find it, you'll find it piled high. If you like it, buy extra. Rhubarb freezes beautifully. Just rinse it, chop it as you'll want it, and throw it in a freezer bag or plastic container to use sometime when those long sturdy stalks seem as elusive as spring.

Shamey's Crisp Topping

MAKES ABOUT 2 CUPS (ENOUGH FOR ONE 9-INCH TART)

Frank always keeps a container of crisp topping in the freezer. That way, he's only a bowlful of fresh, ripe fruit away from a delicious warm dessert. "Recently, I was making a plum tart at home," Frank says. "When I realized our company was coming sooner than expected, I said, Forget rolling out dough. This is going to be a crisp. I only have a big crisp dish, and I realized I didn't have enough plums. I had more apricots, so I decided to use those instead. I went out to the yard and picked a bunch of raspberries." His plum tart was now an apricot-raspberry crisp, which is to say: Fruit desserts are flexible. You can make as much as four times this recipe and throw what you don't need now in the freezer. You can also refrigerate the topping, but because it's all butter, you don't want to store it more than 10 days in the refrigerator.

½ cup unbleached all-purpose flour
½ cup packed light-brown sugar
2 ounces (½ stick) cold unsalted
butter, cut into ¼-inch cubes
¼ cup rolled oats
½ cup walnuts or pecans, coarsely
chopped

1. Dump the flour and the brown sugar into the bowl of the food processor fitted with a metal blade, and pulse until they're just integrated. Add the butter all at once, and use the pulse button to cut butter into flour. Stop pulsing when mixture is the texture of moist crumbs.

2. Remove the blade from the food processor, and dump the crumbs into a big bowl. Add the oats and the nuts. Work them into the crumbs with your fingers until the topping is stuck together into big clumps. It should not be one whole ball of dough but more like . . . well, like crisp topping. Only not cooked.

Black-Plum-and-Honey Tart

MAKES ONE 9-INCH TART

This is one of our most popular tarts. It's simply a tart crust baked with fruit. And it's so beautiful. We use honey instead of sugar because we liked the flowery taste of the honey with the plums.

1. Position your oven racks so that one is in the center, and preheat the oven to 375 degrees.
2. Toss all the ingredients except the crust and the apricot glaze in a big bowl until the honey is evenly distributed over the fruit.
3. Spoon or dump the plum mixture into your tart shell and spread out somewhat evenly. Use a rubber spatula to scrape the sides of the bowl for any extra goop to add to the plums.
4. Place the tart on the center rack in the oven, and bake for 35–40 minutes, until the plums are dark brown at the edges and tender when pierced with a fork. (They will be very soft, but not falling apart.)
5. Remove the tart from the oven, and place it on a wire rack to cool slightly.
6. To remove the tart from the pan, rest it on a big can. Make sure the tart is steady and balanced, then slide the outside ring of the pan down off the tart. Move the tart to your work surface, and slide the tart off the pan bottom onto a rimless serving dish or a cutting board.
7. Use a pastry brush or a scrunched-up paper towel to coat the plums with the apricot glaze. Serve warm or at room temperature with vanilla ice cream or Simple Whipped Cream (page 229).

3 pounds black plums (red or green flesh), rinsed and cut into ½ inch slices

2 tablespoons honey

1½ teaspoons cinnamon

½ teaspoon nutmeg

1½ teaspoons lemon juice (juice of less than ½ lemon)

¼ cup sugar

1 tablespoon unbleached all-purpose flour

1 par-baked Flaky Tart Crust (page 190)

¼ cup Apricot Glaze, melted (page 192, or from a jar)

Variation: Spiced Italian Prune Plum Tart

Italian prune plums are oblong-shaped, black-skinned plums with green flesh. They're meatier than typical black plums and not as juicy when you bite into one. We love them, especially for baking. Plums have a very short season from mid-August to early September, so while they're around we make loads of these tarts—and the black-plum tart, too. Our customers are very curious when they see two plum tarts on the shelf. We have to explain that they are quite different plums, and therefore different tarts. Of course, the word "prune" throws them, too. Prunes aren't exactly the most popular fruit in America. In France, *prune* simply means "plum," and it doesn't carry the negative connotation. To make a tart with Italian prune plums, follow the recipe for the black-plum-and-honey tart, substituting Italian prune plums cut in half straight into a big bowl for the black plums. Add a pinch of ground cloves and a pinch of ground cardamom, and then assemble the plums cut side up into a flowerlike pattern (or concentric circles) from the outside in and bake as you would the black-plum tart.

"I don't bother to pit plums before I slice them. I just hold the fruit in one hand and slice it right off the pit so the slices fall in the bowl. It reminds me of when my mom pulled back a banana peel and sliced the banana directly over a bowl. When the last slice of plum falls into the bowl, I chuck the pit."
—Frank

Peach-and-Blueberry Free-Form Tart

MAKES ONE ROUGHLY 9-INCH TART

We call this tart "free-form" because it isn't confined to a tart pan. We roll out the dough, place it directly on a sheet pan, place the fruit inside, and then fold the edges over the fruit. We sprinkle sugar on the crust, which makes the tart sparkle. It's a very rustic-looking tart, but it's so beautiful that when we put some in the window people come into the store just to ask about them. You can use the same free-form concept and the recipe below to make a nectarine, apricot, apple, or pear tart.

1. Position your oven racks so that one is in the center, and preheat the oven to 425 degrees. Have a 9-inch tart pan or a sheet pan nearby.
2. Cut the peaches in half to remove the pits. Holding a peach half over a big bowl, slice it into four or five wedges, letting the wedges drop into the bowl as you slice. Repeat with the remaining peach halves. Sprinkle the flour, cinnamon, and ⅓ cup sugar over the surface of the fruit. Don't just dump them onto the peaches or you'll have to toss them longer. Longer tossing means mushier fruit. Gently toss the peaches, using your hands or a big spoon, until the peaches are coated with the flour. Add the berries, and toss the fruit gently—again, you don't break up the berries any more than is inevitable.
3. Roll out three-quarters of the tart dough (reserve the rest for another use) to ¼ inch thick, making a roughly circular shape that is 12–13 inches in diameter. Fold the dough in half gently in order to move it to either your tart pan or your sheet pan. Unfold the dough. If you're using a tart pan, let the dough flop over the edges—you are not going to be fitting the dough into the pan.
4. Dump the fruit into the center of the dough and spread the fruit evenly over a

6 big ripe peaches (2–2½ pounds)

2 tablespoons unbleached all-purpose flour

1 teaspoon cinnamon

⅓ cup sugar

1 cup fresh blueberries (or raspberries, blackberries, boysenberries), rinsed and placed on a towel to dry

1 full recipe Flaky Tart Crust dough (enough for 2 regular tarts) (page 190)

1 large egg whisked with 1 tablespoon cream or milk (egg wash)

¼ cup or more granulated or raw sugar for sprinkling

9-inch area. Using a rubber spatula or the edge of your hand, scoop any remaining goop out of the bowl and onto the fruit.

5. Lift the excess dough that is around the edges of the fruit inward to cover the fruit. Don't be alarmed when the flaps of dough don't meet at the top of your tart. You will have a few inches in the center of the tart where the fruit is not covered by dough. The size of the space is inconsequential.

6. Brush the egg wash onto the crust with a pastry brush or a scrunched-up paper towel. Sprinkle the crust with enough sugar to cover the surface.

7. Place the tart on the center rack in the oven, and bake for 15 minutes. Reduce the oven temperature to 375, and continue baking for another hour, until the fruit is soft and bubbling and the crust golden brown.

8. Remove the tart from the oven, and let it rest for at least ½ hour before serving. Slice the tart as you would a pie. This tart is delicious served warm with a scoop of vanilla ice cream.

"No matter how much sugar and spice you add, and no matter how long you cook it, you will never make bad fruit into good food."
—Jerome

Chocolate-Walnut Tart

2 large eggs

¼ cup sugar

¼ cup honey

½ cup plus 2 tablespoons light
corn syrup

2 tablespoons unsalted butter,
melted and cooled to room
temperature

¼ cup light cream

2¼ cups walnut halves

1 prepared (unbaked) Flaky Tart
Crust (page 190)

½ cup semisweet chocolate chips;
or 3 ounces good-quality dark
chocolate, broken into pieces

1 teaspoon solid vegetable shortening

We've never met anyone who didn't love this tart. It's almost candy-like. It you prefer pecans or almonds, you can use those instead of the walnuts.

1. Position your oven racks so that one is in the center, and preheat the oven to 375 degrees.
2. Whisk the eggs and sugar together in a big bowl just enough to combine them. Whisk in the honey and the corn syrup, then stir in the butter, cream, and nuts. Pour this mixture into your tart shell, using a rubber spatula or the edge of your hand to get all the filling out of the bowl and into the tart shell.
3. Place the tart on the center rack in the oven, and bake for 50–55 minutes, until the filling is firm to the touch and the nuts and crust are golden brown.
4. Remove the tart from the oven, and set it on a wire rack to cool slightly.
5. To remove the tart from the pan, rest it on a big can. Make sure the tart is steady and balanced. Slide the outside ring of the pan down off the tart. Move the tart to your work surface, and slide the tart off the pan bottom onto a rimless serving dish or a cutting board.
6. In a double boiler (or a stainless-steel bowl placed over a pot of boiling water), melt the chocolate and shortening together. Pour or spoon the chocolate into a pastry bag, and pipe it onto the cooled tart with a swift back-and-forth motion (page 229). You can really do it in any design you want: circles, random squiggles, "Happy Birthday." You can even forget the pastry bag and pour the chocolate from a glass measuring cup with a spout and handle—the resulting design won't be as delicate, but it'll certainly taste as good. Serve this tart warm or at room temperature.

Coffee-Pecan Tart

MAKES ONE 9-INCH TART

This is the tart rendition of the pecan pie Frank's Aunt Lu makes every Thanksgiving. We substituted coffee where she used Kahlúa, because we don't use any alcohol at the store. At home, we go ahead and throw in the booze.

1. Position your oven racks so that one is in the center, and preheat the oven to 375 degrees.
2. Whisk the eggs to break up the yolks. Add the sugar and the flour, and whisk until the eggs lighten in color. Whisk in the vanilla, coffee (or Kahlúa), corn syrup, and milk. Finally, whisk in the melted butter. Stir in the pecan halves, and pour this filling into your tart shell.
3. Place the tart on the center rack in the oven, being careful that filling doesn't spill over the sides of pan. Bake for 1 hour and 10–15 minutes, until the crust is golden brown and the filling is firm to the touch and doesn't jiggle when you shake the pan. The filling will have puffed up a bit. It will fall back down when it cools.
4. Remove the tart from the oven, and set it on a wire rack to cool slightly.
5. To remove the tart from the pan, rest it on a big can. Make sure the tart is steady and balanced. Slide the outside ring of the pan down off the tart. Move the tart to your work surface, and slide the tart off the pan bottom onto a rimless serving dish or a cutting board. Serve warm or at room temperature with vanilla ice cream or Frank's Simple Whipped Cream (page 229).

2 large eggs

⅓ cup sugar

1 tablespoon unbleached all-purpose flour

½ teaspoon vanilla extract

¼ cup strong brewed coffee at room temperature; or Kahlúa

¼ cup dark corn syrup

½ cup evaporated milk

2 tablespoons unsalted butter, melted and cooled to room temperature

2 cups pecan halves

1 prepared (unbaked) 9-inch Flaky Tart Crust (page 190)

Raspberry-Cranberry Linzer Tart with a Linzer Lattice Crust

MAKES ONE 9-INCH TART

⅓ cup raspberry preserves

⅓ cup dried currants

⅓ cup cranberries, coarsely
chopped

FOR THE LINZER CRUST

1 cup (2 sticks) unsalted butter,
softened

1 cup sugar

2 large eggs

1 cup unbleached all-purpose flour

¼ cup whole-wheat flour

½ teaspoon cinnamon

¼ teaspoon ground cloves

¼ teaspoon salt

1 cup almonds, ground very fine

1 9-inch tart pan with fluted edges
and removable bottom

Jerome loves the nutty crust of a Linzer tart, but he finds the filling unbearably sweet. So he added cranberries, which, by themselves, are unbearably tart, to the traditional raspberry filling. There's no tart shell involved in this one—the Linzer batter is piped directly into a tart pan. We then smear on the jammy fruit filling and pipe on another layer of the batter in a crisscross lattice pattern. What we end up with is something like a giant Linzer cookie. We sell a lot of these around the holidays with the top crust piped around a Christmas-tree cookie cutter, and at Valentine's Day around a heart-shaped cutter.

1. Position your oven racks so that one is in the center, and preheat the oven to 350 degrees.
2. Stir the preserves, currants, and cranberries together in a medium-size bowl.
3. To make the Linzer crust, cream the butter and sugar together in another big bowl, using the whisk attachment of an electric mixer (or a sturdy wire whisk), until they are fluffy and light lemon-yellow in color. Beat in the eggs.
4. In a third, medium-size bowl, whisk the flours, spices, and salt together. Add this to the bowl with the butter, stirring with the paddle attachment of your mixer at low speed or with a wooden spoon or rubber spatula until very little flour remains visible. Add the nuts, and stir until not a trace of flour is left.
5. Dump slightly more than half of the batter into your empty tart pan, and spread the batter over the surface of the pan using a rubber or offset spatula.
6. Spoon the fruit filling into the center of the tart pan on top of the batter. Use

the spatula or the back of the spoon to spread the fruit filling over the surface of the batter, leaving a ¾-inch ring around the outer edge with no filling.

7. Spoon the remaining batter into a pastry bag or a makeshift pastry bag (page 229). Squeeze the batter out of the bag and onto the tart. You can do this in a crisscross pattern, as we do at Once Upon a Tart, with one set of lines at a 60-degree angle to the other. Or you can pipe the batter in a solid mass around a cookie cutter set in the center of the tart. If you use a cookie cutter, leave it in place when you put the tart in the oven.

8. Place the tart on the center rack in the oven, and bake until the top crust is a nice golden brown and the fruit has begun to bubble, 40–45 minutes.

9. Remove the tart from the oven, and place it on a wire rack to cool slightly. Make sure to remove the tart from the pan while it's still warm. Once the the sticky fruit filling dries, it will be impossible to get the tart out without breaking the crust. Remove the cookie cutter from the top of the tart at the same time.

10. To remove the tart from the pan, rest it on a big can. Make sure the tart is steady and balanced. Slide the outside ring of the pan down off the tart. Move the tart to your work surface, and slide the tart off the pan bottom onto a rimless serving dish or a cutting board. Serve at room temperature.

Pumpkin Tart with Sugared Pastry Leaves

MAKES ONE DEEP-DISH 9-INCH TART OR PIE

This tart is made with a classic pumpkin pie filling, complete with evaporated milk, thrown into a tart shell. Granted, we use a deep-dish tart shell so that it holds more filling, which is how Frank likes it. We usually decorate the finished pie with cutouts of maple leaves. But sometimes Frank tops it with the Shamey's Crisp Topping (page 215). He figures, since we've already messed with his beloved pumpkin pie by putting it in a tart shell, he might as well mess with it some more.

1. Position your oven racks so that one is in the center, and preheat the oven to 375 degrees.
2. Whisk the eggs in a big bowl to break up the yolks. Whisk in the pumpkin, molasses, and fresh ginger.
3. In a separate, medium-size bowl, whisk the sugars and spices together. Add this to the pumpkin mixture, and whisk some more. Gradually add the evaporated milk, stirring until the filling is smooth and the milk is fully incorporated into the pumpkin.
4. Pour the pumpkin filling into your deep-dish tart shell, and bake for 35–40 minutes, until the filling is firm to the touch and doesn't jiggle when you shake the pan. Don't worry if the top cracks slightly—that happens. You can cover the cracks with the pastry leaves.
5. Remove the tart from the oven, and place it on a wire rack to cool slightly.
6. To remove the tart from the pan, rest it on a big can. Make sure the tart is steady and balanced. Slide the outside ring of the pan down off the tart. Move the tart to your work surface and slide the tart off the pan bottom onto a rimless serving dish or a cutting board. Cool to room temperature, then refrigerate until serving.

2 large eggs

1 15-ounce can pumpkin purée, or 1¾ cup fresh pumpkin purée

1 tablespoon molasses

1 teaspoon grated fresh ginger (1-inch piece)

½ cup granulated sugar

¼ cup packed light-brown sugar

1 teaspoon ground cinnamon

¼ teaspoon cloves

1 12-ounce can (1½ cups) evaporated milk

1 recipe for Flaky Tart Crust (page 190), rolled into a 9-inch deep-dish tart pan plus the remaining dough chilled (for the leaves)

1 large egg whisked with 1 tablespoon cream or milk (egg wash)

⅛ cup or more granulated or raw sugar for sprinkling

7. Roll out the remaining dough to ¼ inch thick. Use a leaf-shaped cookie cutter to cut out leaves, and score the veins in the leaves with a small knife.

8. Brush the leaves with the egg wash, using a pastry brush or a scrunched-up paper towel, then sprinkle them with enough sugar to coat them. Carefully move the leaves to an ungreased sheet pan or baking sheet. Place them in the oven, and bake until the leaves are golden brown and crispy, 8–10 minutes. Remove the sheet pan from the oven, and allow the leaves to cool slightly.

9. Use a metal spatula to lift the cookies off the pan. Not too long before serving the tart, place the leaves on top of the pumpkin filling in whatever pattern you like. Serve at room temperature or chilled. If you have more leaves than you want to use to decorate your tart, they're delicious with ice cream or nice to serve alongside a slice of a tart.

How to Make and Fill a Pastry Bag

If you're doing fancy piping, which we rarely do at Once Upon a Tart, you need to use a real pastry bag so that you can attach icing tips onto it. For simple uses like those we call for in our recipes, a makeshift pastry bag will work. Take a small plastic sandwich bag. Cut out a triangular-shaped portion of one of the bottom corners. The size of that triangle will depend on how thick or thin you want the lines you're piping out of the bag to be: very small for drizzling chocolate as onto the Chocolate-Walnut Tart or for writing "Happy Birthday," for instance; bigger for piping out Linzer batter for the Raspberry-Cranberry Linzer Tart (page 224). Filling a pastry bag can be trickier than it seems. The bag has no form and it keeps slipping away. The easiest way we've found is to set the bag inside a tall cup and flop the ends of the bag around the edges of the glass. You'll have two hands to spoon the stuff into a bag that is now open and upright.

Frank's Simple Whipped Cream

When I go to a dinner party, I'm often asked to bring dessert. If it's plum season, I bring one of our two plum tarts. In colder months I like to bring Lemon–Poppy Seed or Gingerbread Tea Loaves, pages 286, 287). Regardless of what I bring, come dessert time, I find myself in the kitchen, whipping up some cream.

Knowing how to make whipped cream is a kitchen essential. And making whipped cream is the easiest thing, once you know how. Start with a stainless-steel bowl that you've chilled in the freezer (some people insist on chilling the beaters or whisk, too—that's up to you) and ½ pint (1 cup) very cold heavy whipping cream. I find that ultrapasteurized cream is impossible to whip—it just takes forever, and even then it doesn't whip up like regular pasteurized cream. I like organic cream the very best, not just because it whips up nice and fluffy, but because it has that sweet, fresh cream taste.

Pour your cold cream into the bowl and start beating. You'll notice the cream begin to thicken. If you're using an electric mixer, the beaters will start to leave a trail in their wake. Add a teaspoon of vanilla extract and 1 tablespoon or more confectioners' sugar if you're adding sugar at all. This is really a matter of taste and what you're serving the whipped cream with. If I'm serving whipped cream with something really sweet, like Coffee-Pecan Tart (page 223), I won't put any sugar in it at all.

Stop whipping the cream when it looks like something you'd need to plop, not pour, onto your plate. Lift the still beaters out of the cream. Peaks should form. They may flop at the top, but that's fine—it's cream, not concrete. You don't want to overwhip cream. It will separate. Then you're on your way to making butter.

Cranberry-and-Sour-Apple Tart

1 prepared 9-inch Flaky Tart Crust,
plus ½ recipe dough, chilled
(page 190)

2 12-ounce bags fresh cranberries

⅔ cup packed light-brown sugar

⅔ cup granulated sugar

⅔ cup golden raisins

2 tart apples (such as Granny
Smith), peeled, cored, and diced
fine

½ teaspoon cinnamon

¼ teaspoon ground cloves

1 large egg whisked with 1 teaspoon cream or milk (egg wash)

¼ cup or more granulated or raw
sugar for sprinkling

We make this tart only in the fall and winter, when cranberries are in season. The filling is like a jam, in that we cook the cranberries and apples, along with the spices, before putting it in the tart. It makes the house smell amazing. We top it with a lattice crust, because when it bakes it gets dark, which isn't what we'd call beautiful. It's very tart, so we like it with Frank's Simple Whipped Cream (page 229). You can make the cranberry-apple filling a couple of days in advance and refrigerate in a plastic container with a tight-fitting lid.

1. Position your oven racks so that one is in the center, and preheat the oven to 400 degrees.
2. Roll the chilled dough out onto a sheet of parchment paper to ¼ inch thick and into a roughly round shape that is at least 9 inches in diameter. Place this dough in the refrigerator while you prepare your tart, or for at least 15 minutes.
3. Stir the cranberries, sugars, raisins, apples, and spices together in a heavy saucepan over medium heat, and cook, stirring occasionally with a wooden spoon or a heatproof spatula to prevent them from sticking to the pan. Don't be alarmed when the cranberries begin to pop. That's the idea. But if the mixture begins to boil, lower the heat or the sugar will burn and your tart will be bitter.
4. When about three-quarters of the cranberries have popped, take the pot off the heat and let the filling cool to room temperature before spooning it into your tart shell. If you don't let it cool, the filling will melt the dough. The filling is so thick that it will need to be leveled out with the back of a spoon or spatula before baking.
5. To make your lattice strips, take the rolled-out dough from the refrigerator and,

using a pastry cutter, a pizza cutter, or a small knife, cut it into strips ¾ inch wide (page 11).

6. Lay the strips in parallel lines with 1-inch spaces between them. Lay another set of strips in the opposite direction, at a 60-degree angle. Tuck the ends of the lattice strips into the filling where it meets the edges of the tart. Use a pastry brush or a scrunched-up paper towel to coat the crust with the egg wash, then sprinkle the strips with sugar.

7. Place the tart on the center rack in the oven, and bake about 40–50 minutes until the crust is golden brown all over. Remember, the filling is fully cooked, so the baking is all about browning the crust.

8. Remove the tart from the oven, and set it on a rack to cool slightly. You need to remove the tart from the pan while it is still warm. Any sugar that has melted onto the pan will harden when it cools, and when sugar cools on any surface, well, it gets very sticky. You'd have a tough time getting the tart out without breaking the crust.

9. To remove the tart from the pan, rest it on a big can. Make sure the tart is steady and balanced. Slide the outside ring of the pan down off the tart. Move the tart to your work surface, and slide the tart off the pan bottom onto a rimless serving dish or a cutting board. Cool to room temperature before serving.

"When you're sprinkling a crust with sugar, you can't skimp or it will disappear when you bake the tart. Don't worry about the sugar getting on the filling. It'll melt and disappear in the oven."
—Frank

Once Upon a ...
SCONE

Buttermilk Scones with Dried Currants

Summer Berry Scones

Irish Soda Scones with Dark and Yellow Raisins, Caraway Seeds, and Walnuts

Dried Cranberry Scones with Crystallized Sugar Crust

Variation: Candied Ginger Scones

Spiced Pumpkin Scones with Fresh Cranberries

Toasted Walnut Scones with Raspberry Preserves

Very Lemony Curd

Honey-Cornmeal Scones

Orange Scones with Chocolate Chips

Dried Apricot Scones with Pecans and Shredded Coconut

Drying Your Own Fruit

Cheddar-Parmesan Scones with Fresh Dill

In the beginning, neither of us liked scones. Jerome was introduced to scones during a summer in London, where he went to learn English. The one thing he disliked more than boiled lettuce was scones. "They taste like dust," he says. "I don't understand why anyone eats them."

For Frank, scones were mostly an excuse to eat clotted cream. He believed that clotted cream, which is right between cream and butter, could make just about anything taste good. Back then, you could only get clotted cream in England. Now you can find clotted cream here, but Frank doesn't need it. Not with our scones.

Given our histories with scones, it's kind of ironic that we chose scones to be the first thing to add to our menu when we decided to expand our repertoire past tarts. We had just moved from the wholesale warehouse in Long Island City to our funky café space in SoHo. We were looking for something that would keep people coming in throughout the day. Scones, which are less sweet than muffins and were a bit unusual at the time, seemed like just the right thing.

Of course, our thinking was predicated on our optimism—that we could figure out a way to make scones that we actually liked. Fortunately for us, we were able to. We started with a recipe for classic English scones, which is flour, butter, vegetable shortening, and a leavener. And we began to play around. Our first goal was to overcome the dryness factor. So we added butter. Good butter. And a lot of it (page 313).

As a result of the added butter and buttermilk, which we used in place of the milk in English scones, our dough became more like a batter. We weren't about to roll it out and cut it with a biscuit cutter, the way the English do. So we

You can use a spoon to scoop your scone dough . . . but personally, we love to use our hands.

thought, Hey, these are American scones—wild and free. We decided to drop them—or splash them is more like it, because the batter sticks to your hands—the way you would a typical American drop biscuit.

Scones turned out to be the perfect platform for experimenting, which is probably our favorite thing to do in the kitchen. A lot of our scones are more or less variations on the first one we perfected, which is still our most popular, the Buttermilk Scones with Dried Currants (page 238).

Over the years, about a dozen types of successful scones have risen from our ovens. With the exception of the Irish Soda (page 243) and the Dried Cranberry Scones (page 245), ours are airier than a traditional English scone, with a lighter crumb. We share ours with you here, but also encourage you to have a little fun yourselves. Take chances. Think about what you like, and see how you might integrate these flavors into our scones.

THINGS TO KNOW

Customers, our families, friends . . . They're always asking us why we don't have a store somewhere else. Some gourmet stores in the neighborhood have asked to sell our scones in their stores. But we won't do it. You can't do the same quality when you have more than one store. For our scones to turn out the way they do, we have to make them in small batches, because it has to be done very quickly. You can double a recipe, but anything bigger than that will take too long to mix, and bad things will start to happen.

The trick to making good, flaky scones, if there is one, can be summed up in two words: "quick" and "cold." The primary goal is to keep the butter from melting—*until* it gets into the oven. Butter melting in the scone while it's baking causes the dough to separate into little tiny layers, which results in light, flaky scones.

There are a few tricks to making sure that the butter doesn't melt while you're mixing the dough. One is to start with cold, just-from-the-fridge butter. Another is to make sure not to overwork the dough. Which is why, in the recipes below, you'll see that we've called for you to stop working the butter and flour together—what's known as "cutting" the butter into the flour—as soon as it looks grainy, like coarse meal or moist crumbs. If you keep working the flour and butter until they completely come together and look like dough, that means the butter has melted. When the butter melts before it gets in the oven, the gluten in the flour starts to react to the leavening agents (baking soda or powder), and you'll end up with a tough, dense scone. Maybe this is more than you want to know. Suffice it to say: don't overwork the butter and flour.

We use a food processor, because that's the quickest way to get the job done. If you don't have a food processor, use the paddle attachment of a standing mixer. And if you don't have either, you can do the same thing with a pastry cutter or two knives. Starting with the knives crossed in the center of the bowl, like scissors, pull them away from each other so that they rub against each other and repeat until the butter is cut into the dry ingredients.

Once the butter is cut into the flour and you've got "moist crumbs," you'll add the wet ingredients. Jerome likes to use his hands for this. Frank likes to use a spatula, scraping the dry ingredients from the bottom of the bowl toward his body, and up and over the wet ingredients, and down to the bottom again. Do what you want. Just remember: the less you work the dough, the lighter your scones will be.

At the store, we measure our scones at ½ cup each, but it doesn't matter what size scones you make as long as all the scones on one sheet pan are the same size—otherwise some scones on the pan will burn while others are just getting done. You just need to adjust the cooking time: bake bigger scones longer and smaller ones for less time.

Serious bakers always say not to open the oven door during cooking time. The reason for this is that the temperature drops considerably when you open a 400-degree space onto your 70-degree world. We amend this rule to: Don't open the door during the first two-thirds of cooking time. You may want to open the oven door toward the end of the cooking time, to check for doneness. Another way—besides inserting a toothpick—to test scones for doneness is to press your finger gently into them. If they spring back quickly, they're done. If not, that means they're still soft in the middle and they need a little more time. We figure that a drop in the oven temperature certainly beats dried-out scones.

We recommend you use a timer. "Frank has been known to forget to turn on the timer," Jerome says. "It's the biggest joke at the store. He puts a batch of orange-chocolate chip scones in the oven in the afternoon. He walks away. And the next thing, someone else in the kitchen will notice smoke or a burning smell coming from the oven." Scones are by far best straight out of the oven, but they'll last a few days in an airtight container. You can even freeze them, and just pop them in a 200-degree oven to freshen them up. That's about all you need to know.

"New customers often ask for butter to go with their scones, and we say, 'Take a bite; if you still want butter, we'll give it to you.' They never do."
—Frank

Buttermilk Scones with Dried Currants

4 cups unbleached all-purpose flour

1 tablespoon baking powder

1 teaspoon baking soda

½ teaspoon salt

⅔ cup sugar

20 tablespoons (2½ sticks) cold
    unsalted butter, cut into ¼-inch
    cubes

2 large eggs

1 cup cold buttermilk

1 tablespoon vanilla extract

1 cup dried currants

This was our first scone, and it is still our most popular. We have one customer who comes in every single morning with his two chocolate Labs and he gets two currant-and-buttermilk scones: one for himself, one to split between the dogs. Dried currants, along with their fresh counterparts, are popular in English baking but relatively uncommon here. They're smaller than raisins, and not quite as sweet. You'll find them right between raisins and prunes in the dried-fruit section of most grocery stores.

1. Position your oven racks so that one is in the center, and preheat the oven to 400 degrees. Line a baking sheet with parchment paper.
2. Dump the dry ingredients into the bowl of the food processor fitted with a metal blade, and pulse a few times to mix.
3. Add the butter to the bowl all at once, and run the food processor for 15 seconds. Switch to pulse, and continue pulsing until there are no chunks of butter left and the mixture looks like moist crumbs. Be careful not to overmix the ingredients. Remove the blade from the food processor, and dump the crumbs into a big bowl.
4. In another, small bowl, whisk the eggs to break up the yolks. Whisk in the buttermilk and vanilla. Use the whisk to stir in the currants.
5. Pour the wet ingredients into the bowl with the flour-butter crumbs and stir with a wooden spoon. It will be dry at first, and you may think there is too much flour, but keep mixing and it will come together. Stop as soon as no flour is visible. You don't want to work the dough a moment longer than necessary.
6. Use a ½-cup measuring cup or your hand (eyeballing for size) to scoop the batter out, and plop it onto the baking sheet, leaving 2 inches between the scones.

7. Place the baking sheet on the center rack in the oven, and bake the scones for 25–30 minutes, until the tops are golden brown and a small knife or toothpick inserted into the center of a scone comes out clean.

8. Remove the baking sheet from the oven, and place it on a wire rack to cool for a few minutes. Move the baking sheet off the rack, and use a spatula to transfer the scones from the baking sheet to the rack or to a serving dish. Serve fresh out of the oven or at room temperature.

"If I have a bunch of wet things, like milk and vanilla, I'll measure the milk, throw the measured vanilla on top of that, and then throw the whole mixture into the bowl."
—Frank

What Is Buttermilk?

Traditionally, buttermilk is the liquid left behind after butter is churned. Today, it is made commercially by adding bacteria to nonfat or low-fat milk, which causes the milk to thicken and gives it that characteristic tang. If you don't have buttermilk around, you can improvise for baking purposes by adding a tablespoon of white vinegar or lemon juice to just under a cup of low-fat or skim milk, so that the total equals 1 cup. The flavor and texture of your baked goods may change, but it'll work. What you can't do is substitute regular milk for buttermilk. "We tried," Jerome says. "It doesn't work."

What Is Baking Powder?

Baking powder is baking soda plus an acid, typically cream of tartar. The practical difference between baking powder and baking soda is that baking soda reacts to liquid (like the wet ingredients in scones), whereas baking powder reacts to liquid and then again to the heat of the oven. Thus the "double acting" that you see before the words "baking powder." Baking powder is perishable, so you can't just keep using the same tin you've had in your cupboard forever. If you want to test it, throw a spoonful into boiling water. If it's still good, it will bubble up pretty furiously. It's a good idea to write the date of purchase on your baking powder. Throw it away after a year.

Summer Berry Scones

MAKES 12 SCONES

For these scones, we use whatever summer berries look the freshest and taste the sweetest, in whatever combination we find. Halved and topped with vanilla ice cream or Frank's Simple Whipped Cream (page 229), these make a great mixed-berry shortcake dessert. Berries also freeze well, so you can make these scones year round.

1. Position your oven racks so that one is in the center, and preheat the oven to 400 degrees. Line a baking sheet with parchment paper.
2. Dump the dry ingredients into the bowl of the food processor fitted with a metal blade, and pulse to mix.
3. Add the butter to the bowl all at once, and run the food processor for 15 seconds. Switch to pulse, and continue pulsing until there are no chunks of butter left and the mixture looks grainy, like moist crumbs. Be careful not to overwork the ingredients. Don't let the butter and flour come completely together into something that looks like dough or paste. Remove the blade from the food processor, and dump the crumbs into a big bowl.
4. In a separate, small bowl, whisk the eggs to break up the yolks. Whisk in the buttermilk and extracts. Use the whisk to stir in the preserves and currants.
5. Pour the wet ingredients on top of the flour mixture. Stir them together with a wooden spoon until there is just a slight amount of flour visible.
6. Add the berries and stir gently, being careful not to mash the berries any more than is inevitable, until there's not a trace of flour left.
7. Use a ½-cup measuring cup or your hand (eyeballing for size) to scoop the batter out and plop it onto the baking sheet, leaving 2 inches between scones.
8. Place the baking sheet on the center rack in the oven, and bake the scones for 20–25 minutes, until the tops are golden brown and a toothpick or small knife

4 cups unbleached all-purpose flour

1 tablespoon baking powder

1 teaspoon baking soda

½ teaspoon salt

⅔ cup sugar

20 tablespoons (2½ sticks) cold unsalted butter, cut into ¼-inch cubes

2 large eggs

¾ cup cold buttermilk

1½ teaspoons vanilla extract

1½ teaspoons almond extract

1 tablespoon raspberry preserves

½ cup dried currants

¾ cup blueberries, rinsed and dried on paper towels (page 242)

⅔ cup raspberries, rinsed and dried on paper towels

inserted into the center of a scone comes out clean. Remove the baking sheet from the oven, and place it on a wire rack to cool for a few minutes. Move the baking sheet off the rack, and use a metal spatula to transfer the scones from the baking sheet to the rack, or directly to whatever dish or basket you're serving the scones from. Serve fresh out of the oven or at room temperature.

How to Rinse (and Dry) Berries

Berries don't last long to begin with, but they last even less time once they get wet. Sometimes we don't rinse berries at all—like with really ripe raspberries, which are so delicate. When we do rinse berries, we do it just before we're ready to use them. After rinsing them under a gentle stream of water, we spread them on a sheet pan lined with a towel or paper towels. This way, they are not touching one another so they'll dry more quickly.

Irish Soda Scones with Dark and Yellow Raisins, Caraway Seeds, and Walnuts

MAKES 10 SCONES

The combination of raisins, walnuts, and caraway seeds makes this the scone version of traditional Irish soda bread. The dough is dry enough that it can be rolled and cut with a biscuit cutter if you prefer the cylindrical, cut-edged look of a classic English scone. It's the driest of our scones, but apparently not too dry. We have many customers who eat this every day of the week.

4 cups unbleached all-purpose flour
½ cup packed light-brown sugar
1 tablespoon baking powder
1 teaspoon baking soda
1 teaspoon salt
12 tablespoons cold, unsalted butter (1½ sticks), cut into ¼-inch cubes
2 large eggs
1 cup cold buttermilk
2 tablespoons caraway seeds
1 cup walnuts, coarsely chopped
½ cup golden raisins
½ cup dark raisins

1. Position your oven racks so that one is in the center, and preheat the oven to 400 degrees. Line a baking sheet with parchment paper.
2. Dump the dry ingredients into the bowl of the food processor fitted with a metal blade, and pulse to mix.
3. Add the butter to the bowl all at once, and run the food processor for 15 seconds. Switch to pulse, and continue pulsing until there are no chunks of butter left and the mixture looks like moist crumbs. Be careful not to overwork the ingredients. You can hear when the blade is no longer cutting against the butter. Stop there. Don't let the mixture become one big ball of dough. Remove the blade from the food processor, and dump the mixture into a big bowl.
4. In a separate, small bowl, whisk the eggs to break up the yolks. Whisk in the buttermilk, and use the whisk to stir in the caraway seeds, walnuts, and raisins.
5. Pour the wet ingredients on top of the flour-butter crumbs, and stir with a

wooden spoon until there is no flour visible. Don't work the dough a moment longer than necessary.

6. Use a ½-cup measuring cup or your hand (eyeballing for size) to scoop the batter out and plop it onto the baking sheet, leaving 2 inches between scones.

7. Place the baking sheet on the center rack of the oven, and bake for 20–25 minutes, until the tops of scones are golden brown and a small knife or toothpick inserted into the center of one comes out clean.

8. Remove the baking sheet from the oven, and place it on a wire rack to let the scones cool for a few minutes. Remove the baking sheet from the rack, and use a metal spatula to transfer the scones from the baking sheet to the rack, or directly to whatever you're serving the scones from. Serve the scones fresh out of the oven or at room temperature.

"I never rely on the oven thermostat. I always use an oven thermometer."
—Jerome

"If you're unsure whether your scones are done, pull one out and break it open. Sure—you'll lose one, but it's better than losing the whole batch."
—Frank

Dried Cranberry Scones with Crystallized Sugar Crust

MAKES 8 SCONES

Jerome's grandmother never misses her four-thirty tea. Every day of her life, come late afternoon, she settles down to tea, toast, and jam. When she visits New York, she spends her afternoons at our store, and this scone becomes her teatime staple. We sprinkle it with coarse sugar, to give it texture and sparkle and a little extra sweetness to contrast with the tart cranberries. You can substitute dried sour cherries or candied lemon or orange rind for the cranberries in this recipe.

3 cups unbleached all-purpose flour; plus more to flour your hands to roll out the scones

⅓ cup sugar

1 teaspoon baking powder

¼ teaspoon salt

20 tablespoons (2½ sticks) cold unsalted butter, cut into ¼-inch cubes

2 large eggs

½ cup cold buttermilk

¾ cup dried cranberries

1 large egg whisked with 1 tablespoon cream or milk (egg wash)

1 tablespoon or more granulated or raw sugar for sprinkling

1. Position your oven racks so that one is in the center, and preheat the oven to 400 degrees. Line a baking sheet with parchment paper.

2. Dump the dry ingredients into the bowl of the food processor fitted with a metal blade, and pulse to mix.

3. Add the butter to the bowl all at once, and run the food processor for 15 seconds. Switch to pulse, and continue pulsing until there are no chunks of butter left and the butter and flour are integrated into moist crumbs. Be careful not to mix the butter and flour until they form a dough or paste. Remove the blade from the food processor, and dump the crumbs into a big bowl.

4. In a separate, small bowl, whisk the eggs to break up the yolks. Whisk in the buttermilk, and use the whisk to stir in the cranberries.

5. Pour the wet ingredients into the bowl with flour-butter crumbs. Stir the dough with a wooden spoon until it just comes together and there is no trace of flour visible. You don't want to work the dough a moment longer than necessary.

6. With a little bit of flour on your hands, scoop out a small handful (about ½ cup) of dough with your hand or a big spoon, and roll the dough until it forms a ball.

Drop the dough onto your baking sheet, and press it into a 1-to-1½-inch-thick disk with the heel of one hand. Leave 2-inch spaces between the pressed disks.

7. Use a pastry brush or a scrunched-up paper towel to coat each scone with the egg wash. Sprinkle each scone with a thin layer of sugar.

8. Place the baking sheet on the center rack in the oven, and bake for 20–25 minutes, until the tops of scones are golden brown and a small knife or toothpick inserted into the center of one comes out clean.

9. Remove the baking sheet from the oven, and place it on a wire rack to allow the scones to cool for a few minutes. Lift the baking sheet off the rack, and use a metal spatula to transfer the scones from the baking sheet to the rack, or directly to the dish from which you'll be serving the scones. Serve fresh out of the oven or at room temperature.

"The dried cranberries you find in stores are sweetened. And with good reason, I learned. I tried drying my own. They were so tart I couldn't eat them."
—Frank

Variation: Candied Ginger Scones

Candied ginger adds a complex little snap to baked goods. We started making this scone when the supplier sent us a can of candied ginger by mistake and one of the guys in the kitchen opened it. We couldn't send it back, so we decided to throw some in a batch of scones. The scones were delicious. Add 1 teaspoon ground ginger to your dry ingredients, and substitute a cup of candied ginger (chopped) for the dried currants. We love this with a cup of hot chai tea.

Spiced Pumpkin Scones with Fresh Cranberries

4 cups unbleached all-purpose flour

1 tablespoon baking powder

1 teaspoon baking soda

½ teaspoon salt

1 teaspoon cinnamon

½ teaspoon nutmeg

¼ teaspoon ground cloves

¼ teaspoon ground ginger

½ cup sugar

½ pound plus 6 tablespoons (2¾ sticks) cold unsalted butter, cut into ¼-inch cubes

2 large eggs

¾ cup cold buttermilk

1 cup canned or fresh pumpkin purée

1 teaspoon vanilla extract

1 cup fresh cranberries, coarsely chopped

½ cup walnuts, coarsely chopped

½ cup golden raisins

During the first years we were open, this eccentric old guy from the neighborhood used to come in every day and ask us when we were going to start making pumpkin muffins. We decided on pumpkin scones instead—we were able to get a more intense pumpkin flavor in the scone than we would have in a muffin. And the eccentric old guy was happy.

1. Position your oven racks so that one is in the center, and preheat the oven to 400 degrees. Line a baking sheet with parchment paper.
2. Dump the dry ingredients into the bowl of a food processor fitted with a metal blade, and pulse to mix.
3. Add the butter to the bowl all at once, and pulse until there are no chunks of butter left and mixture looks like moist crumbs. Be careful not to overwork the flour and butter. Remove the blade from the food processor, and dump the crumbs into a big bowl.
4. In another, small bowl, whisk the eggs to break up the yolks. Whisk in the buttermilk, pumpkin purée, and vanilla. Use the whisk to stir in the cranberries, walnuts, and raisins.
5. Pour the wet ingredients on top of the flour mixture. Stir with a wooden spoon until the mixture just comes together, then stop. You don't want to work the dough a moment longer than necessary.
6. Use a ½-cup measuring cup or your hand (eyeballing for size) to scoop the batter out and plop it onto the baking sheet, leaving 2 inches between scones.
7. Place the baking sheet on the center rack in the oven, and bake the scones for

20–25 minutes, until a toothpick inserted into the center of one comes out clean.

8. Remove the baking sheet from the oven, and place it on a wire rack to let scones cool for a few minutes. Lift the baking sheet off the rack, and use a metal spatula to transfer the scones to the rack, or directly to the dish on which you're serving the scones. Serve fresh out of the oven or at room temperature.

"We use canned pumpkin purée. Why go through the trouble of cooking pumpkins and puréeing them ourselves? Canned is good. It's better than a lot of fresh pumpkin I've tasted."
—Frank

Toasted Walnut Scones with Raspberry Preserves

MAKES 12 SCONES

4 cups unbleached all-purpose flour

Just under 1 cup walnuts, toasted
and ground fine

½ cup sugar

1 tablespoon plus 1 teaspoon
baking powder

1 teaspoon baking soda

½ teaspoon salt

½ pound (2 sticks) cold unsalted
butter, cut into ¼-inch cubes

1⅓ cups cold buttermilk

2 teaspoons vanilla extract

1½ cups raspberry preserves

With walnuts ground up into the dough, this is like a scone version of a Linzer cookie. Depending on what you like, or what you happen to have in the cupboard, you can substitute hazelnuts, pecans, pistachio nuts, or almonds for walnuts, and any type of preserves—or even Very Lemony Curd (page 252)—for the jam. And don't be alarmed when you discover there are no eggs in this recipe (trust us, it works).

1. Position your oven racks so that one is in the center, and preheat the oven to 400 degrees. Line a baking sheet with parchment paper.
2. Dump the dry ingredients into the bowl of a food processor fitted with a metal blade, and pulse to mix.
3. Add the butter all at once, and run the food processor for about 15 seconds, then switch to pulse. Continue pulsing until there are no chunks of butter left and the mixture looks like moist crumbs. Be careful not to overwork the mixture. Remove the blade from the food processor, and dump the flour-butter crumbs into a big bowl.
4. In another, small bowl, whisk the buttermilk and vanilla together. Pour them into the bowl with the crumbs, and stir with a wooden spoon until the dough comes together and there is no flour visible. Don't work it a moment longer than necessary.
5. Use a ½-cup measuring cup or your hand (eyeballing for size) to scoop out the dough. Roll each piece of dough into a ball, and place it on your baking sheet, leaving 2 inches between scones. Press down on each scone with the heel of your hand to create a fat disk, 1–1½ inches thick.

6. Press a crater into the center of each scone with a tablespoon or soup spoon dipped in a glass of hot water. Spoon a tablespoon or more of jam into the crater of each scone. The jam should be flush with the rest of the scone. If you pile it higher, it'll drip down the sides of the scone when it cooks.

7. Place the baking sheet on the center rack in the oven, and bake the scones for 20–25 minutes, until the tops are golden brown and a toothpick or small knife inserted into a scone comes out clean. You'll have to poke around the jam, so it won't be the center exactly. Just make sure to insert the toothpick or knife deep into the scone.

8. Remove the baking sheet from the oven, and place it on a wire rack to let the scones cool for a few minutes. Lift the baking sheet off the rack, and use a metal spatula to transfer the scones from the baking sheet to the rack, or directly to whatever you're serving them from. Serve fresh out of the oven or at room temperature.

Jerome on Low-Fat

In the beginning, we tried to lower the calories in our scones, our muffins, our cookies, all of it. Everything tasted terrible. Look: In France, people eat butter all the time. And they aren't obese. Because in France they don't eat all day long. They have breakfast. They have lunch. They have dinner. When people ask me for a low-calorie scone, I hand them a scone and tell them: "Eat half the scone, it's half the calories."

Very Lemony Curd

Lemon curd is very English. It's like a custard that comes in a jar—and it's a requisite part of a classic high tea. They eat it with double cream on their scones—probably because the scones are so dry. We love lemon curd and often use it in place of raspberry preserves on our toasted-walnut scones. We also pour the curd into a prebaked tart shell, or mini–tart shells, which we buy premade from specialty-food stores. You can substitute orange or lime juice and zest for the lemon, to make orange or lime curds. We like to reserve the egg whites, 4 to a container, for Classic Coconut Macaroons (page 321) or Chocolate-Pecan French-Style Macaroons (page 322).

To make the curd, the first thing you want to do, since already-squeezed lemons are nearly impossible to grate, is grate the rind of one lemon. Set this aside. Beat 8 egg yolks in a medium-size bowl to break them up. Pour the yolks through a sieve into a heavy-bottomed saucepan to strain out the white membrane that likely sneaked in with the yolks. (When the curd is cooked, any remaining egg whites will be floating around in the yellow curd like the scrambled egg whites that they are.)

Stir in 1¼ cups sugar and ¾ cup lemon juice (3–4 lemons)

and cook over medium heat, stirring constantly with a heatproof rubber spatula or a wooden spoon in a figure-eight motion (make sure to get around the edges of the pot). You also want to scrape down the sides of the pot occasionally.

Continue cooking until the curd thickens enough to coat the back of your rubber spatula or wooden spoon. Lift the spoon out of the curd, run your finger down the length of the spatula or spoon. If the line left by your finger remains, the curd is thick enough. If the curd quickly runs to cover up the line, it is too runny and needs more cooking time. The first time you make this, you may wonder if the curd is thickening or if it's just your imagination. It's a bit like when you think you hear the phone ringing. You *think* you heard it ring. But when it really rings, you *know* it. When the curd really begins to thicken, you'll know it.

Remove the pan from the heat. Add 10 tablespoons of unsalted butter and your lemon zest all at once, and stir until the butter is melted. Pour the curd into a small bowl, and let cool to room temperature. Cover the cooled curd, and refrigerate until you're ready to use it. Lemon curd will last in the refrigerator for up to 2 weeks.

Honey-Cornmeal Scones

MAKES 12 SCONES

This scone, slightly sweetened with honey, is Frank's homage to the Italian polenta cake that his grandmother used to make just for him. It makes a great midday snack with a cup of flowery tea, such as Earl Grey or jasmine.

1. Position your oven racks so that one is in the center, and preheat the oven to 400 degrees. Line a baking sheet with parchment paper.
2. Dump the dry ingredients into the bowl of a food processor fitted with a metal blade, and pulse to mix.
3. Add the butter to the bowl all at once, and run the food processor for about 15 seconds. Continue to mix, pulsing now so that you have more control, until there are no chunks of butter left and the mixture looks like moist crumbs. Be careful not to mix the ingredients until they come together like dough. Remove the blade from the food processor, and dump the crumbs into a big bowl.
4. In another, small bowl, whisk the eggs to break up the yolks. Whisk in the milk, honey, and vanilla.
5. Pour the wet ingredients into the bowl with the crumbs, and stir with a wooden spoon, stopping as soon as the dough comes together and there is no flour visible. Don't work the dough a moment longer than necessary.
6. Use a ½-cup measuring cup to scoop the batter out and plop it onto the baking sheet, leaving 2 inches between scones. Use a pastry brush or a scrunched-up paper towel to coat each scone with the glaze.
7. Place the baking sheet on the center rack in the oven, and bake the scones for 20–25 minutes, until the tops are golden brown and a toothpick inserted into the center of one comes out clean.
8. Remove the baking sheet from the oven, and place it on a wire rack to let the

3 cups unbleached all-purpose flour

1 tablespoon plus 1 teaspoon baking powder

1½ cups yellow cornmeal

½ teaspoon salt

½ cup packed light-brown sugar

½ pound (2 sticks) cold unsalted butter, cut into ¼-inch cubes

2 large eggs

1 cup cold milk

½ cup honey

1 teaspoon vanilla extract

FOR THE GLAZE

1 large egg, lightly beaten with 1 teaspoon water

scones cool for a few minutes. Lift the baking sheet off the rack, and use a metal spatula to transfer the scones from the baking sheet to the rack, or directly to whatever you're serving the scones from. Serve fresh out of the oven or at room temperature.

Orange Scones with Chocolate Chips

4 cups unbleached all-purpose flour

1 tablespoon plus 1 teaspoon baking powder

1 teaspoon salt

1 cup sugar

1 teaspoon ground ginger

¾ pound (3 sticks) cold unsalted butter, cut into ¼-inch cubes

4 large eggs

2 teaspoons vanilla extract

2 teaspoons grated orange zest (page 297)

½ cup freshly squeezed orange juice

2 tablespoons orange marmalade

1 cup semisweet chocolate chips; or 6 ounces good-quality dark chocolate, broken into pieces

The Silversteins come in every Sunday morning and have from the day we opened. If they don't come, they tell us why. "Sorry we weren't here last week . . ." It's usually because they're down in Florida, visiting their parents. They always want the same thing: the Orange Scones with Chocolate Chips. For a chocolate-on-chocolate experience, replace ¼ cup of the flour with ¼ cup of cocoa powder.

1. Position your oven racks so that one is in the center, and preheat the oven to 400 degrees. Line a baking sheet with parchment paper.
2. Dump the dry ingredients into the bowl of a food processor fitted with a metal blade, and pulse to mix.
3. Add the butter to the bowl all at once, and run the food processor for about 15 seconds. Continue to mix, pulsing now to give you more control, until there are no chunks of butter left and the mixture looks like moist crumbs. Be careful not to overwork. Remove the blade from the food processor, and dump the crumbs into a big bowl.
4. In another, small bowl, whisk the eggs to break up the yolks. Whisk in the vanilla, orange zest and juice, and marmalade. Use the whisk to stir in the chocolate chips.
5. Pour the wet ingredients on top of the crumbs. Stir together with a wooden

spoon until no flour is visible. Don't work the dough a moment longer than necessary.

6. Use a ½-cup measuring cup or your hand (eyeballing for size) to scoop the batter out and plop it onto the baking sheet, leaving 2 inches between scones.

7. Place the baking sheet on the center rack in the oven, and bake the scones for 20–25 minutes, until the tops are golden brown and a toothpick inserted into the center of one comes out clean.

8. Remove the baking sheet from the oven, and place it on a wire rack to let scones cool for a few minutes. Lift the baking sheet off the rack, and use a metal spatula to transfer the scones from the baking sheet to the rack, or directly to whatever you're serving the scones from. Serve fresh from the oven or at room temperature.

"Placing scones (or whatever you're baking) on a wire rack allows them to cool without creating moisture from condensation. Moisture means soggy."
—Frank

Jerome on Baking with Your Hands

I don't feel like I'm baking unless I feel my hands touching dough. I like to use my hands for everything. I use them to mix the wet ingredients into the dry ingredients. I also use them instead of a measuring cup for splashing scone dough onto the baking sheet. It's so sticky, I'll have to use my hands anyway to get it all out of the cup. Besides, splashing the dough gives the scones a nice peaked top.

Dried Apricot Scones with Pecans and Shredded Coconut

MAKES 8 SCONES

2½ cups unbleached all-purpose flour

2 tablespoons baking powder

½ teaspoon salt

½ cup packed light-brown sugar

10 tablespoons (1 stick plus 2 tablespoons) cold unsalted butter, cut into ¼-inch cubes

2 large eggs

¼ cup cold milk

1 teaspoon vanilla extract

½ cup pecans, coarsely chopped

½ cup dried apricots, chopped

¼ cup shredded unsweetened coconut

Dense and packed full of healthy bits of fruits and nuts, these are, we think, the energy bar of scones. Some people say they're a meal by themselves. Dried mango, papaya, and pineapple all work well in place of the apricots.

1. Position your oven racks so that one is in the center, and preheat the oven to 400 degrees. Line a baking sheet with parchment paper.

2. Dump the dry ingredients into the bowl of a food processor fitted with a metal blade, and pulse to mix.

3. Add the butter to the bowl all at once, and run the food processor for about 15 seconds. Switch to pulse, and continue pulsing until there are no chunks of butter left and the mixture looks like moist crumbs. Remove the blade from the food processor, and dump the crumbs into a big bowl.

4. In a separate, medium-size bowl, whisk the eggs to break up the yolks. Whisk in the milk and vanilla. Use the whisk to stir in the nuts, apricots, and coconut.

5. Pour the wet ingredients on top of the flour-butter crumbs, and stir them with a wooden spoon until they come together and there is no flour visible. Don't work the dough a moment longer than necessary.

6. Use a ½-cup measuring cup or your hand (eyeballing for size) to scoop up the dough. Roll each piece of dough into a ball and place it on your prepared baking sheet, leaving 2 inches between pieces. Press down on each dough ball with the heel of your hand so that you have a fat disk (1–1½ inches thick), like a hockey puck.

7. Place the baking sheet on the center rack in the oven, and bake the scones for

20–25 minutes, until the tops are golden brown and a toothpick or small knife inserted into the center of one comes out clean.

8. Remove the baking sheet from the oven, and place it on a wire rack to let scones cool for a few minutes. Lift the baking sheet off the rack, and use a metal spatula to transfer the scones from the baking sheet to the rack, or directly to whatever you're serving the scones from. Serve fresh from the oven or at room temperature.

"We had this customer who was pregnant with twins. She used to call the store to find out what time the Dried Apricot Scones were coming out of the oven. She was crazy for them. We only make them on weekends, so she'd have her husband rush over and buy like one dozen, and she'd keep them in her refrigerator all week."

—Jerome

Drying Your Own Fruit

We've got nothing against raisins, other than to say that dried fruit in American cooking is too often limited to them. There are so many dried fruits available—almost every fruit you eat fresh you can find dried—from apples and pears to stone fruits like apricots, peaches, and plums, to tropical fruits like mango, pineapple, and papaya, and a whole host of berries.

Dried fruit is great for the intense burst of sweetness it adds to both baked goods and savory things, like salads. On a more practical level, dried fruit is always "in season." Keep it in a tightly sealed box at room temperature and it will last longer than you'll ever be able to resist. We like it so much that, when the fresh version of our favorite fruits are in season, we dry our own. To do this, place rinsed fruit, cut according to your preference, in a 200-degree oven for 6 to 8 hours, half that time for berries.

Cheddar-Parmesan Scones with Fresh Dill

MAKES 8 SCONES

A lot of people think this is our scone of scones. We have many customers who refuse to try anything else. Jerome grabs these all day long at the store, when he's too busy to sit down and eat. He likes that they're halfway between sweet and savory. And customers are used to seeing him eating them while he walks around the shop. It's good for business.

1. Position your oven racks so that one is in the center, and preheat the oven to 400 degrees. Line a baking sheet with parchment paper.
2. Dump the dry ingredients into the bowl of a food processor fitted with a metal blade, and pulse to mix.
3. Add the butter to the bowl all at once, and run the food processor for about 15 seconds. Switch to pulse, and continue pulsing until there are no chunks of butter left and the mixture looks like moist crumbs. Be careful not to overwork. Remove the blade from the food processor, and dump the crumbs into a big bowl.
4. In another, small bowl, whisk the eggs to break up the yolks. Whisk in the milk. Use the whisk to stir in the dill and cheeses.
5. Pour the wet ingredients on top of the flour-butter crumbs, and stir with a wooden spoon until no flour is visible. It may seem a bit dry, but keep stirring and it will eventually come together.
6. Use a ½-cup measuring cup or your hand (eyeballing for size) to scoop up the dough and plop it onto the baking sheet, leaving 2 inches between scones.
7. Place the baking sheet on the center rack in the oven, and bake the scones for 20–25 minutes, until the tops are golden brown and a toothpick inserted into the center comes out clean.

2⅔ cups unbleached all-purpose flour

1 tablespoon baking powder

A pinch of cayenne pepper

½ teaspoon salt

8 tablespoons (1 stick) cold unsalted butter, cut into ¼-inch cubes

3 large eggs

½ cup cold milk

2 tablespoons chopped fresh dill (page 162)

2 cups grated cheddar cheese (6 ounces)

⅓ cup grated Pecorino or Parmesan cheese (1½ ounces)

8. Remove the baking sheet from the oven, and place it on a wire rack to let scones cool for a few minutes. Transfer scones with a spatula from the baking sheet to the rack. Serve fresh out of the oven or at room temperature.

"Since you probably have no idea if your oven is properly calibrated, you may want to turn your baking sheet around 180 degrees two-thirds of the way through baking. That way, you won't end up with half your scones (or cookies, or whatever) burned before the other half are even cooked through."
—Frank

Frank on Flour

We use only Hecker's unbleached all-purpose flour. All-purpose flour contains neither the germ nor the bran of the wheat kernel. "Unbleached" means just what it sounds like. You can use bleached and unbleached flours interchangeably. We use unbleached just because we're not wild about the combination of bleach and food.

As for the brand, Hecker's, when we were starting our business I found out through clandestine means that a bakery I really admired used Hecker's exclusively. So that's what we started using. Now I wouldn't even think about using another flour. I'm superstitious about it. Why argue with success?

Once Upon a ...
QUICK BREAD

Banana–Poppy Seed Muffins

Blueberry Muffins with Ground Pecans and Pecan Topping

Pear-Ginger-Raisin Muffins

Apple-Cranberry Muffins

Apple–Oat Bran Muffins

Honey-Corn Muffins

Carrot Cake Muffins with Lemon–Cream Cheese Icing

Variation: Frank's Fruit-and-Nut Carrot Cake

Lemon–Cream Cheese Icing

Raisin Bran Muffins

Zucchini, Walnut, and Raisin Tea Loaves

Chocolate-Banana Tea Loaves

Lemon–Poppy Seed Tea Loaves

Fresh Grated Ginger Gingerbread Tea Loaves

Apple Spice Bundt Cake

Maple-Sugar Glaze

Apple (or Peach) Batter Cake

Skillet Corn Bread

Fresh Berry Coffee Cake with Walnut Crumb Topping

It was pretty obvious from the day we opened Once Upon a Tart that we were going to have to make muffins. "Muffins seem to be a need for American people," Jerome says. "Muffins and bagels. For New Yorkers, anyway." We included loaf cakes in this chapter, too, because muffins, cakes, loaves, are all basically the same thing baked in different-shaped pans.

Even in New York, where there are so many cafés and specialty-food stores, it's rare to find places that make their own muffins. All around town you'll see the same corn-blueberry muffins, the same orange-cranberry muffins—and we know why. Because they're made at the same factory or from the same mix.

Our regular muffin customers each have their favorite, and they eat that favorite muffin every morning of their lives. They're pretty obsessive about it, like they're addicted. Or like their morning simply wouldn't be right without it. If these customers come in—presumably not having had their coffee—and find we don't have their muffin that morning because Frank had the temerity to try something new, well, things can devolve. . . . With muffins, people seem to know what they want and stick with it. There's one woman who's been coming in every morning for we don't know how many years and every morning: "An Apple-Cranberry Muffin, please" (page 274). Jerome tried to get her to taste something else. "A few times I just handed her something different," he says. But she always went straight back to the apple-cranberry. "I love it" is all she says.

When we were coming up with these recipes, we had a few standards as far as our definition of the perfect muffin or loaf.

We wanted them to be moist. We wanted them to have texture—from nuts or seeds, wheat flour, cornmeal, anything to keep them from being like plain ol' cake. And, of course, we wanted to put our own spin on them.

We experimented with different fruits, but there are only so many kinds of fruits you want in a muffin. You could probably make a peach muffin, but if you've got nice peaches, why not split a berry scone in half and make a peach shortcake (page 241)? You could throw some rhubarb in a loaf, but we can think of a lot better things to do with rhubarb, like a Strawberry-Rhubarb Tart with Shamey's Crisp Topping (page 214). So we just took the nuts and fruits we chose to work with and added another flavor dimension to give each of these some kick.

THINGS TO KNOW

What we call muffins and loaves all fall into the category of quick breads. The reason for the name is that they're quick to make. With yeast breads, you have to pound down the dough, wait while the dough rises, then pound it down and let it rise again. Pound and wait and pound and wait. With quick breads, there is no yeast involved. There's no waiting for

dough to rise. The rising happens in the oven, quickly and all by itself with the help of a little baking soda and/or baking powder.

Some of these quick breads are made with butter, others with oil, and we really can't give you any good reason for the distinction other than to say: that's the way it's supposed to be. Carrot cake is always made with oil. Banana bread is always made with butter. Those made with butter (unless it's melted) call for the creaming method, where the softened butter and sugar are creamed together until they're fluffy, which makes for a light and fluffy cake. Oil makes for a denser cake, and is used in instances where the density works, like the Carrot Cake Muffins (page 279) or Pear-Ginger-Raisin Muffins (page 273). "Unless a recipe calls for creaming butter and sugar together,"

Frank says, "I like to make muffins by hand, with a wire whisk—my right hand whisking the whole time, while my left hand adds my premeasured ingredients. It's quick bread. It's supposed to be quick. And this way, it is."

Quick breads are not just quick, they're easy. The one thing you must know, however, is that the leavening agent (baking soda or powder) is activated once it gets wet, but the dough only rises once it's in the oven. Which means that, to get the most rise, the time between the moment the wet and dry ingredients meet and the moment the batter gets in the oven should be as short as possible. For that reason, you don't want to make the batter in advance. But to prepare for, say, a breakfast, where you want to serve your muffins warm, you could do what we do at the store: prepare both the wet and dry ingredients, store them separately (Ziploc plastic bags are great for storing dry mixes), and then combine the wet with the dry just before you're ready to bake the muffins.

All of these recipes call for smearing the muffin tins and loaf pans with butter and dusting the loaf pans with flour. If you do this, they'll easily slide right out of the pan. Get a good chunk of cold or softened butter onto a paper towel or the inside of a butter wrapper, and make sure to get it into the bottom creases of the pan or muffin. You can also use melted butter, brushing it into the pan with a pastry brush or a scrunched-up paper towel. If the recipe calls for dusting with flour, take a handful of flour and flick it into the pan. Pick up the pan and swish the flour around so that it coats the interior surface of the pan. Then hold the pan upside down over the sink and knock on the bottom with your knuckles or a metal spoon, so that any excess flour falls out. You don't want to end up with white powder covering your finished muffins or loaves. When you go to remove your muffins or loaves from their tins, if you find that they're sticking in places, run a knife around the edges between the muffin or loaf and the pan. Get the knife as far down as you can, even underneath the muffin or loaf if possible.

We make big muffins at the café. We prefer the way they look, and our customers tell us they're big enough to call breakfast. We find that filling the cups of the muffin tins almost all the way with batter results in the size muffin we want with a top we like—big enough so that it looks appetizing, but not so that it looks like a giant mushroom cap. We like to use a rubber spatula to scrape down the bowl, but don't make a whole muffin from the scraped-down batter, or that muffin won't have any of the good stuff in it. Use that last bit of batter to top off each muffin. The standard big-muffin tins have space for six. You'll be able to make twelve of the small ones from each muffin recipe if you prefer.

You can double any of these recipes without a problem. And you can make any of them into any shape—a muffin, a loaf, or even a cake. The fact that we make some into muffins and others into loaves is pretty arbitrary. There's no reason the Lemon–Poppy Seed Tea Loaves (page 286) couldn't be made into muffins. And if you smear them with Lemon–Cream Cheese Icing (page 281), you can get away with calling them cupcakes. The cooking time will change, but the formula is pretty basic. The bigger the pan, the longer the baking time, because there's more to bake. So muffins cook the quickest, then loaves, then cakes. If you do decide to make a recipe into a different shape from what we call for, just be careful to test the finished product for doneness. You lose a significant amount of heat every time you open the oven door—but, as we said in the scone chapter, better to lose a little heat than to burn your cake. Insert a toothpick or a small knife deep into the center of the dough, and make sure it comes out totally clean before you take the pan out of the oven. Another good way to test for doneness, especially once you learn to trust your instincts more, is to press your finger into whatever you're baking. If it springs back, it's done. If the indentation from your finger remains, that means you still have some raw batter in the center, and it needs more time. Undercooked dough in the middle will mean a crater in the top once it cools. One more thing: we've found that if you take the muffins out of the tin when they're really hot, it's like they haven't gotten used to their shape. They'll fall apart: the top might fall off, or they might just crumble. On the other hand, if you leave them in too long, the muffins will continue to cook from the heat of the tin; 5–10 minutes is about right. Now get baking.

"When you're mixing the dry ingredients in with the wet, do it gently, almost like folding it, because you want to keep the batter light. If you stir the batter vigorously, it's like you're kneading it, which you don't want to do. It'll give you dense, heavy muffins."
—Frank

Tea loaves make great gifts, especially when they're wrapped nicely. We use kraft paper tied with twine—because that's what we use to wrap everything at the store. Cheesecloth works as well, as do napkins. Or any kind of paper—wrapping paper, wallpaper. If the paper is too heavy to fold easily, wrap it like a tube, leaving the ends open, and tie a string or ribbon around it.

Banana–Poppy Seed Muffins

8 tablespoons (1 stick) unsalted
   butter, softened; plus more for
   smearing in muffin tins
1 cup unbleached all-purpose flour
1 cup whole-wheat flour
1 teaspoon baking powder
1 teaspoon baking soda
¼ teaspoon salt
1 tablespoon poppy seeds
½ cup sugar
4 very ripe bananas, mashed (the
   riper the sweeter; they can even
   be black)
2 large eggs
¼ cup cold milk
2 teaspoons vanilla extract

We used poppy seeds here instead of the usual walnuts because we like the little crunch of poppy seeds and because there are so many people, especially children, who can't eat nuts. It's important to use overripe, or at least ripe, bananas.

1. Position your oven racks so that one is in the center, and preheat the oven to 400 degrees. Smear six big muffin tin cups with butter.
2. Whisk the flours, baking powder, baking soda, salt, and poppy seeds together in a medium-size bowl.
3. In a separate, big bowl, cream the butter and sugar together, using the paddle attachment of an electric mixer or a sturdy wire whisk, until you get a creamy and fluffy texture that is light lemon-yellow in color (about 5 minutes).
4. Add the bananas, and continue mixing at high speed until the bananas are blended with the butter and sugar. If you are doing this with a whisk, mash the bananas with a masher or a fork first. With the mixer speed on low, beat in the eggs one at a time, followed by the milk and vanilla.
5. Gradually add the dry ingredients to the wet, using the paddle attachment of your mixer on low speed (or a wooden spoon) until there's not a trace of flour left. Do not mix longer than necessary.
6. Scoop batter up with a wooden or metal spoon and, using a rubber spatula to scrape batter off the spoon into the cups of the muffin tin, fill each almost to the top. Divide the batter evenly between six cups.

7. Place the muffin tin on the center rack in the oven, and bake the muffins for 35–40 minutes, or until a toothpick or small knife inserted deep into the center of a muffin comes out clean.

8. Remove the tin from the oven and place it on a wire rack until the muffins are cool enough to touch. To remove the muffins, flip the tin upside down and let the muffins fall out onto the rack.

"In the privacy of my own home, when not even my family is watching, I use my right index finger as a spatula. I use it to scrape down the insides of bowls, to get batter off a spoon and into its respective tin, and I use it to level off batter in a pan if I need to. My finger is as flexible and easy to clean as a spatula— and I always know where it is."
—Frank

Blueberry Muffins with Ground Pecans and Pecan Topping

MAKES 8 BIG MUFFINS

We avoided making blueberry muffins for the longest time, because Frank didn't like them. He liked the idea of them all right, but they were never as good as he remembered from childhood. He went through life disappointed in every blueberry muffin he tried. "Not enough flavor," he'd say. "Just a lot of yellow cake." But our customers kept on us over the years to make them, so eventually we started experimenting. We finally got the idea to put ground nuts into the batter, and toasted chopped nuts on top. Frank's happy. Our customers are happy. Make some and you'll be happy.

1. Position your oven racks so that one is in the center, and preheat the oven to 400 degrees. Smear eight big muffin tin cups with butter.
2. Stir topping ingredients together in a small bowl.
3. Whisk the flour, ground pecans, baking powder, and salt together in a medium-size bowl.
4. In a separate, big bowl, whisk the eggs to break up the yolks. Still whisking with one hand, pour in the sugar with the other. Continue to whisk for a few minutes, until the eggs begin to pale in color. Whisk in the milk, vanilla, and melted butter.
5. Gradually add the dry ingredients to the wet, stirring gently with a wooden spoon. When there is still a little flour visible, gently stir in the blueberries, taking care not to break them up any more than is inevitable.
6. Scoop the batter up with a wooden or metal spoon and, using a rubber spatula,

FOR THE PECAN TOPPING
2 tablespoons sugar
2 tablespoons pecans, chopped fine
2 tablespoons rolled oats

FOR THE BATTER
11 tablespoons (1 stick plus 3 tablespoons) unsalted butter, melted and cooled to room temperature; plus more for smearing muffin tins
3½ cups unbleached all-purpose flour
1½ cups coarsely ground (or very finely chopped) pecans (like coarse nut flour; they need to be so small that when you bite into this muffin you should not know there are nuts in it)
2 teaspoons baking powder
½ teaspoon salt
3 large eggs
¾ cup sugar
1 cup cold milk
2 teaspoons vanilla extract
2 cups fresh blueberries, rinsed and dried on paper towels (page 242)

scrape the batter off the spoon into the cups of the muffin tin, filling each almost to the top.

7. Sprinkle the topping evenly over the muffins. You may want to wipe any excess topping off the pan so you won't have to clean the burnt sugar after it bakes.

8. Place the muffin tin on the center rack in the oven, and bake the muffins for 35–40 minutes, until a toothpick or a small knife inserted deep into the center of a muffin comes out clean. The muffins will have risen over the edges of the cups, and the topping will be golden brown.

9. Remove the tin from the oven, and place it on a wire rack. Let the muffins sit for a few minutes in the tin, until they're cool enough to touch. To remove the muffins, flip the tin upside down and let the muffins fall out onto the wire rack.

"If you open up a fruit-filled muffin, like the apple–oat bran muffin, to see if it's done, the dough around the fruit may look wet. That's what makes it a moist muffin. Don't be fooled into thinking it needs to bake longer."
—Frank

"I never use low- or nonfat milk in baking. No reason, other than: why would I? Richness is what baked goods are all about."
—Frank

Pear-Ginger-Raisin Muffins

We had never seen this combination when we came up with it. Over the years, though, we've seen the same or very similar muffins popping up around town. We are flattered. Frank came to this combination when he was deep into a ginger phase. If you really like ginger, substitute a teaspoon of grated fresh ginger for ground in these.

Unsalted butter for smearing muffin tins
2 cups unbleached all-purpose flour
½ cup whole-wheat flour
1 teaspoon baking soda
1 teaspoon ground ginger
½ teaspoon salt
3 large eggs
¾ cup sugar
1 cup vegetable oil
1½ teaspoons vanilla extract
1 large ripe Anjou or Bosc pear, peeled, cored, and cut into ½ inch cubes
½ cup dark raisins

1. Position your oven racks so that one is in the center, and preheat the oven to 400 degrees. Smear six big muffin tin cups with butter.
2. Whisk the flours, baking soda, ginger, and salt together in a medium-size bowl.
3. In a separate, big bowl, whisk the eggs to break up the yolks. Still whisking with one hand, pour in the sugar with the other. Continue whisking for a few minutes, until the eggs begin to pale in color. Whisk in the oil and vanilla.
4. Gradually add the dry ingredients to the wet, stirring gently with a wooden spoon until there is just a little flour visible. Stir in the cubed pear and raisins—gently, so as not to smash the pear—until there is not a trace of flour left.
5. Scoop batter up with your spoon and, using a rubber spatula, scrape the batter off the spoon into the cups of the muffin tin, filling them almost to the top. Divide the batter evenly between the six cups.
6. Place the tin on the center rack in the oven, and bake the muffins for 35–40 minutes, or until a small knife or toothpick inserted deep into the center of one comes out clean.
7. Remove the tin from the oven, and place it on a wire rack. Let the muffins sit for a few minutes in the tin, until they're cool enough to touch. To remove the muffins, flip the tin upside down and let the muffins fall out onto the wire rack to cool. Or, even better, serve warm.

"We use big chunks of fruit in our muffins. You bite into one, you get a huge piece of apple or pear—not just a vague pear flavor."
—Jerome

Apple-Cranberry Muffins

Unsalted butter for smearing muffin
   tins
2 cups unbleached all-purpose flour
¾ teaspoon baking powder
¾ teaspoon cinnamon
½ teaspoon salt
2 large eggs
1 cup sugar
¾ cup vegetable oil
1 teaspoon vanilla extract
1 medium-size tart apple, such as
   Granny Smith, cored (not
   peeled) and cut into ½-inch
   cubes (page 119)
1 cup fresh or frozen cranberries

"We don't peel the apples for our muffins. The peel holds the apple together when it bakes and adds to the texture of the muffin. Of course, if you don't want the texture, by all means peel the apples."
—Frank

This was the first muffin we made. And it's still our most popular. Jerome loves it. He loves the way it smells coming out of the oven. It's the cinnamon, he says.

1. Position your oven racks so that one is in the center, and preheat the oven to 400 degrees. Smear six big muffin tin cups with butter.
2. Whisk the flour, baking powder, cinnamon, and salt together in a bowl.
3. In a separate, big bowl, whisk the eggs to break up the yolks. Still whisking with one hand, pour in the sugar with the other. Continue whisking for a few minutes, until the eggs begin to pale in color. Use the whisk to stir in the oil and vanilla.
4. Gradually add the dry ingredients to the wet, stirring gently with a wooden spoon until there's just a little flour visible. Add the apple and cranberries, and stir gently until there is not a trace of flour left.
5. Scoop the batter up with a wooden or metal spoon and, using a rubber spatula, scrape the batter off the spoon and into your muffin tin cups, filling each almost to the top. Divide the batter evenly between six cups.
6. Place the tin on the center rack in the oven, and bake for 40–45 minutes, or until a small knife or toothpick inserted into the center of a muffin comes out clean.
7. Remove the tin from the oven, and place it on a wire rack. Let the muffins sit for a few minutes in the tin, until they're cool enough to touch. To remove the muffins, flip the tin upside down and let the muffins fall out onto the wire rack to cool completely. Or, better yet, serve warm.

Apple–Oat Bran Muffins

This is one of Frank's favorites. He loves earthy flavors: wheat, oats, brown rice. We made these before the oat-bran craze, so in order to convince people to try it—people not from Berkeley or Seattle, anyway—we decided we had to sort of bribe them, offer them a deal. In this case, the deal included big chunks of apples and loads of raisins.

1. Position your oven racks so that one is in the center, and preheat the oven to 400 degrees. Smear eight big muffin tin cups with butter.
2. Whisk the flour, bran, oats, baking powder, baking soda, salt, and brown sugar together in a medium-size bowl, making sure the brown sugar is broken up and mixed in with the other ingredients.
3. In a separate, big bowl, whisk the eggs to break up the yolks. Whisk in the buttermilk, oil, and vanilla. Stir in the raisins and apple.
4. Gradually add the dry ingredients to the wet, stirring gently with a wooden spoon until there is not a trace of flour left.
5. Scoop the batter up with your spoon. Use a rubber spatula to scrape the batter off the spoon into the cups of the muffin tins, filling each almost to the top. Divide the batter evenly between the eight cups.
6. Place the tin on the center rack in the oven, and bake the muffins for 30–35 minutes, or until a toothpick or small knife inserted into the middle of one comes out clean. These muffins will darken in color, and the tops will have a hard crust.
7. Remove the tin from the oven, and place it on a wire rack. Let the muffins sit for a few minutes in the tin, until they're cool enough to touch. To remove the muffins, flip the tin upside down and let the muffins fall out onto the wire rack to cool. Warm, broken in half, these muffins take particularly well to a thick slice of good butter.

Unsalted butter for smearing in muffin tin cups

2¼ cups unbleached all-purpose flour

1 cup oat bran

1 cup rolled oats

2 teaspoons baking powder

2 teaspoons baking soda

¼ teaspoon salt

¼ cup packed light-brown sugar

2 large eggs

2 cups cold buttermilk

½ cup vegetable oil

2 teaspoons vanilla extract

1½ cups golden raisins

1 medium-size tart apple, such as Granny Smith, cored (not peeled) and cut into ½-inch cubes

Honey-Corn Muffins

4 tablespoons unsalted butter, melted and cooled to room temperature; plus more for smearing in muffin tin cups

1½ cups unbleached all-purpose flour

⅓ cup corn flour

1 cup cornmeal

⅓ cup sugar

1 tablespoon plus 1½ teaspoons baking powder

¾ teaspoon salt

3 large eggs

1½ cups cold milk

½ cup plus 2 tablespoons vegetable oil

3 tablespoons honey

1½ teaspoons vanilla extract

"Microwaves aren't my favorite kitchen appliance—I don't own one. But they sure come in handy for melting butter. And reheating coffee."
—Frank

Frank is simply not allowed to arrive at his Aunt Lu's house without a dozen of these in hand. We sometimes throw in a cup of fresh blueberries or cranberries or, during summer, when the corn is sweetest, a cup of kernels shucked from the cob. For catering jobs, we often bake mini-corn muffins and turn them into sandwiches—with smoked turkey or ham, and honey mustard or chutney.

1. Position your oven racks so that one is in the center, and preheat the oven to 400 degrees. Smear six big muffin tin cups with butter.
2. Whisk the flours, cornmeal, sugar, baking powder, and salt together in a medium-size bowl.
3. In a separate, big bowl, whisk the eggs to break up the yolks. Whisk in the milk, butter, oil, honey, and vanilla.
4. Gradually add the dry ingredients to the wet, stirring gently with the whisk until there's not a trace of flour left. This batter is runny, almost like pancake batter.
5. Using a ladle, pour the batter evenly into the cups of your muffin tin. Wipe off any batter that may have spilled onto the pan.
6. Place the muffin tin on the center rack in the oven, and bake the muffins for 30–35 minutes, or until a toothpick or small knife inserted deep into the center of a muffin comes out clean. These muffins will have a golden-brown, mushroom-shaped top when done.
7. Remove the tin from the oven, and place it on a wire rack. Let the muffins sit for a few minutes in the tin, until they're cool enough to touch. To remove the muffins, flip the tin upside down and let the muffins fall out onto the wire rack to cool completely. Or, better yet, serve warm.

Frank on Eating a Memory

When I was a teenager in New Jersey, we used to go to diners a lot. After the movies or parties, whatever. Midnight would roll around, you'd have nowhere left to go, so you'd go hang out at the diner. I always ordered the same thing: a toasted corn muffin with butter and jam. They cut the muffins down the middle—so both halves had part of the top—and grilled them with tons of butter until they were brown and toasty. I remember them being really good. When I'm feeling decadent, I grill my muffins that way now. I haven't had one of those diner muffins in ages. I'm reluctant to. I'm afraid I'll be disappointed. That's what happens when we eat from memory. Our taste buds change, we experience more and better things. But, even more significant, the memory of how something tasted is wrapped up in the experience. That grilled corn muffin was about being out at midnight as a teenager.

Jerome on Muffin Tops

Everyone knows that the best part of a muffin is the top. When I'm clearing off tables at the café, I find empty cups of coffee and the whole bottoms of muffins left. I have never seen a muffin top left by a customer. The tops are crispier because they're exposed to air when they're baking. The muffin cups hold moisture, so that part of the muffin is softer. I've seen tins, at cooking-supply stores, for making muffin tops only. This is ridiculous. Sure, they have less bottom, but there's still a bottom. If there was no bottom, it wouldn't be a muffin, it would be batter splattered on a flat baking sheet. (We'd call that a scone.) Besides, the fact that there's a finite amount of top—that's what makes the tops so special. Otherwise, it would be like too much of a good thing. If there were no bottoms, nobody would appreciate the tops.

Jerome on the Muffin Myth

I hate to break this to you, but muffins are cake. They're mini-cakes. Same with loaves. Loaves are cakes shaped like bread. Americans think French people are crazy to eat croissants. "So much butter," they say. Meanwhile, they're eating *cake* for breakfast. When my parents come to visit, they have to split a muffin at our store—and ours aren't even the biggest muffins out there. But Americans are convinced that muffins are breakfast food. I figure: whatever helps them get up in the morning.

Carrot Cake Muffins with Lemon–Cream Cheese Icing

MAKES 6 BIG MUFFINS

It seems like everyone has a carrot cake recipe that they insist is better than yours. Well, we insist ours is better than anyone's. Frank begged the recipe off a restaurant called Elephant & Castle that was located around the corner before the neighborhood got fancy and the rents got so high that they had to move. The recipe called for thirteen eggs. "That cracked me up," Frank says. "Whoever heard of a recipe with thirteen eggs? It made me love the recipe as much as the cake." Of course, the recipe we give here is much smaller, and calls for only three eggs.

1. Position your oven racks so that one is in the center, and preheat the oven to 400 degrees. Smear six big muffin tin cups with butter.
2. Whisk the flours, baking powder, baking soda, cinnamon, nutmeg, and salt together in a medium-size bowl.
3. In a separate, big bowl, whisk the eggs to break up the yolks. Still whisking with one hand, pour in the sugar with the other. Continue whisking for a few minutes, until the eggs begin to pale in color. Whisk in the oil and applesauce. Stir in the carrots and walnuts.
4. Gradually add the dry ingredients to the wet, stirring gently with a wooden spoon until there's not a trace of flour visible. This batter will be very runny.
5. Scoop the batter up with a glass measuring cup or a ladle, and pour it evenly into the six cups of your prepared muffin tin. Wipe off any batter that may have spilled onto the pan.
6. Place the muffin tin on the center rack in the oven, and bake the muffins for

Unsalted butter, cold or softened, for smearing in muffin cups
1 cup unbleached all-purpose flour
¼ cup whole-wheat flour
¼ teaspoon baking powder
¼ teaspoon baking soda
¾ teaspoon cinnamon
¾ teaspoon nutmeg
1½ teaspoons salt
3 large eggs
1 cup sugar
½ cup vegetable oil
¼ cup applesauce or canned or fresh chopped pineapple
2 cups (½ pound) shredded carrots
⅔ cup walnuts, coarsely chopped
1 recipe Lemon–Cream Cheese Icing (page 281)

35–40 minutes, until they begin to darken and a toothpick or small knife inserted deep into the center of a muffin comes out clean.

7. Remove the tin from the oven, and place it on a wire rack. Let the muffins sit for a few minutes in the tin, until they're cool enough to touch. To remove the muffins, flip the tin upside down and let the muffins fall out onto the wire rack to cool completely.

8. Just before you're ready to serve these, spread a nice thick layer of lemon–cream cheese icing on top with a rubber or offset spatula.

"I discovered muffins here in America. Now there are stores in Paris that make them. But to me, I look at a muffin and it says: 'Welcome to America.' "
—Jerome

"If my baking soda or powder has gotten lumpy (as it does after a humid summer), I 'sift' it through a tea strainer before adding it to the flour."
—Frank

Variation: Frank's Fruit-and-Nut Carrot Cake

During the holidays, I turn our carrot cake batter into fruitcakes that I make for family and friends. I double the recipe, and then I just start throwing stuff in—toasted chopped pecans, walnuts, or filberts, dark and golden raisins, dried cranberries, dried apricots, dried figs. The batter can handle up to 4 cups of added fruits and nuts. I then pour the batter into a 9-inch round cake pan, and bake it the same as the carrot muffins, only a lot longer. Of course, I wouldn't even consider skipping the Lemon–Cream Cheese Icing (below). Believe me when I tell you that this is a fruitcake people will actually eat.

Lemon–Cream Cheese Icing
MAKES ENOUGH FOR 6 BIG MUFFINS

The carrot cake muffins were for the longest time the only thing we iced. We're not into goopy, saucy baked goods, but we felt very strongly that it would be wrong to have carrot cake without cream cheese icing. It's essential that your butter and cream cheese be soft for making icing. Otherwise, you'll have lumps in your icing that are impossible to smooth out.

8 tablespoons (1 stick) unsalted butter, softened
6 ounces cream cheese, softened
2 cups confectioners' sugar
Grated zest of 1 lemon (page 297)
1 tablespoon lemon juice
¼ teaspoon vanilla extract
A pinch of salt

1. Beat the butter and cream cheese together in a big bowl, using the whisk attachment on an electric mixer on high speed (or a sturdy wire whisk and a lot of elbow grease), until they're smooth and creamy and totally combined.

2. Gradually sift the sugar over the bowl (or pass the sugar through a sieve), beating all the while, until there are no lumps left. Add the remaining ingredients, and beat until the icing is smooth. If you find that while you were making icing the butter melted and made the icing thin, you may want to put the icing in the refrigerator before using it.

Raisin Bran Muffins

4 tablespoons (½ stick) unsalted
butter, melted and cooled to
room temperature; plus more for
smearing in muffin cups

2 large eggs

1 cup cold buttermilk

¼ cup vegetable oil

¼ cup honey

½ cup unprocessed bran

1½ cups bran cereal (such as All-
Bran)

1 cup whole-wheat flour

¼ cup packed light-brown sugar

1 teaspoon baking powder

1 teaspoon baking soda

½ teaspoon salt

¾ cup dark raisins

Unlike a lot of bran muffins that have the taste and texture of a Duraflame log, this one is really moist and loaded with honey and raisins. Frank thinks it's the best bran muffin he's ever tasted.

1. Position your oven racks so that one is in the center, and preheat the oven to 400 degrees. Smear six big muffin tin cups with butter.
2. Whisk the eggs in a big bowl to break up the yolks. Whisk in the buttermilk, melted butter, oil, and honey. Add the bran and cereal, and let sit for 5–10 minutes, so that the liquids soften the cereal.
3. Whisk the flour, brown sugar, baking powder, baking soda, and salt together in a separate, medium-size bowl.
4. Stir the raisins into the wet ingredients. Gradually add the dry ingredients to the wet, stirring gently with a wooden spoon until there is no flour visible.
5. Scoop the batter up with your spoon, and use a rubber spatula to scrape the batter off the spoon, filling the cups of your muffin tin almost to the top. Divide the batter evenly between the six cups.
6. Place the muffin tin on the center rack in the oven, and bake the muffins for 30–35 minutes, or until the muffins darken around the edges and a toothpick or small knife inserted deep into the center of one comes out clean.
7. Remove the tin from the oven, and place it on a wire rack. Let the muffins sit for a few minutes in the tin, until they're cool enough to touch. To remove the muffins, flip the tin upside down and let the muffins fall out onto the wire rack to cool completely. Or, better yet, serve warm.

Zucchini, Walnut, and Raisin Tea Loaves

MAKES TWO 5-BY-9-INCH LOAVES (8–10 SLICES EACH)

This is Frank's mother's recipe, with whole-wheat flour added for texture. Dusting the pan with cornmeal gives the crust a nice little crunch. This loaf is just as moist the second and third days.

1. Position your oven racks so that one is in the center, and preheat the oven to 350 degrees. Smear two 5-by-9-inch loaf pans with butter, and dust them lightly with cornmeal.
2. Whisk the flours, cinnamon, baking powder, baking soda, and salt together in a medium-size bowl.
3. In a separate, big bowl, whisk the eggs to break up the yolks. Still whisking with one hand, add the sugar with the other, and whisk until the eggs begin to pale in color. Whisk in the oil and vanilla. Use the whisk to stir in the zucchini, raisins, and nuts.
4. Gradually stir the dry ingredients into the wet ingredients, using a rubber spatula or wooden spoon, until there is not a trace of flour left.
5. Use a rubber spatula to scrape the batter into the prepared loaf pans. Make sure to divide the batter equally between the two loaves, so that they require the same baking time.
6. Place the loaf pans side by side on the center rack in the oven, and bake for 60–70 minutes, or until a small knife or toothpick inserted deep into the center of each loaf comes out clean.
7. Remove the loaves from the oven, and set them on a wire rack to cool. To remove a loaf from a pan, place the rack over the top of the pan and quickly flip it so the loaf falls out onto the rack. Allow the loaves to cool a bit before slicing. These are best served at room temperature, and even better the next day or the day after that.

Unsalted butter for smearing in loaf pans
Cornmeal (for dusting loaf pans)
2½ cups unbleached all-purpose flour
1 cup whole-wheat flour
1 teaspoon cinnamon
1½ teaspoons baking soda
¾ teaspoon baking powder
1 teaspoon salt
4 large eggs
2 cups sugar
1 cup vegetable oil
1½ teaspoons vanilla extract
2 medium zucchini (¾ pound), coarsely grated
1 cup dark raisins
1 cup walnuts, coarsely chopped

"I like to break walnuts by hand instead of chopping them, so I bite into an actual chunk of nut in a slice of zucchini cake."
—Jerome

Chocolate-Banana Tea Loaves

12 tablespoons (1½ sticks)
unsalted butter, softened; plus
more for smearing in loaf pans

1¼ cups unbleached all-purpose
flour; plus more for dusting loaf
pans

¾ cup cocoa powder

1½ teaspoons baking soda

¾ teaspoon salt

1½ cups sugar

3 large eggs, lightly beaten

6 very ripe bananas, mashed (the
riper the sweeter; they can even
be black)

1 cup cold sour cream

This is by all definitions a cake shaped like a bread. And without icing. It is so rich and moist from sour cream, it doesn't need icing. Frank often serves this as dessert at home, in which case he undercooks the batter by 10 minutes. When he slices into the loaf, it spills all over, like half cake, half goopy chocolate dessert, which he serves with vanilla ice cream or Frank's Simple Whipped Cream (page 229). We even slightly undercook our "fully cooked" loaves, making them almost fudgy.

1. Position your oven racks so that one is in the center, and preheat the oven to 400 degrees. Smear two 5-by-9-inch loaf pans with butter, and dust them lightly with flour.

2. Whisk the flour, cocoa powder, baking soda, and salt together in a medium-size bowl.

3. In a separate, big bowl, cream the butter and sugar together, using the whisk attachment of a standing or handheld electric mixer on high speed (or a sturdy wire whisk), until the mixture is creamy and fluffy and a light lemon-yellow in color. With the mixer on low, beat in the eggs. Add the banana, and continue mixing at low speed until it is completely incorporated into the batter.

4. Stir half of the sour cream into the wet ingredients with the paddle attachment of the mixer (or with a wooden spoon). Fold in half the dry ingredients. Repeat, until all the ingredients are combined and not a trace of flour remains.

5. Use a rubber spatula to scrape the batter into the prepared loaf pans. Make sure to divide the batter equally between the two loaves, so they will require the same baking time.

6. Place the loaf pans side by side on the center rack in the oven, and bake for

70–75 minutes. We like to take these out before they're totally done, so the toothpick test is a bit tricky. A toothpick or small knife inserted into the edge of each loaf will come out clean. Inserted deep into the center, it will come out with a little bit of wet batter stuck to it. When the loaves are ready to come out of the oven, they will have split on top and pulled away from the sides of the pans.

7. Remove the loaves from the oven, and set them on a wire rack for a few minutes, until they are cool enough to touch. Don't worry when the lovely mounds on the top of the loaves fall, within minutes after coming out of the oven. This cake does that. To remove a loaf from its pan, place the rack over the top of the pan and quickly flip the pan so the loaf falls out onto the rack. Allow to cool a bit before slicing. Serve warm or at room temperature. If you are undercooking, as we indicated in the introduction to this recipe, don't remove the loaf from the pan at all. Just slice it and serve it hot.

"We use a European, Dutch-processed cocoa powder for these loaves. ('Dutch-processed' means it's been treated with alkali to reduce the cocoa's acidity.) That said, I've also made them with Hershey's cocoa powder and they turned out delicious."
—Frank

"Varying the speed of the blender is not a mystery. You cream the butter at high speed because you want it to get fluffy. You lower the speed when you add other ingredients, especially liquids, because you don't want them to splash all over the place."
—Jerome

Lemon–Poppy Seed Tea Loaves

½ pound (2 sticks) unsalted butter, softened; plus more for smearing in loaf pans

2 cups unbleached all-purpose flour; plus more for dusting loaf pans

1½ teaspoons baking powder

½ teaspoon salt

2 tablespoons poppy seeds

1½ cups sugar

3 large eggs, lightly beaten

1 tablespoon grated lemon zest (page 297)

¼ cup freshly squeezed lemon juice

½ cup cold milk

We worked long and hard to get this loaf as moist and as lemony as it is.

1. Position your oven racks so that one is in the center, and preheat the oven to 400 degrees. Smear two 5-by-9-inch loaf pans with butter, and dust them lightly with flour.

2. Whisk the flour, baking powder, salt, and poppy seeds together in a medium-size bowl.

3. In a separate, big bowl, cream the butter and sugar together, using the whisk attachment of a standing or handheld electric mixer on high speed (or a sturdy wire whisk), until they are fluffy and light lemon-yellow in color. With the mixer speed low, beat in the eggs, continuing with the lemon zest and juice. Don't worry if the batter looks lumpy, like there's cottage cheese in it; the lemon juice causes the batter to "break."

4. Using the paddle attachment of your mixer (or a wooden spoon), stir half the milk into the wet ingredients. Stir in half the flour. Stir in the remaining milk. Add the remaining flour, and stir until no flour is visible.

5. Scrape the batter into the prepared loaf pans with a rubber spatula. Make sure to divide batter evenly between the two pans, so that they require the same baking time.

6. Place the loaves side by side on the center rack in the oven, and bake them for 55 minutes to 1 hour, or until the tops are a very light golden brown and a toothpick or small knife inserted deep into the center of each loaf comes out clean.

7. Remove the loaves from the oven, and set them on a wire rack for a few minutes, until loaves are cool enough to touch. To remove a loaf from its pan, place the rack over the top of the pan, and quickly flip the pan so the loaf falls out onto the rack. Allow the loaves to cool a bit before slicing. Serve at room temperature.

Fresh Grated Ginger Gingerbread Tea Loaves

MAKES TWO 5-BY-9-INCH LOAVES (8–10 SLICES EACH)

We love the zingy flavor of fresh ginger, so we decided to try it in place of powdered ginger in our gingerbread. We loved it. So much that when you see how much ginger we call for, you might think it's a typo. It's not. This loaf makes a not-too-sweet dessert served warm with fresh berries and Frank's Simple Whipped Cream (page 229) or Very Lemony Curd (page 252).

½ pound (2 sticks) unsalted butter, softened; plus more for smearing in loaf pans

3 cups unbleached all-purpose flour; plus more for dusting loaf pans

2 teaspoons baking soda

1 teaspoon salt

1 cup packed light-brown sugar

½ cup molasses

½ cup dark corn syrup

2 large eggs

6 ounces fresh ginger (2 6-inch pieces), peeled and finely grated (page 75)

¼ cup orange marmalade

1 cup cold sour cream

1. Position your oven racks so that one is in the center, and preheat the oven to 350 degrees. Smear two 5-by-9-inch loaf pans with butter, and dust them lightly with flour.

2. Whisk the flour, baking soda, and salt together in a medium-size bowl.

3. In a separate, big bowl, cream the butter and sugar together, using the whisk attachment of a standing or handheld electric mixer at high speed (or a sturdy wire whisk), until they are fluffy and light lemon-yellow in color.

4. With the mixer on low, beat in the molasses and corn syrup. Continue mixing on low speed, and beat in the eggs, one at a time, then the ginger and the marmalade.

5. Using the paddle attachment of your mixer (or a wooden spoon), gently stir half the sour cream into the wet ingredients. Stir in half the dry ingredients until only a little flour remains visible. Stir in the remaining sour cream. Add the rest of the dry ingredients, and stir until there is no flour visible.

6. Use a rubber spatula to scrape the batter into the prepared loaf pans. Make sure to distribute the batter evenly between the two pans, so that they require the same baking time.

7. Place the loaves side by side on the center rack in the oven, and bake them for 55 minutes to 1 hour, or until a toothpick or small knife inserted deep into the cen-

ter of each loaf comes out clean. Be sure to cook these all the way through. If your toothpick or knife comes out the least bit wet, or if the center of the loaf tops appear wet or shiny, close the oven door and wait 10 minutes before checking them again.

8. Remove the loaves from the oven, and set on a wire rack for a few minutes, until they are cool enough to touch. To remove a loaf from its pan, place the rack over the top of the pan and quickly flip the pan so the gingerbread falls out onto the rack. Allow to cool before slicing. Serve warm or at room temperature.

Apple Spice Bundt Cake

MAKES ONE 9-INCH BUNDT CAKE

We make this very spiced cake only in the fall. At home, Frank covers it with Maple-Sugar Glaze.

1. Position your oven racks so that one is in the center, and preheat the oven to 350 degrees. Smear a Bundt pan with butter, and dust lightly with flour.
2. Whisk the flour, baking soda, cinnamon, nutmeg, cloves, and salt together in a medium-size bowl.
3. In a separate, big bowl, cream the butter and sugars together, using the whisk attachment of a standing or handheld electric mixer on high speed (or a sturdy wire whisk), until they're creamy and fluffy. With the mixer speed low, beat in the eggs one at a time, then the vanilla.
4. Using the paddle attachment of your mixer (or a wooden spoon), stir half the buttermilk into the butter mixture. Add half the dry ingredients, and stir until just a little visible flour remains. Stir in the remaining buttermilk. Add the rest of the dry ingredients, and stir until they are almost combined. Add the apples, and stir until no flour is visible. Don't worry if the batter looks very thick and heavy; that's the way it is. Try not to mix it any more than necessary. Scrape the batter into the Bundt pan using a rubber spatula to get it all out.
5. Place the pan on the center rack in the oven, and bake the cake for 50 minutes to 1 hour, or until a small knife or toothpick inserted into the center of the cake comes out clean.
6. Remove the cake from the oven, and set it on a wire rack. Let the cake rest for a few minutes.
7. To remove the cake from the pan, place a serving plate on top of the pan and quickly flip the pan so the cake falls out onto the plate.

½ pound (2 sticks) unsalted butter, softened; plus more for smearing in Bundt pan

3½ cups unbleached all-purpose flour; plus more for dusting Bundt pan

1½ teaspoons baking soda

1 tablespoon cinnamon

1 teaspoon nutmeg

1 teaspoon ground cloves

1½ teaspoons salt

1½ cups granulated sugar

1½ cups packed light-brown sugar

4 large eggs

2 teaspoons vanilla

1½ cups cold buttermilk

4 large tart apples, chopped (not peeled)

1 recipe Maple-Sugar Glaze (page 290), optional

"To make a Bundt cake out of any of the loaves, double the recipe and increase the baking time by 10–15 minutes."
—Frank

8. If you're using the glaze, drizzle it evenly over the top of the cake while it's still warm or after it has cooled to room temperature. The only difference is that the glaze will spread farther down the sides of a warm cake. Serve warm or at room temperature.

"Sometimes a nice ribbon is all you need to make a box of baked goods look special. We use seam binding at the store—it's soft and shiny and comes in all different colors. (And it's cheap.) Wander around a fabric or notions store for ideas. Or go to flea markets for vintage ribbons, wallpaper, dish towels, funky tin boxes, buckets. That's what I do."
—Frank

Maple-Sugar Glaze

2 tablespoons unsalted butter, softened
½ cup confectioners' sugar, sifted or passed through a
    mesh sieve
2 tablespoons maple syrup

In a small bowl, beat 2 tablespoons softened butter with confectioners' sugar until they are smooth and creamy. Beat in the maple syrup. Keep the glaze at room temperature until you're ready to use it. Chilled glaze won't drizzle.

Apple (or Peach) Batter Cake

This cake is so easy to make. All you do is throw the apples (or peaches) in the bottom of a cake pan, whip up a simple batter, pour it on top, and bake. The apples (or peaches) caramelize on the bottom of the pan, and the batter browns on the top. Flip it over, and what you have is something like a pineapple upside down cake.

1. Position your oven racks so that one is in the center, and preheat the oven to 350 degrees. Smear a 9-inch round cake pan with a generous amount of butter.
2. Toss the apple slices (or peach wedges) with the cinnamon and 1 tablespoon of the sugar. Spread the fruit evenly over the bottom of the cake pan.
3. Whisk the remaining sugar and the flour together in a big bowl. Whisk in the egg and melted butter until just a bit of flour remains visible. Stir in the walnuts, and continue stirring until no flour is visible. Pour the batter evenly over the fruit, using a rubber spatula or your finger to get it all out.
4. Place the pan on the center rack in the oven, and bake the cake for 40–45 minutes, or until top is golden brown and a toothpick or small knife inserted into the center comes out clean.
5. Remove the pan from the oven, and place it on a wire rack. Let the pan sit for a few minutes, until it is cool enough to touch. To remove the cake from the pan, put a serving plate over the top of the pan and quickly flip the pan over. The cake should come right out. If it doesn't, slide a table knife around the edges to loosen up any bits that are stuck. Serve warm or at room temperature.

12 tablespoons (1½ sticks) unsalted butter, melted and cooled to room temperature; plus more, cold, softened, or melted, for smearing in cake pan

5 or 6 medium-size tart apples (such as Granny Smith), peeled, cored, and cut into ¼-inch slices; or 5 big ripe peaches, peeled and cut into ½-inch wedges

1 tablespoon cinnamon

1 cup plus 1 tablespoon sugar

1 cup unbleached all-purpose flour

1 large egg, lightly beaten

1½ cups walnuts, coarsely chopped

Skillet Corn Bread

MAKES ONE 9- OR 10-INCH ROUND CORN BREAD (8 WEDGE-SHAPED SLICES)
OR ONE 5-BY-9-INCH LOAF

Frank eats this for breakfast, with softened butter and honey or maple syrup. It's denser than our corn muffins, and also sweeter. If you like a really sweet corn bread, you can add ⅓ cup of sugar to this recipe without doing any collateral damage to the bread. We bake this in a 9- or 10-inch cast-iron skillet, but it's also nice as a loaf.

1. Position your oven racks so that one is in the center, and preheat the oven to 450 degrees. Smear a cast-iron skillet (or 5-by-9-inch loaf pan) with butter.
2. Whisk the egg in a big bowl to break up the yolk. Whisk in the milk and butter.
3. In a separate, medium-size bowl, whisk the flours, cornmeal, sugar, baking powder, and salt together.
4. Gradually add the dry ingredients to the wet, stirring gently with a wooden spoon until there is no flour visible. Pour the batter into your skillet (or loaf pan), scraping down the sides of the bowl with a rubber spatula. Use the spatula to level the batter in the pan.
5. Place the skillet on the center rack in the oven, and bake the corn bread for 25–30 minutes, until the top is completely browned and a small knife or toothpick inserted deep into the center comes out clean.
6. Remove the skillet (or loaf pan) from the oven, and set it on a wire rack to cool slightly. Serve warm or at room temperature, sliced like a pie, straight from the skillet.

5 tablespoons unsalted butter, melted and cooled to room temperature; plus more, cold, softened, or melted, for smearing in skillet (or loaf pan)

1 large egg

1⅓ cups cold milk

1⅓ cups unbleached all-purpose flour

¼ cup whole-wheat flour

1 cup cornmeal

1 cup sugar

1 tablespoon plus 1 teaspoon baking powder

½ teaspoon salt

Fresh Berry Coffee Cake with Walnut Crumb Topping

This is not your average coffee cake, where you're lucky to get one bite of fruit with a big chunk of yellow cake. This one's loaded with fruit. In the fall and winter, we make it with apples or pears, but we like it best in the summer, because we like it best with fresh berries. The crumb topping sinks into the berries, the berries sink into the cake—it really is the perfect coffee cake. To make this with apples or pears, substitute 1½–2 pounds fruit, peeled and cut into small cubes, for the berries.

1. Position your oven racks so that one is in the center, and preheat the oven to 350 degrees. Smear a 13-by-9-inch cake pan with butter, and dust it lightly with flour.

2. Toss the topping ingredients into the bowl of a food processor fitted with a metal blade, and pulse until the topping looks moist and crumbly—like coffee-cake topping. Don't pulse it so much that it all comes together into a big ball of dough. Refrigerate the topping until you're ready to use it.

3. In a big bowl, cream the butter and sugar together, using the whisk attachment of a standing or handheld electric mixer on high speed (or a sturdy wire whisk), until they become fluffy and light lemon-yellow in color, about 5 minutes. Reduce the mixer speed to low, and beat in the eggs, one at a time, then the extracts.

4. Whisk the flour and other dry ingredients together in a separate, medium-size bowl.

5. Stir half the buttermilk into the wet ingredients with the paddle attachment of

FOR THE TOPPING

1 tablespoon unbleached all-purpose flour

½ cup walnuts, chopped fine

½ teaspoon cinnamon

½ cup packed light-brown sugar

2 tablespoons cold unsalted butter, cut into ½-inch cubes

¼ cup almond paste (page 211)

FOR THE CAKE

8 tablespoons unsalted butter (1 stick), softened; plus more, cold or softened, for smearing in cake pan

¾ cup granulated sugar

2 large eggs

1 teaspoon vanilla extract

½ teaspoon almond extract

2 cups unbleached all-purpose flour; plus more for dusting cake pan   *continued*

1 teaspoon baking powder

¼ teaspoon baking soda

½ teaspoon cinnamon

¼ teaspoon ground ginger

¼ teaspoon salt

½ cup cold buttermilk

1 cup fresh raspberries, rinsed and dried on paper towels (page 242)

1 cup fresh blueberries, rinsed and dried on paper towels

1 cup fresh strawberries, rinsed and dried on paper towels, and cut into pieces about the same size as other berries

your mixer on low speed (or with a wooden spoon). Stir in half the dry ingredients. Repeat until all the ingredients are combined and no flour is visible.

6. Use a rubber spatula to scrape the batter into the cake pan. Run the spatula over the batter in the pan to level it. Cover the batter with the fresh fruit. Sprinkle the topping in an even layer over the fruit.

7. Place the pan on the center rack in the oven, and bake the cake for 50 minutes to 1 hour, or until a toothpick or small knife inserted deep into the center of the cake comes out clean. The topping will be golden brown, and the cake itself will have risen through the gaps between the fruit.

8. Remove the pan from the oven, and place it on a wire rack for a few minutes to cool before cutting the cake into squares.

"If you have access to fresh local berries in the summer, chances are there'll be a short window wherein they're pretty affordable. Take advantage of this by buying extra. Just rinse the berries, dry them, throw them in Ziploc plastic bags, and freeze them."
—Frank

How to Grate Lemons (and Oranges and Limes)

"Zest" refers to the outermost, bright-colored layer of the peel of citrus fruits. This is where the aromatic oils and flavor are. Zest does *not* include the lighter, pithy part of the skin. That's the rind, and it tends to be bitter. So, when a recipe calls for the "grated zest of 1 lemon," you just want to make one pass around the lemon—taking off only the bright-colored top layer.

There's actually a special tool called a "citrus zester" that pulls about five tiny strips of zest from the skin all at once. These strips are bigger—and definitely prettier—than plain ol' gratings. Neither of us owns one of these tools. If you happen to have one, or if you like decorating your food, put the strips of lemon zest on any lemony dessert, like the Baked Lemon Tart (page 207), or the Carrot Cake Muffins with Lemon–Cream Cheese Icing (page 279).

Remember, if you're going to need both the zest and juice of the citrus, you need to grate them *before* you squeeze the juice out of them. Frank uses one of those old-fashioned glass cone-shaped things where you squeeze the juice out with your hand. He thinks his is really special because it strains out the bigger pulp and seeds.

Jerome on the Importance of Fat

We do not make nonfat muffins at Once Upon a Tart. And I'm sure we suffer the consequences of that. Many people don't want to eat fat. "You have nothing nonfat?" they'll ask. They'll just have a tea, and I'm sure they don't come back. One of our regular customers bugged us for a long time to make nonfat muffins. Even though I was opposed to the idea of a nonfat muffin, I did play around with them for a while. I tried using purées, like applesauce, to give them moisture without adding fat. And I used egg whites, but no yolks. I threw some ginger and raisins in there, trying to add flavor. But they were all disgusting. They all had a weird rubbery texture you get from using only egg whites in a muffin. And they just didn't taste good. Which is why we use butter. And cream. And eggs.

Once Upon a ...
COOKIE

Chewy Oatmeal-Raisin-Walnut Cookies

Crunchy Dried Cranberry–Chocolate Chip Cookies

My Mother's Are Better Ginger Cookies

Our Original Very Ginger Cookies

Raisin-Spice Cookies with Sugar Icing

Best Big Chocolate Chip Cookies

Variation: The Cookie Frank Is Most Likely to Bake on a Rainy Day

Rosie's Peanut Butter Cookies

Classic Coconut Macaroons

Chocolate-Pecan French-Style Macaroons

Hazelnut Meringues

Honey Madeleines

Crispy Sugar Cookies

Variation: Dark-Chocolate Sugar Cookies

Royal Icing

Chocolate Chip–Hazelnut Biscotti

Almond-Raisin Biscotti

Pumpkin-Cranberry Biscotti

Cornmeal-Almond Biscotti

Pine Nut Cookies

Fudgy Brownies

When we began making cookies, shortly after we opened the store, we started with the three American classics: oatmeal raisin, chocolate chip, and peanut butter.

"In France," Jerome says, "our cookies are very tiny, very thin, very delicate, very buttery, and very simple. They are sold by weight and usually served with ice cream. You don't have the big cookies like you have here. I like chocolate chip cookies, but I don't love them. Now, Frank, he *loves* them." And Frank, he got his way.

We had no idea at the time how convenient cookies would be in terms of our production needs. If we had to make every item in the store from flour to finish the moment we needed it (like we do with muffins and scones, for instance), we'd need an army of bakers in the kitchen. And we'd need a much bigger kitchen! The great thing about cookie dough, which many of you might know from your slice-and-bake days, is that it can be made in advance. We now keep a full repertoire of prepared doughs in the refrigerator. When we are running low on cookies at the store, we reach for our dough, throw some on the baking sheet, and 30 minutes later our jars are full of fresh warm cookies.

The recipes in this chapter are our standards, refined through years of experimenting. "Each variation on an ingredient changes the taste and texture of the cookie so much," Frank says. (This kind of thing excites him.) "Like putting in more butter, or more brown sugar, changing honey for sugar . . ." Frank will tinker for hours until he gets just the texture he wants. Hey, he changed his *mother's* Peanut Butter Cookie recipe.

At one point, Frank had so many jars of cookies in the store that we couldn't fit them all on the counter. Since then, Jerome has made a rule: for every new thing we make, we have to take one away. Otherwise, he thinks, we'll offer so many random items that we'll lose our identity. The rule is more like a goal. "Sometimes we just can't help ourselves," Frank confesses. Like in the case of the Cornmeal-Almond Biscotti (page 341). "We made them. We put them out there. And then we couldn't take them away. They were just too popular." Still, none of them is as popular as those first three, the classics. That's why classics are classics. People love them, and come back to them.

THINGS TO KNOW

Many of our cookie recipes are hand-me-downs from friends, family, and customers. Cookies are like that. Everyone has a recipe that he or she loves. Even people who don't bake are likely to have a standby cookie that they'll whip up when they have an unexpected domestic urge, or when the weather turns cold. It's those smells, wafting through the house, warding off the weather outside, as much as the finished product itself, that people find comforting.

The fact that cookies are quick and easy to make is probably what makes them so popular. The only things you need to keep in mind are some basic principles of baking. Things like: read the recipe through and get all your ingredients out before starting; preheat your oven; measure carefully, using dry measuring cups for dry ingredients and liquid measuring cups for wet ingredients. And, of course, a basic understanding and respect for the creaming method.

What with the word *method* stuck on there, creaming sounds like more than it is. The creaming method simply refers to the step in making cookie dough (and sometimes cake batter) where butter and sugar are whipped together. The most common error here is to simply whip the two until they're mixed. But, in fact, they should be whipped and whipped and whipped—using an electric mixer or a sturdy wire whisk and a whole lot of wrist work—until they are transformed into something light and fluffy in both texture and color. The concept behind this creaming is that the excessive beating incorporates air into the mix, which somehow makes the cookies what we want them to be in the end—chewy on the inside and not caky at all. We believe deeply in the creaming method where it is appropriate.

Cookies can be divided into a few categories, each of which is based on different techniques. Sugar cookies fall into the category of rolled cookies, because they're rolled out, then cut with a cookie cutter.

Drop cookies are those whose dough is dropped on a baking sheet. These include chocolate chip, oatmeal, and peanut butter. Drop cookies spread out and flatten when they're baked. We press ours down with the heel of our hand before baking, because we make ours big—and big cookies tend be doughy in the middle, or caky if you don't do this. If you make the drop cookies small, it's not necessary to flatten the dough unless, like us, you prefer a thinner cookie. In this case, simply press down on each ball of dough with the back of the spoon you dropped it with.

Another kind of cookie that we make is biscotti. Biscotti means "cookies" in Italian. In English, "biscotti" refers to a very specific kind of Italian cookie. A cookie that is baked first in a log, then sliced, then baked again. A cookie that is, therefore, quite hard. In Italy, biscotti are traditionally dipped in either espresso or wine, which is why they are so hard. Ours aren't so hard, which isn't to say they wouldn't be perfect for dipping in either espresso or wine. We've also taken the liberty of adding all kinds of crazy things that Italians wouldn't dare add to their biscotti—chocolate chips, cornmeal, pumpkin! Some people might think we're excessive. We're simply interested in making things taste better. You can do the first baking of biscotti on one day and cut them, and do the second baking another day. We often do that at the store. Biscotti are cut on the diagonal because the cookies are longer that way.

The last type of cookie we make is characterized by egg whites that have been whipped up to form stiff peaks: meringues and macaroons. Most Americans think that the word "macaroon" refers only to the coconut lumps, and in fact those *are* macaroons, but not *our* macaroons. Technically speaking, macaroons are cookies made with egg whites—no yolks—and often ground nuts, while meringues are made only of stiffly beaten egg whites and sugar.

The secret that makes baking cookies convenient for us can make them convenient for you at home. That is: You can make the dough in advance. You can also double any of these recipes without a problem, baking what you want and refrigerating or freezing the rest. If you're going to freeze dough, you'll want to roll it into logs. That way, when the urge to bake strikes, you don't have to wait for the dough to thaw completely. You can simply use a big sharp knife to, well, . . . slice and bake. Back to the beginning.

There's a big difference between softened and melted butter when you're making cookies. If a recipe calls for softened and you don't have time to let the butter soften at room temperature, resist the temptation to melt it on the stove or throw it in a microwave. Better to cut the butter into very small pieces and use an electric mixer to break it up before adding even the sugar to it. "At home, I often end up doing it this way," Frank says, "because I don't get inspired to bake far enough in advance. When I want to make cookies, I want to make them *now*."

We like to use parchment paper to line baking sheets. For cookies it's not necessary, but using parchment paper makes it easier to clean the pan and to remove the cookies from the pan. It also saves time: you can slide the whole thing off— parchment paper and cookies together—while the cookies are still hot, enabling you to use the pan for the next batch without having to wait for that batch of cookies to cool.

If you're using more than one baking sheet and you can only fit one on each oven rack, switch the sheets midway through baking to make sure the cookies bake evenly. At home, Frank says, "I work in a rotation. I put one baking sheet on the higher rack, then make the rest of the cookies. Before I put the second sheet in the oven, I switch the one already baking to the lower rack, then place the new batch on the higher rack, and on the cycle goes." From our experience with customers, we've found that some like their cookies soft and chewy, others prefer them crispy, so baking times will vary. Make them how you like them. And if you don't know how you like them, experiment with different baking times to find out.

Cookies make great gifts. Everyone loves cookies. And they're easy to package in a creative way. We like an assortment of cookies best—a vintage lunchbox filled with the classics: peanut butter, chocolate chip, and oatmeal. Or a bakery box filled with all kinds of cookies, all made about the size of a quarter. Brown coffee-bean bags also make great packages for cookies. If that's not fancy enough for you, stamp the bag first, or wrap a ribbon around the bag that's as wide as the bag itself.

Chewy Oatmeal-Raisin-Walnut Cookies

MAKES 20 BIG COOKIES (OR 5 DOZEN SMALLER COOKIES)

½ pound (2 sticks) unsalted butter, softened

1¾ cups packed light-brown sugar

2 large eggs

⅓ cup honey

1½ cups unbleached all-purpose flour

4 cups rolled oats (not quick-cook or instant)

1½ teaspoons ground cinnamon

½ teaspoon salt

1½ cups walnuts, coarsely chopped

1½ cups dark raisins

"I love baking with honey. Because it doesn't just sweeten—it adds flavor."
—Frank

We put honey in these to make them chewier (and also because Frank's obsessed with honey). For the same reason, we undercook them ever so slightly.

1. Position your oven racks so that one is in the center, and preheat the oven to 400 degrees.
2. Cream the butter and sugar together in a big bowl, using the whisk attachment of an electric mixer at high speed (or a sturdy wire whisk), until they are fluffy and light lemon-yellow in color, about 5 minutes. With the mixer speed on low, beat in the eggs one at a time, then the honey.
3. Whisk the flour, oats, cinnamon, and salt together in a separate, medium-size bowl. Gradually add these dry ingredients to the wet ingredients, using the paddle attachment of your mixer on low speed (or stirring with a wooden spoon) until there is no flour visible. Then stir in the walnuts and raisins.
4. To make big cookies, use a ⅓-cup measuring cup or your hand (eyeballing for size) to scoop out the dough for each cookie. Roll the dough into a ball between your hands. Have some flour handy to dust your hands in case the dough is too sticky to work with. Place the balls on the baking sheet, leaving 3 inches between them, then flatten them all with the heel of your hand until they are ⅓ inch thick and about 4 inches in diameter. To make smaller cookies, use a teaspoon to scoop up the dough, and your finger to scrape it onto the baking sheet. Drop the cookies with 1½ inches between them—no flattening necessary.
5. Place the baking sheet on the center rack in the oven, and bake for 16–18 minutes (10–12 minutes for small cookies), until the edges of the cookies are brown and the centers no longer look like raw dough. You don't want to overcook

these, or they'll be hard and crispy when they cool, rather than moist and chewy, the way we like them.

6. Remove the baking sheet from the oven, and place it on a rack to let the cookies cool slightly. Lift the baking sheet off the rack, and use a metal spatula to transfer the cookies to the rack to cool completely. If you're using parchment paper, there's no need to let the cookies cool on a rack. Slide the paper with the hot cookies off the baking sheet and onto a flat surface to cool.

"A great way to tell if cookies are done is to lift one up with a metal spatula. If it's brown underneath, it's done. Or touch one—it will be soft, because it's warm, but it shouldn't be goopy-soft, like there's raw dough inside."
—Frank

Crunchy Dried Cranberry–Chocolate Chip Cookies

MAKES 2 DOZEN BIG COOKIES (OR 6 DOZEN SMALLER COOKIES)

½ pound (2 sticks) unsalted butter, softened

1 cup granulated sugar

1 cup packed light-brown sugar

2 large eggs

1 teaspoon vanilla extract

1 cup plus 2 tablespoons unbleached all-purpose flour

½ cup wheat germ

3 cups rolled oats (not quick-cook or instant)

1 teaspoon baking powder

1 teaspoon baking soda

½ teaspoon salt

½ cup semisweet chocolate chips; or 3 ounces good-quality dark chocolate, broken into pieces

½ cup dried cranberries

1 cup walnuts, coarsely chopped

This is Jerome's favorite cookie—he eats at least one a day. We got the recipe from an editor at *Martha Stewart Living*. She asked Jerome for a recipe for a French cookie to publish in the magazine. He gave it to her, and as a thank-you she gave us this: her nanny's recipe, and her childhood cookie favorite. The wheat germ gives it a unique, airy kind of crunch.

1. Position your oven racks so that one is in the center, and preheat the oven to 350 degrees.
2. Cream the butter and sugars together in a big bowl, using the whisk attachment of an electric mixer on high speed (or a sturdy wire whisk), until they are fluffy and light lemon-yellow in color, about 5 minutes.
3. With the mixer speed low, beat in the eggs one at time, then the vanilla.
4. In a separate, medium-size bowl, whisk the flour, wheat germ, oats, baking powder, baking soda, and salt together.
5. Gradually add the dry ingredients to the wet ingredients, using the paddle attachment of your mixer on low speed (or stirring with a wooden spoon) until no flour is visible. Then stir in the chocolate chips, cranberries, and nuts.
6. To make big cookies, use a ⅓-cup measuring cup or your hand (eyeballing for size) to scoop out the dough. Roll the dough for each cookie between your hands into a ball. Have some flour handy to dust your hands in case the dough is too sticky to work with. Place the balls on your baking sheet, leaving 3 inches between them, and flatten them all with the heel of your hand until they are about 4 inches in diameter. To make smaller cookies, use a teaspoon to scoop up

the dough, and your finger to scrape it onto the baking sheet. Drop the cookies 1½ inches apart—no flattening necessary.

7. Place the baking sheet on the center rack in the oven, and bake the cookies for 18–20 minutes, or until cookies are golden brown all over (10–12 minutes for small cookies). You don't want to undercook these; they're best crispy.

8. Remove the baking sheet from the oven, and place it on a wire rack to let the cookies cool slightly. Lift the baking sheet off the rack, and use a metal spatula to transfer the cookies to the rack to cool completely. If you're using parchment paper, there's no need to let the cookies cool on a rack. Slide the paper with the hot cookies off the baking sheet and onto a flat surface to cool.

My Mother's Are Better Ginger Cookies

MAKES 18 BIG COOKIES (OR 66 SMALLER COOKIES)

2 cups sugar, plus more for rolling
cookies

2 large eggs

½ cup molasses

1½ cups solid vegetable shortening, melted and cooled to room
temperature

4 cups unbleached all-purpose flour

1 tablespoon cocoa powder

1 teaspoon ground ginger

1 teaspoon ground cloves

2 teaspoons cinnamon

2 teaspoons baking soda

1 teaspoon salt

We had a customer who came into the store about a year after we opened and said something like: "Your ginger cookies are great, but my mother's are better." Then she gave us the recipe. We did a taste test that day with our customers. We often do this when we're trying something new: offer samples to our customers, then poll them for results. Well, our customers voted on the woman's mom's cookies. We give you both recipes here and invite you to conduct your own taste test. (This is the new recipe—the one we sell at the store now.)

1. Position your oven racks so that one is in the center, and preheat the oven to 350 degrees.

2. In a big bowl, beat the sugar and eggs together, using the whisk attachment of an electric mixer on high speed (or a sturdy wire whisk), until they are light yellow in color. With the mixer on low speed, beat in the molasses, then the shortening.

3. In a separate, medium-size bowl, whisk the flour, cocoa powder, spices, baking soda, and salt together. Gradually add this to the wet ingredients, using the paddle attachment of your mixer on low speed (or stirring with a wooden spoon) until no flour is visible.

4. To make big cookies, use a ⅓-cup measuring cup or your hands (eyeballing for size) to scoop out the dough. Roll the dough for each cookie between your hands into a ball. Pour a handful of sugar onto a small plate. Roll the ball of dough in the sugar so that it is coated all the way around. Place the balls on your baking sheet, leaving 3 inches between them, and flatten them all with the heel of your hand until they are about 4 inches in diameter. To make smaller cookies, use a teaspoon to scoop up the dough, drop the cookies 1½ inches apart, and sprinkle with sugar—no flattening necessary.

5. Place the baking sheet on the center rack in the oven, and bake the cookies for 18–20 minutes (10–12 minutes for smaller cookies), or until they're a deep-brown color.

6. Remove the baking sheet from the oven, and place it on a wire rack to let the cookies cool slightly. Lift the baking sheet off the rack, and use a metal spatula to transfer the cookies to the rack to cool completely. If you're using parchment paper, there's no need to let the cookies cool on a rack. Slide the paper with the hot cookies off the baking sheet and onto a flat surface to cool.

"There's a rule in baking, When you smell it, it's done. I don't know about the science here. But it's a good indicator. If you're in the other room enjoying the nice smells of your cookies, you better get up and take them out!"
—Frank

Our Original Very Ginger Cookies

12 tablespoons (1½ sticks)
    unsalted butter, softened

2 cups sugar

2 large eggs

½ cup molasses

½ teaspoon balsamic vinegar

3¾ cups unbleached all-purpose
    flour

1½ teaspoons baking soda

2 tablespoons ground ginger

½ teaspoon cinnamon

¼ teaspoon ground cloves

Once in a while, we still make our original ginger cookies just to please ourselves. "I love this cookie," Jerome says. "Because I love ginger—I like it candied, pickled, I love piles of it. I love ginger fresh, and I love it in cookies." So that settles that. The balsamic vinegar in the recipe enhances the already very gingery flavor.

1. Position your oven racks so that one is in the center, and preheat the oven to 350 degrees.

2. Cream the butter and sugar together in a big bowl, using the whisk attachment of an electric mixer on high speed (or a sturdy wire whisk), until they are light lemon-yellow in color. Don't worry if the mixture seems a bit dry; it's supposed to be that way. With the mixer on low speed, beat in the eggs, one at a time, then the molasses and the vinegar.

3. In a separate, medium-size bowl, whisk the flour, baking soda, and spices together. Gradually add these dry ingredients to the wet, using the paddle attachment of the mixer on low speed (or stirring with a wooden spoon) until no flour is visible.

4. To make big cookies, use a ⅓-cup measuring cup or your hand (eyeballing for size) to scoop out the dough. Roll the dough for each cookie between your hands into a ball. Have some flour handy to dust your hands in case the dough is too sticky to work with. Place the balls on your baking sheet, leaving 3 inches between them, and flatten them with the heel of your hand until they are about 4 inches in diameter. To make smaller cookies, use a teaspoon to scoop up the dough and your finger to scrape it onto the baking sheet. Drop the cookies 1½ inches apart—no flattening necessary.

5. Place baking sheet on the center rack in the oven, and bake the cookies for

18–20 minutes (10–12 minutes for small cookies), until they are cooked through and crackly on the top. If you're going to overcook any cookie slightly, this is the one. These are nice hard, like gingersnaps.

6. Remove the baking sheet from the oven, and place it on a wire rack to let the cookies cool slightly. Lift the baking sheet off the rack, and use a metal spatula to transfer the cookies to the rack to cool completely. If you're using parchment paper, there's no need to let the cookies cool on a rack. Slide the paper with the hot cookies off the baking sheet and onto a flat surface to cool.

"I use unsalted butter in baking and cooking, so that I can control the amount of salt I put in my food. I use salted butter for toast. That's it."
—Frank

Raisin-Spice Cookies with Sugar Icing

½ pound (2 sticks) unsalted butter, softened

2 cups packed light-brown sugar

2 large eggs

½ cup cold sour cream

½ cup cold milk

4 cups unbleached all-purpose flour

1 tablespoon plus 1 teaspoon baking powder

2 teaspoons cinnamon

½ teaspoon nutmeg

½ teaspoon ground cloves

¼ teaspoon salt

2½ cups dark raisins

FOR THE ICING

1 teaspoon light cream

A drop of vanilla extract

2 tablespoons confectioners' sugar

These cookies are very soft and have a big spice flavor. They're a winter thing. A Christmas cookie, actually. We can't bring ourselves to make them in the summer, for philosophical as well as practical reasons: the icing melts.

1. Position your oven racks so that one is in the center, and preheat the oven to 350 degrees.
2. Cream the butter and sugar together in a big bowl, using the whisk attachment of an electric mixer at high speed (or a sturdy wire whisk), until they are fluffy and light lemon-yellow in color, about 5 minutes. With the mixer on low speed, beat in the eggs, one at a time.
3. Whisk the sour cream and milk together in a small bowl. Add this to the butter mixture, beating at low speed so the liquid doesn't fly out of the bowl.
4. In a separate, medium-size bowl, whisk the flour, baking powder, cinnamon, nutmeg, cloves, and salt together. Gradually add this to wet ingredients, using the paddle attachment of your mixer on low speed (or stirring with a wooden spoon) until no flour is visible. Then stir in the raisins.
5. Cover the dough and refrigerate it for at least an hour to harden it. (If you want to skip this step, you can. It just means stickier dough, to be splattered onto the baking sheet.)
6. To make big cookies, use a ⅓-cup measuring cup or your hand (eyeballing for size) to scoop out the dough. Roll the dough for each cookie between your hands into a ball. Place balls on baking sheet, leaving 3 inches between them, and flatten them with the heel of your hand until they are about 4 inches in diameter. (To make smaller cookies, use a teaspoon to scoop up the dough and

your finger to scrape it onto the baking sheet. Drop the cookies 1½ inches apart—no flattening necessary.)

7. Place the baking sheet on the center rack in the oven, and bake the cookies for 18–20 minutes (10–12 minutes for small cookies), or until the cookies are golden brown and puffy and no longer look the least bit wet.

8. Remove the baking sheet from the oven, and place on a wire rack to allow the cookies to cool slightly. Lift the baking sheet off the rack, and use a metal spatula to transfer the cookies off the baking sheet and onto the rack to cool to room temperature. Don't be alarmed if they fall as they cool—they're supposed to do that. If you're using parchment paper, there's no need to let the cookies cool on a rack. Slide the paper with the hot cookies off the baking sheet and onto a flat surface to cool.

9. Whisk the cream and vanilla together in a small bowl. Add the confectioners' sugar through a sieve or sifter, and whisk until the icing is smooth. Use a pastry brush to top each cookie with the icing. (If you don't have a pastry brush, spoon the icing onto the cookie and use the back of the spoon to spread it over the tops.)

Jerome on Butter

The quality of the butter makes a difference in our cookies and other baked goods. At Once Upon a Tart, we only use Grade AA butter. Look on the package: it tells you if the butter is AA. In France, butter is treated as a special thing, not a packaged thing. You buy butter at the cheese shop. It makes sense, doesn't it? They scoop it from a big crate that has red-and-white fabric around the inside. Even the modern grocery store in France has only good-quality butter. I eat a lot of butter. Someday, get yourself some Lescour butter. It's so good. A slice of butter on a piece of bread—you really get the taste of butter.

Best Big Chocolate Chip Cookies

20 tablespoons (2½ sticks)
unsalted butter, softened

1½ cups packed light-brown sugar

2 large eggs

1 teaspoon vanilla extract

3¼ cups unbleached all-purpose
flour

1½ teaspoons baking soda

1½ teaspoons salt

2 cups semisweet chocolate chips;
or 12 ounces good-quality dark
chocolate, broken into pieces

Everyone loves chocolate chip cookies, so we didn't set out to do anything unusual to this one. We did load it with chocolate chips. They are, hands down, our best-selling cookies. We never have even a single one left at the end of the day.

1. Position your oven racks so that one is in the center, and preheat the oven to 350 degrees.
2. Cream the butter and sugar together in a big bowl, using the whisk attachment of an electric mixer on high speed (or a sturdy wire whisk), until they are fluffy and light lemon-yellow in color, about 5 minutes. With the mixer on low speed, beat in the eggs one at a time, then the vanilla.
3. In a separate, medium-size bowl, whisk the flour, baking soda, and salt together. Gradually add this to wet ingredients, using the paddle attachment of your mixer on low speed (or stirring with a wooden spoon) until no flour is visible. Then stir in the chocolate chips.
4. To make big cookies, use a ⅓-cup measuring cup or your hand (eyeballing for size) to scoop out the dough. Roll the dough for each cookie between your hands into a ball. Have some flour handy to dust your hands in case the dough is too sticky to work with. Place the balls on your baking sheet, leaving 2 inches between them, and flatten each with the heel of your hand until it is about 4 inches in diameter. To make smaller cookies, use a teaspoon to scoop up the dough and your finger to scrape it onto the baking sheet. Drop the cookies 1½ inches apart—no flattening necessary.
5. Place the baking sheet on the center rack in the oven, and bake the cookies for 18–20 minutes (10–12 minutes for smaller cookies), or until the cookie centers no longer have the shiny look of raw dough.

6. Remove the baking sheet from the oven, and place on a wire rack to cool slightly. Lift the baking sheet off the rack, and use a metal spatula to lift the cookies off the sheet and onto the rack to cool completely. If you're using parchment paper, there's no neeed to let the cookies cool on the rack. Slide the paper with the hot cookies off the baking sheet and onto a flat surface to cool.

"When I bake, I'm constantly dipping my hands into the three jars—raisins, chocolate chips, and walnuts—making my own little trail mix to snack on as I wait for that first cookie."
—Frank

Variation: The Cookie Frank Is Most Likely to Bake on a Rainy Day

MAKES 4 DOZEN COOKIES

Making cookies reminds Frank of Christmas, when all his Italian aunts would form a production line in the kitchen, making crescent cookies and rum balls and pine nut cookies and deep-fried bows and knots with icing. More than his own family's Italian cookies, though, he loved chocolate chip cookies. The same friend's mother who introduced Frank to Wonder bread could be counted on to pull a batch of warm chocolate chip cookies out of the oven just as the boys walked in the door after school. "To this day," Frank insists, "I stop by to visit and there she is, taking a sheet of chocolate chip cookies out of the oven." Someday the neighborhood kids will probably say the same thing about Frank, though he throws everything but the kitchen sink into his chocolate chip cookies.

Prepare the dough and drop and bake the cookies in same way as our Best Big Chocolate Chip Cookies (page 314). Frank always makes small cookies at home. He fills the cookie jar, and, barring any unforeseen indulgences, they last the week.

2 cups unbleached all-purpose flour
1 teaspoon baking soda
¾ teaspoon salt
½ pound (2 sticks) unsalted butter, softened
½ cup granulated sugar
1 cup packed light-brown sugar
2 teaspoons vanilla extract
2 large eggs
1½ cups semisweet chocolate chips; or 9 ounces good-quality dark chocolate, broken into pieces
2 cups rolled oats (not quick-cook or instant)
½ cup pecans, coarsely chopped
½ cup dark raisins

Rosie's Peanut Butter Cookies

MAKES 16 BIG COOKIES (OR 4 DOZEN SMALLER COOKIES)

½ pound (2 sticks) unsalted butter,
  softened
½ cup granulated sugar
1½ cups packed light-brown sugar
1½ cups commercial peanut butter
  (we use smooth, but if you like
  crunch, use crunchy)
2 large eggs
1 teaspoon vanilla extract
2½ cups unbleached all-purpose
  flour
1½ teaspoons baking soda
½ teaspoon salt

Frank's mother, Rosie, is famous for her peanut butter cookies. When we were developing our cookie menu, we figured, why mess with success? Of course, Frank still had to make adjustments; he's just that way. Because he's big on texture, when he makes these at home he throws in a handful of chopped roasted and salted peanuts. We don't do this at the store, because our customers would be unhappy if we monkeyed with something as standard as a peanut butter cookie. These are cookies you should bake only as you want to eat them: the peanut butter taste seems to fade with time.

1. Position your oven racks so that one is in the center, and preheat the oven to 350 degrees.
2. Cream the butter and sugars together in a big bowl, using the whisk attachment of an electric mixer on high speed (or a wire whisk), until they are fluffy and light lemon-yellow in color, about 5 minutes. Add the peanut butter, and continue beating at high speed until it is incorporated with the butter. With the mixer on low speed, beat in the eggs, one at a time, then the vanilla.
3. In a separate, medium-size bowl, whisk the flour, baking soda, and salt together. Gradually add these dry ingredients to the wet, stirring with a wooden spoon (or the paddle attachment of your mixer on low speed) until no flour is visible.
4. To make big cookies, use a ⅓-cup measuring cup or your hand to scoop out the dough. Roll the dough for each cookie between your hands into a ball. Have some flour handy to dust your hands in case the dough is too sticky to work with. If it is still too sticky, which it may be, refrigerate the dough for an hour. Place the balls on your baking sheet, leaving 2 inches between them, and flatten them with the heel of your hand until they are about 4 inches in diameter. To

make smaller cookies, use a spoon to scoop up the dough and your finger to scrape it onto the baking sheet. Drop the cookies 1½ inches apart—no flattening necessary.

5. We always make our peanut butter cookies with crosshatching. Because the diameter of these cookies is longer than your average fork, we press the fork in and then drag it along the length of the big cookies, or simply press down on the smaller cookies.

6. Place the baking sheet on the center rack in the oven, and bake the cookies for 18–20 minutes (10–12 minutes for small cookies), or until cookies are golden brown around the edges.

7. Remove the baking sheet from the oven, and place it on a wire rack to let the cookies cool slightly. Lift the baking sheet off the rack, and use a metal spatula to transfer the cookies to the rack to cool completely. If you're using parchment paper, there's no need to let the cookies cool on the rack. Slide the paper with the hot cookies off the baking sheet and onto a flat surface to cool.

"If you're working with dough that is chilled, or if you want thin cookies, pat the cookies down with the back of a spoon or your hand. I do this with all my drop cookies. But that's me: I like thin cookies."
—Frank

Classic Coconut Macaroons

MAKES 14 BIG COOKIES (OR 42 KISS-SIZE COOKIES)

One weekend, we had to make a bunch of cookies for a photo shoot for a Martha Stewart commercial. We had way more work than we could handle, and so one of our regular customers—a lawyer who lives in the neighborhood and whose fantasy it is to own a bakery—volunteered to help us. She refused to take any money. And when it was over, she left us this recipe which we still make. These couldn't be any easier or quicker to make.

4 large egg whites, at room
   temperature
½ cup sugar
4 cups unsweetened shredded
   coconut
½ cup unbleached all-purpose flour
½ teaspoon almond extract
1 teaspoon vanilla extract
3 tablespoons honey

1. Position your oven racks so that one is in the center, and preheat the oven to 350 degrees. Line a baking sheet with parchment paper.
2. Beat the egg whites in a big bowl, using the whisk attachment of an electric mixer at high speed (or a sturdy wire whisk), until peaks form. Slowly add the sugar, and continue beating a few more minutes.
3. In a separate, medium-size bowl, mix the coconut and flour together, then dump this into the bowl with the egg whites, and stir gently using the paddle attachment of your mixer on low speed (or a wooden spoon). Add the extracts and the honey, and mix until all the ingredients are combined.
4. To make big cookies, dip a ¼-cup measuring cup in a cup of hot water before using it to scoop out the batter. Use a strong flick of the wrist to get the batter out of the cup and onto the baking sheet. Dip the cup in the hot water again before scooping again, and continue until you've used up all the batter, dropping the cookies 2 inches apart. To make kiss-size cookies, dip a teaspoon in a cup of hot water, then scoop up the dough. Scrape the dough off the spoon and onto your baking sheet, leaving 1½ inches between them. For large or small cookies, use your fingers to pinch each macaroon into the shape of a chocolate kiss.
5. Place the baking sheet on the center rack in the oven, and bake the macaroons

for 18–20 minutes (7–8 minutes for small cookies), or until the edges of the cookies are golden brown.

6. Remove the baking sheet from the oven, and place it on a wire rack to allow the cookies to cool slightly. Lift the baking sheet off the rack, and slide the parchment paper, cookies and all, onto the rack to let the macaroons cool completely.

Chocolate-Pecan French-Style Macaroons

MAKES 14 BIG COOKIES (OR 42 SMALLER COOKIES)

4 large egg whites, at room
temperature
1½ cups sugar
1 cup plus 2 tablespoons cocoa
powder
3 cups pecans, ground fine

"Egg yolks left over from macaroons and meringues are a great excuse to make lemon curd."
—Frank

At the store, we keep the jar of these right next to the cash register. People often grab one with their afternoon coffee or tea. They consider these cookies less of a commitment than our big cookies. Meanwhile, these are as rich as anything we make. And what's more: people become addicted to them. They're crispy on the outside and, being slightly underbaked, chewy and gooey on the inside. They're really rather extraordinary.

1. Position your oven racks so that one is in the center, and preheat the oven to 350 degrees. Line a baking sheet with parchment paper.

2. Beat egg whites in a big bowl, using the whisk attachment of an electric mixer at high speed (or a sturdy wire whisk), until peaks form. Add the sugar to combine. Stop the mixer and use the spatula to fold in the cocoa powder and the pecans, scraping down the sides of the bowl as you go, until there's not a trace of dry cocoa powder left and the cocoa looks like it's evenly blended with the egg whites. Don't worry if this batter looks wet. It's because there's no flour in it, and it's supposed to be that way.

3. Dip a ¼-cup measuring cup in a cup of hot water, then use it to scoop out the batter. Knock the cup against the baking sheet to get the batter out. Dip the mea-

suring cup in the hot water again before scooping out more dough, and continue this process, leaving 2 inches between cookies, until you've used up all the batter. To make smaller macaroons, use a teaspoon, also dipped in hot water, to scoop up your dough, and your finger to drop it onto your baking sheet, leaving 1½ inches between them. Use your fingers to pinch the cookies (large or small) into the shape of a chocolate kiss.

4. Bake the cookies for 10 minutes, or until a very thin crust has formed on the outside. It's important to undercook these slightly, and not to let them dry out, as with other egg-whites-only cookies. We recommend testing. Take one out of the oven with a metal spatula and open it up. The inside should be wet and look a bit raw—but not so much that the insides pour out.

5. Remove the baking sheet from the oven, and place it on a wire rack to allow the cookies to cool slightly. Lift the baking sheet off the rack, and slide the parchment paper, cookies and all, onto a rack to let the cookies cool completely.

"The easiest way to remove an eggshell from your bowl of eggs is to use the half-shell itself to scoop it out."
—Frank

How to Beat Egg Whites

We suggest beating egg whites with an electric mixer. You could use a sturdy wire whisk or a manual egg beater. But be forewarned: beating egg whites manually until they form stiff peaks takes some serious wrist work. Egg whites take less time to beat at room temperature, so take the eggs out of the refrigerator before you're ready to use them. (Eggs are also easier to separate when they're at room temperature.) It is possible to overbeat egg whites— overbeaten whites begin to look dry. If you're using an electric mixer, check the whites occasionally to see if they're done. Turn the beaters off and lift them straight up out of the whites; if the whites hold the stiff shape of a peak, they're done.

Hazelnut Meringues

3 large egg whites, at room
  temperature
¼ teaspoon cream of tartar
½ cup sugar
½ teaspoon vanilla
½ cup hazelnuts, chopped fine

When we first opened, we were one of a few new businesses moving into a very old Italian neighborhood. Another was a restaurant around the corner (since closed), appropriately called Frontier. The neighborhood was quiet back then, and we were all sort of struggling. So we helped each other out in whatever ways we could. The chef at Frontier baked his Thanksgiving pies in our deck ovens. We often borrowed ice from him on hot iced-coffee and iced-tea days. And back and forth it went. We even shared recipes. This is his mother's hazelnut-meringue recipe.

1. Position your oven racks so that one is in the center, and preheat the oven to 325 degrees. Line a baking sheet with parchment paper.
2. Beat the egg whites in a big bowl with the cream of tartar, using the whisk attachment of an electric mixer on high speed (or a sturdy wire whisk), until they form stiff peaks (page 323).
3. Slowly pour in the sugar, beating all the while. Continue beating until the whites hold a peak. With the mixer on low speed, beat in the vanilla.
4. Use a rubber spatula to fold in the hazelnuts, scraping down the sides of the bowl as you go.
5. Use a ¼-cup measuring cup to scoop out the meringue. Bang the cup against the baking sheet to knock the meringue out of the cup. Leave 2 inches between meringues; they will spread slightly. Use your fingers to pull up on the top of each meringue to form the shape of a chocolate kiss.
6. Lower the oven heat to 250 degrees. Putting the meringues into a hot oven helps them keep their shape; we lower the oven temperature just before putting them in so that we can cook them for a long time to dry them out. Place the baking

sheet on the center rack in the oven, and bake the meringues for 50–60 minutes, or until they are a light-golden color and feel dry to the touch.

7. Turn the oven off, and let the meringues sit in the oven for about an hour to further dry them out.

8. Remove the baking sheet from the oven, and place it on a wire rack until the meringues cool completely, 10–15 minutes. Peel the cooled meringues off the parchment paper. They may stick a bit, but not enough so that they will break when you try to remove them from the paper. Store them in an airtight container.

"Moisture is the enemy of meringues. The whole concept of meringue is to dry it out in your oven. If meringues get wet, they get grainy and eventually start to disintegrate. They will last awhile if you store them in an airtight container in a cool, dry place."
—Frank

Honey Madeleines

The very first article about our café wasn't even a food review. It was a "Talk of the Town" piece in *The New Yorker* by a woman who lived on Park Avenue, which, in the context of New York City neighborhoods, is nowhere near our café. She came in with her husband the first time, and after that continued to come in, always bringing in new people. And always coming for the same thing: our madeleines. Madeleines are delicate, light cookies, or more like little sponge cakes made in a scalloped mold. Fresh out of the oven, they are divine. The *New Yorker* writer called them "peerless."

The truth is, at the time, in New York City anyway, our madeleines didn't have any peers. The only people who even knew what madeleines were back then had either fallen in love with them in France, or had fallen in love with the idea of them from Proust's description in *Remembrance of Things Past:* "I raised to my lips a spoonful of the cake," meaning the madeleine. ". . . A shudder ran through my whole body and I stopped, intent upon the extraordinary changes that were taking place."

Neither of us had quite *that* strong a feeling for madeleines. But we did like them, and we were pleased when they became one of our signature cookies. We make at least 120 madeleines a day now, and we never, ever have one left over. We don't sell them all. We pop a lot of them in our own mouths when they're still warm. And we give a lot of them away. It's kind of a neighborhood ritual. You come in with a child, we hand the child a madeleine. Parents like madeleines for children because they're not too big, and not too sweet. And grown-ups like madeleines for themselves.

"If you haven't had homemade madeleines before, you're in for a treat. Remember: eat them warm."
—Jerome

Madeleines are so delicate and subtle that when customers ask us what they are, we never know quite how to describe them. Technically, we could say something like "a soft, honey-sweetened tea cake from Normandy." But we're more likely just to hand one over the counter for the person to try.

You need a specific piece of equipment—a madeleine mold—to make these. There's just no way around it.

4 tablespoons unsalted butter; plus
  more, melted, for brushing in
  madeleine molds
1 tablespoon honey
½ teaspoon vanilla or almond
  extract
2 large eggs
⅓ cup granulated sugar
1 tablespoon packed light-brown
  sugar
¾ cup unbleached all-purpose flour
1 teaspoon baking powder
A pinch of salt
Confectioners' sugar for dusting
  madeleines

1. Melt the 4 tablespoons butter in a small saucepan over low heat, being careful not to burn or brown the butter. Remove pot from the stove. Stir in the honey and the extract, and let cool to room temperature.

2. Beat the eggs and sugars together in a big bowl, using the whisk attachment of an electric mixer on high speed (or a wire whisk), until the eggs are foamy and light in color.

3. In a separate, small bowl, whisk the flour, baking powder, and salt together. Slowly fold these dry ingredients into the wet, using the paddle attachment of your mixer on low speed (or stirring with a wooden spoon), stopping as soon as no flour is visible. Pour in the cooled butter-honey, and continue mixing until all the ingredients are combined. Cover the bowl, and refrigerate for at least 30 minutes, until the batter is chilled.

4. Before removing the dough from the refrigerator, position your oven racks so that one is in the center and preheat the oven to 425 degrees. Brush your madeleine molds with melted butter.

5. Take a spoonful of batter and, pushing it off with your finger (or piping through a plastic bag), fill each mold to three-quarters full. Madeleines rise a lot, so don't overfill the molds. The goal is to have the cookies retain their perfect little scallop shape.

6. Place the mold on the center rack in the oven, and bake the madeleines for 8–10 minutes, or until they are puffed up above the edge of the mold and each madeleine has a bump on it, like the hump on a camel. You don't want to overbake these; take them out when the edges have turned golden brown.

7. Remove the mold from the oven, and set it on a wire rack for a few minutes, to cool enough so that it's easy to work with. Don't let it cool for too long. Ideally you want to eat the cakes while they're still warm. Lift the mold off the rack, and set it on your work surface. Place the rack on top of the mold and flip it upside down. The madeleines will fall right out.

8. If you are not serving the madeleines warm, once they've cooled to room temperature use a strainer to sprinkle a thin dusting of confectioners' sugar on the seashell side of the madeleines. They're so pretty this way that it almost makes up for the fact that they're not still warm.

"At the store, we use a canister with shaker holes to sprinkle confectioners' sugar on things like tarts and madeleines. At home, I use a sieve or sifter, basically whatever I find first."
—Frank

Crispy Sugar Cookies

We make sugar cookies year-round—in different shapes and sizes, depending on the season. Trees at Christmastime, leaves during fall, pencils and letters at back-to-school time. A fancy little hotel around the corner from Once Upon a Tart has a standing order for our sugar cookies. We cut them into little squares and rounds and sprinkle them with sugar, and the hotel uses them as "turndown" treats, in place of squares of chocolate. This recipe has a very high yield because we find that when we make sugar cookies at home, it's more often than not for a special occasion—a birthday party, Christmas. The dough also freezes well, for up to 2 months. Feel free to cut the recipe in half if you wish.

20 tablespoons (2½ sticks) unsalted butter, softened
2 cups sugar
2 large eggs
1½ teaspoons vanilla extract
4½ cups unbleached all-purpose flour
1¼ teaspoons baking powder
1 teaspoon salt

1. Cream the butter and sugar together in a big bowl, using the whisk attachment of an electric mixer on high speed (or a sturdy wire whisk), until they are fluffy and light lemon-yellow in color, about 5 minutes. With the mixer switched to low speed, beat in the eggs, one at a time, then the vanilla.

2. In a separate, medium-size bowl, whisk the flour, baking powder, and salt together. Add these dry ingredients to the wet, using the paddle attachment of your mixer on low speed (or stirring with a wooden spoon) until the dough forms a ball. The dough will be a bit sticky, but it should clean itself off the sides of the bowl once all the flour is incorporated. If the dough is too wet and sticky to form a ball, add a tiny bit more flour. Wrap the ball of dough in plastic wrap, and chill 1–2 hours before rolling it out.

3. When you are ready to make your cookies, position your oven racks so that one is in the center, and preheat the oven to 350 degrees. Line a baking sheet with parchment paper.

4. To roll out your dough, clear a large flat surface—kitchen counter or cutting board—and dust it with a generous amount of flour. Cut the dough ball into quarters. Starting with one chunk of the dough, roll it into a ball and set it in the center of your work area. Dust your rolling pin with flour, and set it on top of the dough. Gently press on the pin and begin rolling out the dough to ¼ inch thick, working from the center out toward the edges, and dusting more flour over your work surface, your dough, and your pin whenever the dough gets too sticky.

5. The goal when cutting the dough with your cookie cutters is to get the most cookies out of each sheet of rolled-out dough. So cut your cookies as close to one another as you can, like pieces of a puzzle.

6. Gently lift the cut dough onto your prepared baking sheet with a metal spatula. Arrange same-size cookies on the same baking sheet, so that they require the same amount of baking time, leaving a 1-inch space between the cookies.

7. Place the baking sheet on the center rack in the oven, and bake the cookies until the edges are a very light golden-brown, 10–12 minutes for 2–3-inch cookies (baking time will vary significantly, depending on the size you cut the cookies). You do not want the entire cookie golden brown. The cookies will crisp up when they cool, but they'll be hard if you overbake them. A couple minutes of baking time can mean the difference between an undercooked, too-soft sugar cookie and a perfectly crisp, sweet, buttery-tasting one. Lift it up; if the underside is light golden brown, the cookies are done. If it's almost as pale as raw dough, they need more time.

8. Remove the baking sheet from the oven, and place it on a wire rack to let the cookies cool slightly. Lift the baking sheet off the rack and slide the parchment paper off the baking sheet and onto the rack, being careful not to break the cookies. Let the cookies cool completely before icing them or sprinkling them with sugar.

Variation: Dark-Chocolate Sugar Cookies

These are a chocolate version of our Crispy Sugar Cookies. Be careful not to over-bake these cookies—the cocoa will burn, and the cookies will turn out bitter. Substitute 1 cup of cocoa powder plus ⅛ cup sugar for 1 cup of the flour. Omit the vanilla. Otherwise, prepare these just like the Crispy Sugar Cookies (page 331).

Royal Icing

Generally, we don't ice our cookies. But we make an exception for sugar cookies. We have one woman at the store, a baker-cum-artist, who does nothing but paint these cookies. She often even makes her own cutters, twisting a piece of tin until it is just the right shape—a fish or spider or whatever she has in her imagination that day. This icing can be used for piping as is. If you want to brush it on your cookies, thin it with a little water or an additional unbeaten egg white stirred into the finished icing.

MAKES ENOUGH ICING TO DECORATE 1 BATCH OF CRISPY SUGAR COOKIES (PAGE 331)
4 large egg whites, at room temperature
1 pound confectioners' sugar

1. Beat the egg whites and the sugar, using the whisk attachment of an electric mixer on low speed (or a sturdy wire whisk) so the sugar doesn't fly around. Once the sugar is moistened by the egg whites, turn the mixer up to high speed and continue beating for another 7–10 minutes, until the icing is thick and shiny.
2. Divide the icing among separate ramekins or small bowls, and use food coloring to mix your own palette of colors.
3. Pretend you're Picasso.

Chocolate Chip–Hazelnut Biscotti

MAKES 25 BISCOTTI

6 tablespoons (¾ stick) unsalted
    butter, softened

1¼ cups sugar

3 large eggs

2 tablespoons strong brewed coffee,
    at room temperature

2 teaspoons vanilla extract

4⅔ cups unbleached all-purpose
    flour

2¼ teaspoons baking powder

1½ teaspoons cinnamon

¼ teaspoon nutmeg

⅛ teaspoon salt

¾ cup whole hazelnuts

1¼ cups semisweet chocolate
    chips; or 7½ ounces good-
    quality dark chocolate, broken
    into pieces

These are great dipped in espresso. They're denser and sweeter than traditional Italian biscotti.

1. Position your oven racks so that one is in the center, and preheat the oven to 350 degrees. Line a baking sheet with parchment paper.
2. Cream the butter and sugar together in a big bowl, using the whisk attachment of an electric mixer on high speed (or a sturdy wire whisk), until they are fluffy and light lemon-yellow in color, about 5 minutes. With the mixer on low speed, beat in the eggs, one at a time, then the coffee and vanilla.
3. In a separate, medium-size bowl, whisk the flour, baking powder, spices, and salt together to mix. Slowly add these dry ingredients to the wet, stirring with the paddle attachment of your mixer on low speed (or a wooden spoon) until they are almost combined. Add the nuts and the chocolate chips, and continue to mix until the dough comes into a ball.
4. Place the dough on a flour-dusted work surface. Dust your hands with flour, and roll the dough into a log 4 inches in diameter about 14 inches long.
5. Carefully lift the log, and place it on a baking sheet. If the log is too long, cut it in half and place each half on a separate baking sheet; the dough will spread when it bakes.
6. Place the baking sheet on the center rack in the oven—side by side if you're using two baking sheets—and bake for 35 minutes, or until the top of the log is golden brown and feels firm when you press it with your finger.
7. Remove the baking sheet from the oven, and place it on a wire rack to cool to room temperature.
8. Pick the log up with your hands, and move it to a cutting board. Using a serrated knife, cut the log on a slight diagonal into ½-inch slices. (If the log isn't

"When we make biscotti for cocktail parties, we slice perpendicular to the log. The cookies turn out half the length as when they're sliced on the diagonal. It's an aesthetic choice. Slice them however you want."
—Frank

cooled, the melted chocolate will make a mess of your biscotti as you're cutting them.) Line up the slices on a baking sheet cut side down. The biscotti can be touching one another, because the sides that are touching are already cooked.

9. Return the biscotti to the oven, and bake for another 30 minutes, or until they are crisp and golden brown throughout.

10. Remove the baking sheet from the oven, and place it on a wire rack to let the biscotti cool on the sheet. Biscotti are best after they've cooled completely and hardened.

Almond-Raisin Biscotti

For these, we melt the butter instead of creaming it. The resulting cookies are denser than traditional biscotti.

1. Position your oven racks so that one is in the center, and preheat the oven to 350 degrees. Line a baking sheet with parchment paper.
2. Whisk the flour, baking powder, and salt together in a medium-size bowl.
3. In a separate, big bowl, beat the egg yolks with roughly half the sugar, using the whisk attachment of an electric mixer on high speed (or a sturdy wire whisk), until the sugar dissolves and the yolks become pale yellow and frothy.
4. Rinse the beaters and, in a third, medium-size bowl, beat the egg whites until they form stiff peaks. With the mixer still on high speed, beat in the remaining sugar.
5. Using the paddle attachment of your mixer on low speed (or a wooden spoon), fold the egg whites into the egg yolk mixture. Gently stir in the butter, vanilla, anise, almonds, and raisins.
6. Gradually stir the dry ingredients into the wet, until the dough forms a ball.
7. Place the dough on a flour-dusted work surface. Dust your hands with flour, and roll the dough into a log 4 inches in diameter (about 14 inches long).
8. Carefully pick up the log, and place it on a baking sheet. If the log is too long to fit on the baking sheet, cut it in half and place each half on a separate baking sheet; the dough will spread when it bakes.
9. Place the baking sheet on the center rack in the oven (side by side if you're using two sheets), and bake for 45 minutes, until the top of the log is golden brown and feels firm when you press it with your finger.
10. Remove the baking sheet from the oven, and place it on a wire rack to cool the log completely.

4 cups plus 2 tablespoons unbleached all-purpose flour
¾ teaspoon baking powder
⅛ teaspoon salt
3 large eggs, at room temperature, separated
1¼ cups sugar
8 tablespoons (1 stick) unsalted butter, melted and cooled to room temperature
¼ teaspoon vanilla extract
¾ teaspoon aniseed
½ cup almonds, coarsely chopped
½ cup golden raisins

"Yes, biscotti are supposed to be hard."
—Frank

11. Lift it with your hands to a cutting board. Using a serrated knife, cut log on a slight diagonal into ½-inch slices. Line the slices up on your baking sheet with one cut side down. It's okay if the biscotti are touching one another, because the sides that are touching are already cooked.

12. Return the biscotti to the oven, and bake for another 12–15 minutes, until they are crisp and golden brown throughout.

13. Remove the baking sheet from the oven, and allow the biscotti to cool on the sheet. Biscotti are best after they've cooled and hardened.

"If an original recipe calls for an odd number of eggs and you want to cut the recipe in half, whisk one egg, then pour half of that into a cup. You now have half an egg."
—Frank

Pumpkin-Cranberry Biscotti

MAKES 25 BISCOTTI

We first made these as a special for Thanksgiving. Now we make them year-round, because we're in the business of giving the people what they want. And they want these year-round.

1. Position your oven racks so that one is in the center, and preheat the oven to 350 degrees. Line a baking sheet with parchment paper.
2. Whisk the flour, baking powder, salt, and spices together in a medium-size bowl.
3. In a separate, big bowl, beat the egg yolks with roughly half the sugar, using the whisk attachment of an electric mixer on high speed (or a sturdy wire whisk), until the sugar dissolves and the eggs become pale yellow and frothy. Add the pumpkin purée and vanilla, and stir to blend.
4. Rinse the beaters and, in a third, medium-size bowl, beat the egg whites until they form stiff peaks. With the mixer still on high speed, beat in the remaining sugar.
5. Using the paddle attachment of your mixer on low speed (or a wooden spoon), fold the egg whites into the egg yolk mixture. Gently stir in the butter, nuts, cranberries, and raisins.
6. Gradually stir the dry ingredients into the wet ingredients, until the dough comes together into a ball.
7. Place the dough on a flour-dusted work surface. Dust your hands with flour, and roll the dough into a log 4 inches in diameter and about 14 inches long. This is wet and sticky dough, so you'll probably need to flour your hands and work surface continually as you roll the dough into a log.
8. Carefully pick up the log with your hands, and place it on your baking sheet. If

4½ cups unbleached all-purpose flour

1 teaspoon baking powder

⅛ teaspoon salt

¾ teaspoon cinnamon

¼ teaspoon ground ginger

¼ teaspoon nutmeg

⅛ teaspoon ground cloves

3 large eggs, at room temperature, separated

1⅓ cups sugar

¾ cup canned or fresh pumpkin purée

¼ teaspoon vanilla extract

8 tablespoons (1 stick) unsalted butter, melted and cooled to room temperature

1 cup pecans, chopped

½ cup fresh cranberries

⅓ cup golden raisins

the log is too long, cut it in half and place each half on a separate baking sheet, because the dough will spread when it bakes.

9. Place the baking sheet on the center rack in the oven, and bake for 50 minutes, or until the top of the log is golden brown and feels firm when you press it with your finger.

10. Remove the baking sheet from the oven, and place it on a wire rack to allow the log to cool to room temperature.

11. Pick up the log, and place it on a cutting board. Using a serrated knife, cut the log on a slight diagonal into ½-inch slices. Line the slices on the baking sheet with one cut side down. The biscotti slices can be touching one another, because the sides that are touching are already cooked.

12. Return the biscotti to the oven, and bake for another 25–30 minutes, until they are crisp and golden brown throughout.

13. Remove the baking sheet from the oven, and place it on a wire rack. Allow the biscotti to cool completely on the sheet. Biscotti are best after they've cooled and hardened.

Cornmeal-Almond Biscotti

These are by far our most popular biscotti. The cornmeal gives them crunch. And they're not too sweet, so they make a perfect snack.

1. Position your oven racks so that one is in the center, and preheat the oven to 350 degrees. Line a baking sheet with parchment paper.
2. Cream the butter and sugar together in a big bowl, using the whisk attachment of an electric mixer on high speed (or a sturdy wire whisk), until they are fluffy and light lemon-yellow in color, about 5 minutes. With the mixer on low speed, beat in the eggs, one at a time, then beat in the almond extract.
3. In a separate, medium-size bowl, whisk the flour, cornmeal, anise seeds, baking powder, and salt together to mix. Slowly add these dry ingredients to the wet, stirring with the paddle attachment of your mixer on low speed (or a wooden spoon) until they are almost combined. Add the almonds, and stir until the dough comes together into a ball.
4. This dough is sticky and not very stiff; for that reason, we roll it directly on the parchment paper. So cut a piece of parchment paper the same size as your baking sheet, and lay it on your work surface. Dust it with flour, and place your dough on the flour-dusted parchment. Dust your hands with flour, and roll the dough into a log 4 inches in diameter and about 14 inches long.
5. Lift the parchment and let the loose flour fall onto your work surface before placing the dough log, parchment and all, on your baking sheet. If the log is too long, cut it in half (parchment, too) and place the halves on two separate baking sheets, because the dough will spread when it bakes.
6. Place the baking sheet on the center rack in the oven, and bake for 35–40 minutes, or until the top of the log is golden brown and feels firm when you press it with your finger.

12 tablespoons (1½ sticks) unsalted butter, softened

1½ cups sugar

3 large eggs

1 tablespoon plus 1½ teaspoons almond extract

3 cups unbleached all-purpose flour

¾ cup cornmeal

2½ tablespoons aniseed

2½ teaspoons baking powder

⅛ teaspoon salt

1¾ cups almonds, toasted and coarsely chopped (page 76)

7. Remove the baking sheet from the oven, and place it on a wire rack to allow the log to cool completely.
8. Pick up the cooled log with your hands, and place it on a cutting board. Using a serrated knife, cut the log on a slight diagonal into ½-inch slices. Lay the slices flat on your baking sheet. The biscotti slices can be touching one another, because the sides that are touching are already cooked.
9. Return the baking sheet to the oven, and bake the biscotti for another 30 minutes, until they are crisp and golden brown throughout.
10. Remove the baking sheet from the oven, and place it on a wire rack. Allow the cookies to cool completely on the sheet. Biscotti are best after they've cooled and hardened.

Pine Nut Cookies

This recipe comes from a friend of Frank's mother. These cookies are often called Italian macaroons, because, like all macaroons, they are made with egg whites only. We make them at Christmastime.

½ cup granulated sugar
½ cup confectioners' sugar
¼ cup unbleached all-purpose flour
⅛ teaspoon salt
8 ounces almond paste (page 211)
2 large egg whites, at room temperature, lightly beaten
½ cup pine nuts

1. Whisk the sugars, flour, and salt together in a small bowl to mix.
2. In a separate, big bowl, break up the almond paste with your fingers. Add the egg whites, and beat the whites and almond paste together, using the whisk attachment of an electric mixer at high speed (or a sturdy wire whisk), until they form a smooth mixture.
3. Gradually add the dry ingredients to the egg white mixture, and stir them with the paddle attachment of your mixer on low speed (or a wooden spoon) until no flour is visible. Cover the bowl with plastic wrap, and refrigerate for 1–2 hours, or until dough is chilled through.
4. When you're ready to bake the cookies, position your oven racks so that one is in the center, preheat the oven to 350 degrees, and line a baking sheet with parchment paper.
5. Use a teaspoon to scoop up the dough, and your finger to drop it onto your baking sheet, leaving an inch between cookies. Place a few pine nuts on top of each cookie, and press each cookie down with the palm of your hand until it is ¼ inch thick.
6. Place the baking sheet on the center rack in the oven, and bake the cookies until they are golden brown, 20–25 minutes.
7. Remove the baking sheet from the oven, and place it on a wire rack. Allow the cookies to cool slightly. Lift the baking sheet off the rack and, using a metal spatula, transfer the cookies off the sheet and onto the rack to cool completely.

Fudgy Brownies

Frank's brother, John, came to visit from Los Angeles to help us open the store. Not that he knows a thing about baking. But he was a pair of hands, and he was willing to work for free. John is somewhat of a brownie addict, and thus took it upon himself to make what he considered the perfect brownie: moist, fudgy, and nutty. After a week of serious experimentation and Frank's over-the-shoulder input, he did what he'd set out to do.

1 pound (4 sticks) unsalted butter, plus more to grease pan

1½ cups semisweet chocolate chips; or 9 ounces good-quality dark chocolate, broken into pieces

2 cups sugar

8 large eggs

1 teaspoon vanilla extract

2 cups unbleached all-purpose flour

¼ teaspoon salt

2 cups walnuts, very coarsely chopped, or broken up with your fingers

1. Position your oven racks so that one is in the center, and preheat the oven to 350 degrees. Smear a 13-by-9-inch baking pan with butter.

2. Melt the 4 sticks butter and chocolate together in a heavy-bottomed saucepan over low heat. Stir frequently with a wooden spoon or heat-proof spatula in a figure-eight motion to prevent the chocolate from sticking and burning. Even slightly burned chocolate will give the brownies a bitter taste.

3. When the butter and chocolate are combined, add the sugar and cook, stirring constantly, for 2 more minutes. Don't worry if the chocolate appears grainy; the sugar won't dissolve completely, but this doesn't mean you will end up with grainy-textured brownies. Remove the pot from the heat and scrape the chocolate mixture into a big bowl using a heat-proof rubber spatula.

4. Allow the chocolate mixture to cool for 5–10 minutes before adding the eggs; otherwise, the heat of the chocolate will cook the eggs, and you'll end up with little scrambled bits of egg in your brownie batter. Whisk in the eggs one at a time, then whisk in the vanilla.

5. In a separate, medium-size bowl, stir the flour and salt together to mix. Dump the flour into the bowl with the chocolate, and stir until almost no flour remains visible. Stir in the walnuts.

6. Pour the batter into your prepared baking pan. Place the baking pan on the center rack in the oven, and bake the brownies for 40–45 minutes. We undercook these slightly, which is what makes them fudgy and moist. So a fork inserted in the middle will not come out clean. To test for doneness, open the oven and shake the pan; if the batter jiggles, it needs more time.

7. Remove the pan from the oven, and place it on a wire rack. Let the brownies cool to room temperature before cutting them into 2½-inch squares.

"Stirring in a figure-eight motion is a good way to make sure you're touching everything—including the edges of the pot."
—Frank

Jerome on Holiday Cookies

Frank got this crazy idea one year to make all the traditional Christmas cookies and package them together in baskets and boxes. Crescents, rum balls—we didn't make any of these cookies. Now we do holiday-cookie boxes, but mostly from the cookies we already make. If you're doing a bunch of these as gifts, make the dough one day. Any of these cookie doughs can be kept for at least a month in an airtight container in the freezer. Then, closer to holiday time, bake them on another day.

For the boxes themselves, which are much less expensive than baskets, and we think more stylish, use regular bakers' boxes. You can get them at a bakery-supply store. We fold them inside out, so the brown cardboard is on the outside, rather than the shiny white surface. It's more the Once Upon a Tart look. At Christmastime, we cut a window out of the tops of our bakers' boxes and glue in a sheet of clear plastic from the inside. Frank got the idea from the boxes Christmas bulbs come in. Then we stamp each box with our logo. There are a lot of cute stamps out there that you could use to decorate your boxes. Remember to pack the cookies in something soft so they don't break. We use shredded brown kraft paper. It also works to crumple up some wrapping or tissue paper and make a bed out of that. Close up the box, tie a ribbon or bakers' string around it. Just keep things simple. Simple looks better.

Some Favorites for a Holiday Box

Raisin-Spice Cookies with Sugar Icing (page 312)—made golf-ball size for easy packing

Pumpkin-Cranberry Biscotti (page 339)—because they last awhile and they don't break

Pine Nut Cookies (page 343)—traditional for an Italian Christmas

Chocolate-Pecan French-Style Macaroons (page 322)—rich and decadent and last awhile

Crispy Sugar Cookies (page 331)—cut into the smallest of stars or trees

Dark-Chocolate Sugar Cookies (page 333)—cut into the smallest of stars or trees

Our Original Very Ginger Cookies (page 310)—rolled to ⅛ inch and cut into the smallest little men and women

THE END

One of the things we like most about the cooking process is the presentation. And, yes, we consider presentation to be part of the same process. Cooking starts with going to the market and ends with serving. We talked a lot about ingredients in this book—about how your food will only taste as good as the ingredients you make it with. We also believe that your food will only taste as good as it looks. Of course, there are exceptions. We all know that some of our mothers' best casseroles wouldn't exactly win a prize for style.

Nevertheless, we want to urge you to keep thinking and caring about your food even after you turn the stove off—or toss your salad or dump your muffins out of the tin. How you present your food, whether it's for a picnic or a dinner party or for yourself, makes a difference. Throughout the chapters, we included suggestions for our favorite ways of presenting things. But use your imagination. It's mostly a matter of thinking about what you're serving, to see how the items all work together, then looking around—at your bowls and platters, pots of herbs, and leftover ingredients. I guess you could say it's one of our "secrets."

One of our customers came to us recently; he had just taken a cooking and baking course for amateurs and he'd loved it. We asked him what he loved about it. What he learned. He said that, more than anything, he felt less intimidated by the whole idea of cooking. And more comfortable trying new things in the kitchen. We hope this book has done the same for you, because we believe that the primary reason for cooking—especially now, when you can buy good-quality foods already made—is to enjoy yourself while you're doing it.

Happy cooking.

Frank and Jerome

ACKNOWLEDGMENTS

The authors wish to thank:

Ansell and **Matthew**, who endured

Julie Audureau—the storefront wouldn't be the same without you

Jacqueline and **Kurt** for their support

Mom and **Aunt Lu** for their love and sharing of their recipes

Maura McEvoy for her guidance

Julie Dunbar for all her help with recipe testing

Chantal Rey for keeping it all going

Paul Bogaards and **Judith Jones** for believing in Once Upon a Tart . . .

Janis Donnaud for her confidence in us and for eating lots of cheddar-dill scones

Carolynn Carreño for turning our thoughts and words into this book

Jee Levin for her beautiful food styling and professionalism

Stephen Brown for all his help

Homegoods in Margaretville, New York

Peter Andersen for his patience and talents and making this a beautiful book

Carol Devine Carson for her encouragement

Jane and **Carlynn** for their efforts

Claudia for always being there

our staff who continue to create consistent, quality food and finally

our customers who keep coming back

INDEX

eggplant
caponata, 172–3
goat cheese sandwich with, 90
tuna sandwich with, 102
frittata, 45
how to deal with, 38
penne salad with, 147–9
tart
ratatouille, 37–8
with tomato and basil, 32–3
electric mixer, 302
emulsion, 171
English muffins, 103
equipment, xix–xxii

fennel, 41
penne salad with, 147–9
tart, 40–1
feta cheese, cucumber-and-watercress
salad with, 146
figs, fresh, brie cheese sandwich with, 99
flour, 261
cutting butter into, 6, 8
focaccia, 85
food processor, xix
four-sided grater, xxi
frangipane, 210–11
French baguette, 84
frisée, pork loin sandwich with, 111
frittata
potato-and-onion, 43–4
sandwich, 45
variations, 45
fruit
crisps, topping for, 215
drying your own, 257

-and-nut carrot cake, 281
poached, 197
tart with vanilla cream, 208–9
see also specific types of fruit

garlic
how to deal with, 23
and roasted red pepper soup,
66–7
-rosemary aïoli, 178
gazpacho, 79
salad, 150
ginger
candied, scones, 247
cookies, 308–9
original, 310–11
fresh
gingerbread tea loaves, 287–8
how to deal with, 75
sweet pea soup with, 74–5
-pear-raisin muffins, 273
vinaigrette
curry, 167
soy, 183
goat cheese sandwiches, 90
with marinated artichoke hearts,
89
grains, how to cook, 115
graters, xxi
greens, how to rinse and dry, 103
grill pan, xxi
Gruyère, 27
onion soup baked with, 55
potato tart with, 26–7
Provençal tart with, 18–19
turkey sandwich with, 100

handheld grater, xxi
haricots verts, 143
and corn salad, 142–3
three-bean salad, 151–2
hazelnut
biscotti, 334–5
meringues, 324–5
heavy-bottomed pots and pans,
xxii
herbes de Provence, 18
herbs, fresh, 162
mustard with, 161
holiday cookies, 347
honey
-balsamic vinaigrette, 170
-cornmeal
muffins, 276
scones, 253–4
madeleines, 327–9
mustard, 161
horseradish mustard, 161
hummus, 181
sandwich, 88

icing
lemon–cream cheese, 281
royal, 333
sugar, 312–13
immersion blender, xxi, 58
Irish soda scones, 243–4
Italian bread, 85
Italian sausage, goat cheese sandwich with,
90

jicama slaw, 120
julienne, 152

A NOTE ABOUT THE AUTHORS

Frank Mentesana has spent ten years as owner of Once Upon a Tart. He is the creator of several cooking curricula for children, and has recently broadened his involvement with food to include food styling, photography, and gardening. He holds a degree in hotel management and met partner Jerome Audureau while working as a food and beverage director for the French Accor Hotel Group. Frank learned to cook from his Italian grandmother and learned to love food during long forays through meat, cheese, and produce markets with his father. His proudest achievement by far is his son, Matthew. Frank lives in New Jersey.

Jerome Audureau grew up in Avignon, France. While running a summer business as part of his studies at Maxine's Hotel and Restaurant School in Paris, he developed an idea for a café dedicated to tarts. He brought this idea with him when he came to the United States and, along with partner Frank Mentesana, made it into Once Upon a Tart. Jerome is still responsible for running the café, remembering which customer likes which cookie, and generally making people feel good. Jerome lives in Long Island City.

Carolynn Carreño is a writer living in New York City.

A NOTE ON THE TYPE

The text of this book was set in a typeface called Bulmer. This distinguished letter is a replica of a type designed and cut by William Martin about 1790 for William Bulmer of the Shakespeare Press. In design, it is all but a modern face, with vertical stress, sharp differentiation between the thick and thin strokes, and nearly flat serifs.

Composition and color separations by North Market Street Graphics, Lancaster, Pennsylvania
Printing and binding by Tien Wah Press, Singapore
Design by Peter A. Andersen